THE 100 GREATEST BASEBALL *Autographs*

THE 100 GREATEST
BASEBALL
Autographs

Tom Zappala & Ellen Zappala

with John Molori & Steve Grad

Foreword and Contributions by Joe Orlando

Peter E. Randall Publisher
Portsmouth, New Hampshire
2016

© 2016 by Tom Zappala and Ellen Zappala

ISBN: 978-1-937721-29-9

Library of Congress Control Number: 2016935510

Produced by Peter E. Randall Publisher

Box 4726, Portsmouth, New Hampshire 03802
www.perpublisher.com

Book design: Grace Peirce

Photography credit: © Images Anthony Dube/White Point Imaging 2015
www.whitepointimaging.com

Original player portraits provided by renowned sports artist, Arthur K. Miller.
www.artofthegame.com

Autograph images and player card images provided by Professional Sports Authenticator PSA.
www.psacard.com

Signed memorabilia on cover photo and inside art photos provided by Memory Lane Inc.
www.memorylaneinc.com

Additional images provided by Heritage Auctions
www.ha.com

Unsigned photo images of players provided by RMY Auctions.
www.rmyauctions.com

Tribute to Lou Criger multi-signed image provided by Love of the Game Auctions.
www.loveofthegameauctions.com

Vintage baseball equipment provided by Brett Lowman of Play OK Antiques.
www.playokantiques.com

"Jimmy Collins' Wake" by the Dropkick Murphys quoted with permission.

Additional copies available from: www.greatestbaseballautographs.com

Printed in China

Dedicated to our little All-Stars

Lucy, Emmie, Anna, Johnny, and Tommy

An Appreciation
Lou Criger

We want you to know, old pal, that none of us could forget you, that we were all thinking of you and praying for you as we gathered here in Boston for one more good time together.

God in his wisdom has seen fit to give us various burdens. Yours has been heavy, but we know that you are giving it a grand and gallant fight, and we know you'll come thru, for Lou Criger always fought it out until the last strike was called.

The only shadow on the day was the fact that you couldn't be here, but since you couldn't we, your old team mates, and the boys you played against, send you this expression of our affection.

[signatures of players including Cy Young, Ty Cobb, Harry Hooper, Bill Carrigan, and others]

The Boston Post Old Timers Baseball Game Braves Field, Boston, Mass. September 8th 1930

Contents

★ ★ ★ ★ ★ ★ ★ ★ ★ ★ ★ ★ ★ ★ ★

Foreword by Joe Orlando viii

Acknowledgments x

Introduction xi

Chapter 1
The Most Wanted 1

Chapter 2
The Early Years 43

Chapter 3
Baseball's Golden Age 115

Chapter 4
The Modern Era 159

Player Index 208

Authors & Contributors 210

Foreword

★ ★ ★ ★ ★ ★ ★ ★ ★

Autograph collecting has been around for decades, and while hobbyists have been building all types of collections during that time, there is no doubt baseball autographs reign supreme. There are those who chase the signatures of actors or rock-and-roll icons and others who seek presidential penmanship. However, Marilyn Monroe, Elvis Presley, and Abraham Lincoln all take a back seat to the Sultan of Swat—Babe Ruth—when it comes to autographs.

Even within the world of sports autographs, baseball is dominant. Is it the rich history? Is it the abundance of fascinating personalities? Is it the wonderful simplicity of the most desired medium of all—the signed ball—that draws people in? All of these factors and more contribute to the unrivaled allure of baseball autographs. When it comes to autograph popularity, there are major standouts in other sports—like Muhammad Ali, Michael Jordan, Walter Payton and Wayne Gretzky—but these athletes transcend sports. They are the exception, not the rule.

In the autograph world, baseball rules.

With so many collectibles available, what is it specifically about collecting autographs that appeals to so many people? When it comes to trading cards, hobbyists love to build complete sets and imagine the journey that each tiny piece of cardboard went through to land in their collection today. If we're talking about equipment such as professional model bats, gloves, or jerseys, there is certainly something very cool about owning a tangible piece of history. For those who collect tickets, each one is like a time capsule that can be used to recall a historic moment.

All of these collectibles, and more, offer something attractive for the hobbyist, but there's something about the appeal of autographs that differs from other types of items. First, collectors are often drawn to the personal touch that an autograph possesses. By definition, autographs *require* a personal touch that is absent in collectibles like trading cards or tickets. No matter what type of medium is used or when it was signed, at some point, the signer spent a moment of their life to place their autograph on that item.

Furthermore, an autograph will often tell a story about the person to whom it belongs. For example, if you were to compare a rookie-era autograph of Mickey Mantle to one penned much later in his career and life, you can see the evolution of not only his signature style, but also of his personality. What was once a very simplistic signature early in his career developed into one of the most recognizable and stylish autographs in the entire hobby. Mantle went from being a small-town phenomenon to the starting center fielder of the most popular team on the planet—the New York Yankees.

If you follow the changes in his autograph, you can see Mantle's rise to stardom. As he blossomed into a superstar on the field, more people asked for his autograph. As more people requested his autograph, Mantle had time to perfect it and his confidence grew as an athlete. You can sense the confidence in his seasoned signature. It is bold and definitive, much like those of fellow baseball legends like Ted Williams, Joe DiMaggio, and Babe Ruth. Their signatures provide a window into their personalities.

This window isn't limited to the style of autograph, but the habits of the signer can also reveal something about the person behind the autograph. As most of you know, Babe Ruth was a gregarious person who loved big crowds and all the attention that came with it. His teammate, and slugging icon, Lou Gehrig was the exact opposite. Ruth would often sign the sweet spot of the baseball and assume that spot was, in essence, reserved for him when signing team balls. Gehrig would often sign the side panel and, in almost submissive fashion, leave the sweet spot open for Ruth on team balls. It was just his nature, and you can see that nature in plain view based on his signing habits.

There are also many mysteries in the autograph world, especially as it relates to baseball. For instance, while it certainly isn't always the case, why does it seem like the signatures of great hitters are often much more visually appealing than those penned by pitchers? Is it superior hand-eye coordination? Is there a general personality difference between position players and pitchers that manifests itself via the autograph? Have you seen Greg Maddux's autograph? Hall of Fame pitcher Don Drysdale, who happened to be an excellent hitter, had a very stylish autograph. Maybe there is something to that theory, but, then again, maybe not.

In baseball, comparing players from different eras is a favorite pastime of fans and collectors. With such a rich history, it's hard not to do, especially when great talents come along. The same can be said of comparing autographs from different generations. There definitely seems to be a difference in the legibility, care, and pride between baseball players of the past and present, but there is a pretty logical explanation for at least part of it.

You have to remember that many legends of the past earned far more money after their careers by signing autographs than they ever did playing the game that made them famous. If you were a star player of the 1950s or 1960s, for example, that was certainly the case. As a result, many of those stars took their time in perfecting their autograph because they had to. They were paid to take their time and place a nice signature on baseballs, bats, and photos once their playing days were over. That certainly doesn't explain why so many vintage autographs were far more aesthetically pleasing *prior* to the hobby boom of the 1980s, but it explains part of it.

Today, the average back-up player makes more money in one season than the legends of the past did in their entire careers. In other words, what financial incentive do most modern-day athletes have to slow down and apply a beautiful autograph to an item? The average level of compensation has changed so dramatically in sports that the need for athletes to participate in private or public signings has virtually disappeared. You can still get many athletes to provide a quick version of their signature at the ballpark, but there is no doubt that the standard of care has changed.

All you have to do is look at some of the superstar autographs of today. Mike Trout and Clayton Kershaw are two of the brightest young talents in the game and they also appear to be two genuinely nice guys, but their autographs look like some sort of primitive cave etching. You can barely decipher the letters used in their signature. The point here is that they are not alone. That is just the way it is today. Certainly not all athletes or baseball players sign their names using some form of hieroglyphics, but so many of them do.

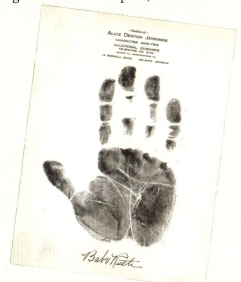

While collecting baseball autographs didn't emerge in a major way until about 1920, right around the time Babe Ruth revolutionized the sport, the endeavor was more prevalent in other genres before that time. During the pre-1920 era, collecting autographs of famous entertainers and Presidents had already gained some measure of traction, but it seems as if fewer people chose to pursue baseball autographs. It just wasn't part of the culture, which explains why many autographs from that period are so rare today. It's not just about survival, it's about the lack of autograph generation in the first place.

As we look into the future, you can make the argument that acquiring some current athletes' signatures may become more difficult than acquiring the autographs of past greats. It simply comes down to supply and demand. Without the financial incentive that was present for prior generations of ballplayers, the forecast may present some real challenges. Ironically, this challenge may enhance the need for the hunt, and the hunt plays a big part in the endeavor of collecting.

No matter what challenges lie ahead, autograph collecting has evolved into one of the most intriguing segments of the hobby. The personal touch that the autograph embodies gets the collector closer to the legends of the game, and it opens a tiny window into the personality of each icon. All collectors know…it's the story that drives us. The autograph, in its own unique way, tells a story about every figure who graced an item with their signature. Collecting them is a story that keeps writing itself and has no end as long as you are having fun.

Acknowledgments

This project could not have been completed had it not been for the combined efforts of many talented individuals.

First and foremost, we would like to thank our dear friend Joe Orlando, president of Professional Sports Authenticator (PSA) and PSA/DNA Authentication Services, for his involvement in just about every aspect of this publication. From writing the foreword to advising us on the finer points of the autograph hobby, Joe's contribution was immeasurable.

We would also like to thank Steve Grad, principal authenticator at PSA/DNA Authentication Services and authentication expert for the History Channel's hit show *Pawn Stars*. His analysis and background of each player's autograph provide valuable insight for the collector. A special shout out also goes to Quality Autographs for their contributions.

Kudos to Jackie Curiel from PSA/DNA for her outstanding support throughout this entire project. Her quick, efficient turnaround and positive attitude was greatly appreciated and made our work on this project much easier.

This has been our second opportunity to collaborate with our good friend and talented colleague, John Molori. Once again, his witty yet folksy writing style and sharp baseball analysis blend for a fun, informative read. Thanks John, for your help and friendship. We greatly appreciate it.

Renowned sports artist Arthur K. Miller allowed us to use his work as player illustrations in this book. In addition to the Hall of Fame in Cooperstown, his paintings are seen in galleries across the country and on his *Art of the Game* website. Thank you, Arthur. Your work is magnificent.

The beautiful cover photo and full-page art photos inside the book are the work of the immensely talented Tony Dube of White Point Imaging. Tony's images also appear in *The T206 Collection: The Players & Their Stories* and *The Cracker Jack Collection: Baseball's Prized Players*, and we are pleased to once again showcase his work.

We would like to thank the folks at Memory Lane Inc. for supplying most of the signed memorabilia that appears on the cover and full page photos inside the book. Thanks for entrusting us with these wonderful treasures. They offer a great visual history of our National Pastime.

Thanks also to our friend and East Coast collector, Joe Mariano, for allowing us to use memorabilia from his private collection for the art photos as well.

Brett Lowman, owner of Play OK Antiques, once again supplied the vintage baseball equipment used for the cover photo and inside art photos. Brett's collection can also be seen in *The T206 Collection: The Players & Their Stories* and *The Cracker Jack Collection: Baseball's Prized Players*. Brett, we sincerely thank you.

Special thanks to the wonderful staff at Heritage Auctions for providing many of the outstanding autograph images used throughout the book.

Thank you to RMY Auctions for permitting us to use several historic unsigned black and white photos of players that appear in this book.

We would like to thank Love of the Game Auctions, for allowing us to use the image from the tribute to Lou Criger. This remarkable piece was signed by a number of players and captures the essence of what autograph collecting is all about.

Thank you to PSA/DNA Authentication Services for providing some of the exceptional autograph images used for each player included in the book.

We would also like to thank our good friends Dick Johnson, Curator of the Sports Museum in Boston, and Ken Casey, vocalist for our favorite Boston band, the Dropkick Murphys; for allowing us to use the lyrics to "Jimmy Collins' Wake." Dick penned the lyrics, and Kenny and his crew wrote the music. Thanks guys!

Thank you to Deidre Randall and the talented staff at Peter E. Randall Publisher for another outstanding publication. The design and layout expertise of Grace Peirce and the careful editing of Zak Johnson have helped us win national awards with our first two books. Let's hope the streak continues!

Finally, thanks to all of you for the tremendous support we have received for this series of books. We are happy that you are happy! Our goal is to help perpetuate this wonderful hobby while celebrating the lives of the men who made baseball the greatest game in the world.

Introduction

When I was asked to write this book, I took on the project not quite realizing how extensive the baseball autograph industry really is. After all, for the last twenty-five years I have been focused on upgrading my T206 collection, enjoying my little cardboard addiction in between writing assignments. As a matter of fact, I personally own one single autograph. No, it isn't Babe Ruth, Ty Cobb, or Honus Wagner, but rather Stuffy McGinnis. Why Stuffy McGinnis? Because I loved his name, and he was part of the Athletics famous $100,000 infield along with three other great names: Eddie "Cocky" Collins, Frank "Home Run" Baker, and Jack "Black Jack" Barry. That is the extent of my personal autograph collection.

However, back in 1992, my eleven-year-old son accumulated some very nice autographs by painstakingly sending out requests, every day, with a self-addressed, stamped envelope to just about every Major League player on the face of the earth. He was able to get his hands on one of those handbooks that lists the home address of every living Major League player, and as a result, he was able to put together a pretty neat autograph collection of players who were stars between 1940 and 1990.

As I delved into researching the player stories and the story behind their autographs, it became apparent that collecting premium baseball autographs takes quite a bit of knowledge, and a keen eye if you are not standing right in front of the person signing the autograph.

Without a doubt, it is a great hobby because the "hunt" for that rare autograph is similar to the hunt for that rare baseball card. It's both challenging and fun.

In the following pages, we decided to rank the top 100 baseball autographs in the hobby. From Babe Ruth to Roberto Clemente to Derek Jeter, many familiar names are here along with some rarities that might surprise you. We used a combination of criteria such as popularity, historical importance, and scarcity to select and rank these special signatures. On each page you will find interesting background on the subject and, with the help of hobby experts Joe Orlando and Steve Grad, terrific insight about the autograph, too. How does your list match up with ours? Take the visual tour to learn more about the baseball autographs that collectors desire most. The combination of the story about the player as well as the story about the signature will make it a fun journey. Enjoy!

Tom Zappala

1

The Most Wanted

★ ★ ★ ★ ★ ★ ★ ★ ★ ★ ★ ★

This first chapter highlights the twenty baseball autographs that are the most desirable in the collecting world along with background information about the player and insight about the autograph. These sought-after signatures were selected and ranked based on popularity, historical importance, and scarcity. You'll probably find a few surprises here. Players from just about every baseball era are included.

Here is our "Most Wanted List."

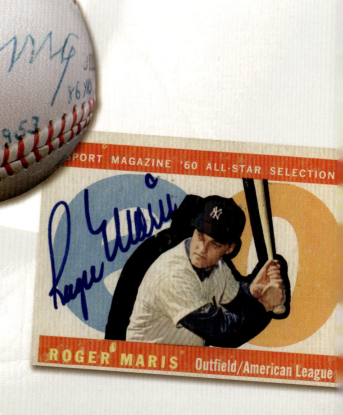

Babe Ruth

"He hits a ball harder and further than any man I ever saw."

– Bill Dickey, New York Yankees

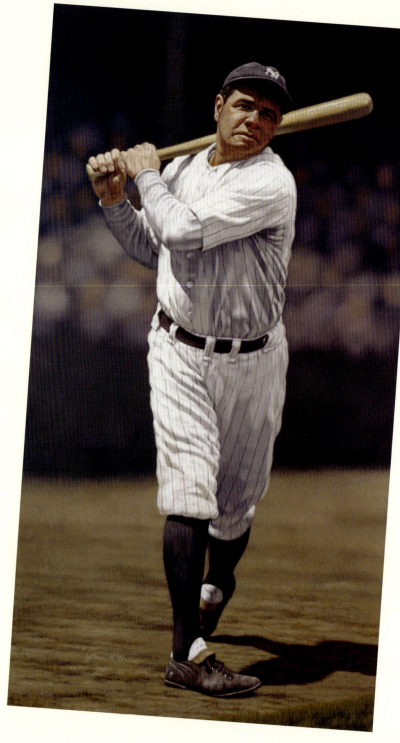

To say that George Herman Ruth was one of the most memorable figures in American history is no exaggeration. A man identified by mere words and numbers—Sultan, 60, Swat, 714, Bambino, 3—Babe Ruth transcended sports to become a cultural icon of the highest caliber. His persona is so massive, it is easy to forget his legend began on the field. Not just a five-tool player, Ruth had an entire workshop of skills. His numbers are staggering, as was his unique ability to hit the ball harder and more frequently than almost anyone ever born. Oh yeah, he could pitch a little, too. In 1916 and 1917 with the Red Sox, Ruth posted 23 and 24 wins, respectively, and led the American League with 1.75 ERA in 1916. Ruth won 94 games in a pitching career that was cut short by his epic offensive prowess.

In 1920, after a celebrated deal that sent him to the Yankees, Ruth clouted a then-record 54 home runs. The game of baseball shifted from small ball to long ball, and a sports dynasty was born. The equation was simple: Ruth + New York = Legend, and this legend was fortified not only with runs, but with rum. Ruth dominated the Big Apple's Roaring Twenties social scene as much as he did opposing pitchers. He was, indeed, the most lethal member of New York's Murderers' Row. Hardly an all-or-nothing slugger, Ruth batted .342 for his career, and is the all-time leader in slugging percentage (.690) and OPS (1.164). He slugged over .700 nine times, including two times over .800. In 22 seasons, Ruth hit

The Bambino

714 career home runs, including a then-unthinkable 60 in 1927. His legend grew with his offensive totals and mythical mystique highlighted by the still-debated called home run shot in the 1932 World Series. Despite his iconic status, Ruth never achieved his goal of managing in the Bigs and was unceremoniously dumped by the Yankees in 1935. He finished his playing career back in Boston with the Braves that season. His womanizing, carousing, eating, and drinking binges were as colossal as his home runs, and in the long run, even more damaging. In 1948 at age 53, Ruth succumbed to cancer of the liver, lungs, and kidneys. Part of baseball's original 1936 Hall of Fame class, Ruth was more than a ballplayer, bon vivant, and superstar. He was, and remains, a national treasure.

PSA/DNA Authentication Services Says:

Not only the king of baseball, the Sultan of Swat is also the king of autographs. If you were to pick one signature to represent autograph collecting, it would be a Ruth single-signed baseball. Ruth completely changed the autograph landscape. Prior to his arrival in the major leagues, signing autographs was not commonplace. Ruth went out of his way to be accessible to fans of all ages. His social nature endeared him to the public and it presented infinite opportunities for Ruth to sign. He also signed numerous items for charity and giveaways throughout his life. On rare occasions, those items were penned by someone other than Ruth. For example, as part of a Sinclair Oil promotion in 1937, a secretary signed "Sincerely Babe Ruth" on the baseballs sent to all contest winners. A clubhouse attendant would occasionally sign items on Ruth's behalf in the 1920s, but Ruth was more active than any player of his generation. Compared to his very early signature style, the one he developed while with the Yankees was confident and bold. During this evolution, Ruth started placing quotation marks around "Babe," but eventually ceased this practice in the late 1920s. You will encounter many variations of Ruth's signature on a variety of mediums, from "George Herman Ruth" to "George H. Babe Ruth" to "G.H. Ruth" to "Babe Ruth." It is important to note that while his health was declining in the late 1940s, a large number of items sent through the mail were actually signed by his nurse. Despite his incredible appetite for signing autographs, Ruth remains one of the heavily-forged names in the hobby, along with fellow Yankee legend, Mickey Mantle.

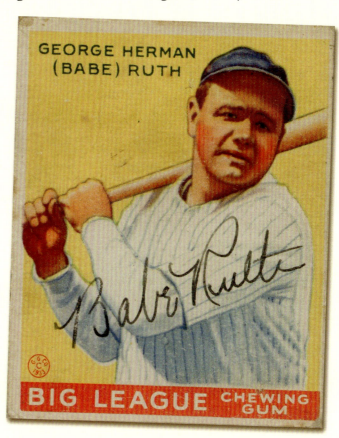

Christy Mathewson

The ultimate ace of the Deadball Era, Christy Mathewson put together one of the most brilliant pitching careers in baseball history. In 1902, Mathewson won 14 games for the New York Giants. It would be the last time he would win fewer than 22 games until 1915. This incredible run included four seasons of 30 or more victories and an ERA that never rose higher than 2.97. He led the National League in wins four times and in ERA five times. Overall, Mathewson finished with a

career record of 373–188 and an ERA of 2.13. He set NL records in wins for a season and career, and even today is firmly ensconced on the Mount Rushmore of big league pitchers. However, statistics do not tell the whole story of the man they called Matty.

The legend of Mathewson began at Bucknell University, where the class president excelled in football as a fullback, punter, and kicker. Mathewson's baseball career took a few years to blossom. He was just 2–13 in 1899, his first professional season in Taunton, Massachusetts. As a young player, the Giants actually tried Mathewson at first base and outfield before legendary manager John McGraw set him off on a run of mound mastery. The 6-foot, 1-inch and 195 pound, chiseled All-American boy quickly became a Madison Avenue darling, endorsing everything from underwear to sports equipment, all the while befuddling batters and racking up records. Most of all, Mathewson was about winning. He led the Giants to pennants in 1905, 1911, 1912, and 1913, and while he had just a 5–5 postseason record, his ERA was a microscopic 0.97 and he surrendered just 11 earned runs in over 100 innings pitched.

In 1916, after 17 years with the Giants, Mathewson was traded, by request, to the Reds. He wanted to be a manager and Cincinnati was in dire need of some star power to change their luck. Unfortunately, luck was in short supply for Mathewson. He contracted influenza

4   THE MOST WANTED

Matty

while serving in France with the U.S. Army's Chemical Warfare Division, and returned to find the Reds had replaced him as manager. Mathewson rejoined the Giants in 1919 as McGraw's assistant manager, but in 1921, he was diagnosed with tuberculosis, the same disease that killed his brother Henry four years earlier. Back in good health, Mathewson became president of the Boston Braves in 1923, but soon relapsed and passed away in 1925, at age 45. Eleven years later, Christopher Mathewson was inducted into of the Hall of Fame with the inaugural class.

PSA/DNA Authentication Services Says:

Christy Mathewson's autograph is one of the most desirable in the hobby because of its scarcity, beautiful appearance, and his legendary status. Mathewson's signature style changed several times throughout his life. Many existing examples feature a full-name signature, but you will encounter examples where Mathewson abbreviated his first name to a simple *C* within his autograph. While you may find an occasional signed baseball or photograph, most of the known Mathewson signatures are found on documents such as checks and contracts. In fact, after his death in 1925, Mathewson's wife would sometimes send signed checks in response to those seeking old examples of his autograph through the mail. Today, high-end examples of Mathewson's signature on a baseball often command north of $100,000 in the marketplace.

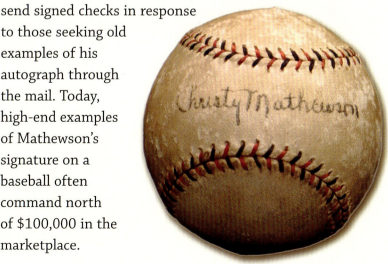

3 Josh Gibson

If the baseball gods were to construct the perfect ballplayer, they might just create a mold called Joshua Gibson. At 6-foot, 1-inch, and 215 pounds, Gibson was a lethal combination of athleticism, power, and speed. Because his Negro League stats are incomplete, talking about Gibson statistically is a somewhat futile endeavor. In addition, because of the racism disguised as a "gentlemen's agreement," among Major League Baseball owners, Gibson never got the chance to show his wares at the highest level. He was, however, the most dominant offensive force in that bastion of baseball talent known as the Negro Leagues.

Gibson played a reported 16 seasons, most of them with the legendary Homestead Grays franchise. He was known for his prodigious home runs, many approaching or even surpassing 600 feet depending on which legend you choose to believe. Gibson was also a rock as a catcher. He was strong, steely tough, had a keen eye, and a mighty swing. It is one of sports' great injustices that Gibson, as well as many of his Negro League teammates and foes, never got to play in the majors. It was truly baseball's loss. Think of the many clubs whose fates might have been altered if they had the gumption to break from the prejudiced pack and sign Gibson. He played between the years 1930 and 1946. Would the Boston Red Sox have broken their World Series curse long before 2004 with Gibson and Ted Williams in the lineup together? Would perennial cellar dwellers like the Phillies or Browns have risen to glory with Gibson clouting tremendous taters? Would any pitcher in either league have as good a lifetime ERA if they had to face Gibson multiple times each season?

In 2000, the *Sporting News* rated Gibson #18 on their list of the 20th century's 100 greatest players. The Georgia native had a ninth-grade education, but was a baseball genius, a man who drew gasps of awe from

The Black Babe Ruth

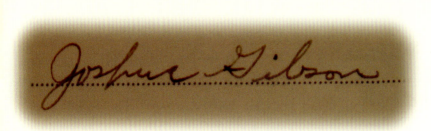

legends such as Satchel Paige and Sam Jethroe. In 1947, Jackie Robinson broke MLB's color barrier just months after Josh Gibson suffered a fatal stroke at age 35. Twenty-five years later, in 1972, Robinson passed away just months after Gibson was elected to the Baseball Hall of Fame. Both men were baseball luminaries, but only one got the opportunity to shine.

> "*I played with Willie Mays and against Hank Aaron. They were tremendous players, but they were no Josh Gibson. You saw him hit, and you took your hat off. It makes me sad to talk about Josh, because he didn't get to play in the Major Leagues, and when you tell people how great he was, they think you are exaggerating.*"
>
> – Monte Irvin, Hall of Famer

PSA/DNA Authentication Services Says:

Josh Gibson autographs are among the great rarities in the hobby. Gibson not only failed to sign often during his career, but his early death further contributed to the clear lack of authentic examples in the marketplace. On legal documents, such as contracts from his playing time in Cuba, the legendary slugger would often sign "Joshua" Gibson in more formal fashion. On other mediums, such as album pages, photos, or baseballs, you may see either "Josh" or just the initial J in place of his full first name. Much like the autographs of fellow "Top 20" member Shoeless Joe Jackson, Gibson autographs are desirable and valuable regardless of the medium as advanced collectors are often trying to fill the hole created by such a scarce signature.

4 Joe Jackson

> *"He was the finest natural hitter in the history of the game."*
>
> – Ty Cobb

Volumes have been written about whether or not Joe Jackson was involved in the most infamous scandal to rock Major League Baseball, but let's take a look at Shoeless Joe Jackson, the player. Shoes, no shoes, Sox, no Sox, he is simply one of the greatest hitters in baseball history. After two seasons with the Athletics, Jackson was off to the races when, in 1911 with the Cleveland Naps, he hit .408 with 41 stolen bases. The 23-year-old outfielder also had a cannon for an arm. From that point on, people came from all over to see the unassuming young phenom.

The South Carolina native was the oldest of eight children and worked from a young age to help support the family. He was never able to attend school to learn to read and write. When he went to Philadelphia to play for the Athletics in 1908 and 1909, Jackson had difficulty adjusting to life in the north. His teammates teased him for his country ways and illiteracy, but Jackson's skill with his favorite bat, "Black Betsy," quieted them down. To this day, Jackson's career average of .356 is the third-highest batting average in MLB history. During his 13-year career with the Athletics, Naps, and White Sox, Jackson led the American League in triples, hits, total bases, and OBP at one time or another.

It all came to an abrupt end in 1920 when, along with seven White Sox teammates, Jackson was banned from baseball for life for allegedly fixing the 1919 World Series. Although he maintained his innocence, his career was over. Jackson continued to play semi-pro ball in the South, sometimes under an assumed name. He also owned a liquor store in Greenville, South Carolina. In *Shoeless Joe and Ragtime Baseball*, Harvey Frommer tells about a day in 1946 when Ty Cobb and sportswriter

Shoeless Joe

Grantland Rice visited Jackson's liquor store. Jackson didn't acknowledge them, and Cobb asked, "Don't you know me, Joe?" Jackson responded, "I do know you, Ty, but was not sure if you wanted to know me. A lot of them don't." Joseph Jefferson Jackson died of a heart attack in 1951 at age 63, just months after he was inducted into the Cleveland Indians Hall of Fame. Legend, myth, and scandal aside, pure and simple, Joe Jackson was one of the best.

PSA/DNA Authentication Services Says:

Much has been written about Joe Jackson's virtual illiteracy. As a result, Jackson autographs are extremely rare. Even authentic examples have a very drawn appearance. You can tell that Jackson struggled to form the letters of his own name. Autographs that were signed during Jackson's playing days are even harder to find than those signed after his banishment.

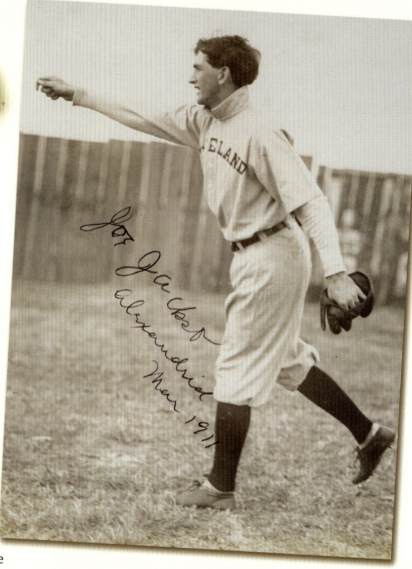

His wife, Katie, signed for Joe most of the time after his career was over. Some of the less than two dozen authentic Jackson autographs known to exist appear on documents, while others are scrawled on a simple piece of paper. At the time of this writing, only one Jackson signed photo is known to exist. Regardless of the medium, all authentic Jackson autographs have tremendous value.

> "*Regardless of what anybody says, I was innocent of any wrongdoing. I gave baseball all I had.*"
>
> – Joe Jackson

5 Lou Gehrig

Imagine a mythical family portrait of the New York Yankees. The photographer would probably struggle to wrangle his subjects into position. Babe Ruth and Mickey Mantle would likely sit front-row-center, smiling and cutting it up with everyone. In the center of the back row, probably with his arms around Derek Jeter and Joe DiMaggio, would be the quiet unassuming "big brother" of the clan, Lou Gehrig.

With a career spanning 17 glorious seasons, Henry Louis Gehrig set the record when he played in 2,130 consecutive games over 15 of those seasons, a streak that earned him the nickname "The Iron Horse." That moniker seems ironic today. Although he appeared invincible, the 37-year-old Gehrig succumbed in 1941 to amyotrophic lateral sclerosis (ALS), now known as Lou Gehrig's disease. On July 4, 1939, Lou Gehrig Day, the Yankees paid tribute to their ailing teammate. Gehrig marked that day with his unforgettable, inspirational "Today, I consider myself the luckiest man on the face of the earth" speech, which still resonates in the hearts of fans to this day.

Considered by many to be the greatest first baseman of all time, Gehrig's litany of baseball heroics is matched by few men. He won six World Series with the Yankees, was a two-time American League MVP, and won the AL Triple Crown in 1934. As part of the legendary "Murderers' Row Yankees," Gehrig was voted MVP for the first time in 1927, with 52 home runs and 173 RBI to go with his .373 batting average. Despite those gaudy numbers, Gehrig took a back seat to Ruth's quest for 60 home runs, which captivated fans that year. In 1931, Gehrig drove in an American League record 184 runs to go along with 46 homers.

Along with Yankee teammates Ruth, and later, Joe DiMaggio, Gehrig dominated the American League. After Ruth left the Yankees in 1935, Gehrig became

The Iron Horse

Henry Louis Gehrig (Player)

captain, a position he held through the end of his career. Solid and dependable, he led by example, and was one of the most respected players of the day. "Larrupin' Lou" was unanimously elected to the Hall of Fame in 1939, the year of his retirement, and was the first player in baseball history to have his number retired. He is ranked by *Sporting News* as one of the top ten greatest players of all time. Truly gifted to fans across the country by the baseball gods, Lou Gehrig was an amazing athlete and an American hero. Although his life was cut short, his legend lives on.

PSA/DNA Authentication Services Says:

Out of respect for Babe Ruth, Lou Gehrig very rarely signed his autograph on the sweet spot of a baseball. Gehrig felt that it was Ruth's place to be on the sweet spot because, after all, "The Bambino" was the biggest star in the game. It was Gehrig's nature to play "Robin" to Ruth's "Batman." It was not until Ruth retired as a player that Gehrig's signature began to appear more frequently on the sweet spot, but single-signed baseballs of "The Iron Horse" are infinitely harder to find than those of his boisterous teammate. After July of 1939, Gehrig signed infrequently because of his deteriorating condition, and as Gehrig's disease advanced, most items were signed by his wife, Eleanor, or applied by a secretary. Some authentic Gehrig autographs were signed during this period, but they are few and far between.

" *His greatest record doesn't show in the book. It was the absolute reliability of Henry Louis Gehrig. He could be counted upon. He was there every day at the ballpark bending his back and ready to break his neck to win for his side.*"

— John Kieran, sportswriter, *The New York Times*

THE MOST WANTED 11

6 Roberto Clemente

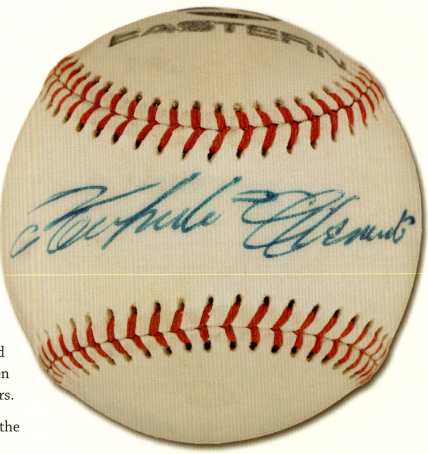

Much more than a 12-time All-Star, National League MVP, 12-time Gold Glove winner, member of the 3,000 hit club and four-time NL Batting Champ, Roberto Clemente did more in his short 38 years than most could do in two lifetimes. Clemente was a flawless outfielder with a howitzer for an arm, who could effortlessly track a fly ball. During his 18 years with the Pittsburgh Pirates, he batted over .300 thirteen seasons, hitting .320 or better 8 times. Not a power hitter, he did hit 240 career home runs, with a career-high 29 homers in 1966. The highlight of Clemente's great career was the 1971 World Series. He hit safely in all seven games, topped off by a home run in the fourth inning of Game Seven to seal the championship and earn Series MVP honors.

Off the field, Clemente dedicated himself to helping the underprivileged. Proud of his Puerto Rican heritage, he took advantage of his celebrity to help the needy at home and elsewhere in Latin America. His free baseball clinics for children in Puerto Rico inspired many future athletes.

His last at-bat took place on September 30, 1972, when he reached the 3,000 hit pinnacle. That December, a devastating earthquake struck Nicaragua in an area Clemente had recently visited. He raised donations in Puerto Rico and decided to accompany the aid flight on New Year's Eve to personally oversee distribution of the medical supplies, food, and clothing in Nicaragua. Sadly, the DC-7 was overloaded with aid supplies causing it to crash almost immediately over the coast of Puerto Rico. Roberto Clemente's body was never found.

After his death, when many of his charitable endeavors came to light, people realized that baseball had lost a very special human being. Numerous awards in Clemente's name have been established, including the prestigious Roberto Clemente Award, which is given out during the World Series to a player selected for ability, sportsmanship, and community involvement. Clemente became the first Latin American player to be inducted to the Hall of Fame after a special election in 1973. Interestingly, at the time of this writing, the Catholic Church is investigating healings of the sick attributed to Clemente as part of the process of considering him for sainthood. Farfetched? Most likely, but don't count out Roberto Clemente. After all, he was bigger than life.

Sweetness

PSA/DNA Authentication Services Says:

Is it Roberto or Phil? That's the million-dollar question when it comes to Clemente autographs, one of the most unique-looking autographs you will ever see. Roberto was diligent about signing throughout the 1950s until about 1960. From that point right into the early 1970s, Clemente's good friend Phil Dorsey started signing a portion of autograph requests, with Roberto's blessing. Phil's signature was so good that it went undetected in the hobby for many years. As a result, while they were non-malicious in nature, the market was infiltrated by forged Clemente autographs. With Roberto Clemente passing away in 1972, the authentic Clemente autographs today are in very high demand, especially on signed trading cards.

" *Anytime you have an opportunity to make a difference in this world and you don't, then you are wasting your time on earth.*"

– Roberto Clemente

Mel Ott

A great baseball talent evaluator, Giants manager John McGraw decided to look at a short, sturdy 16-year-old Louisiana kid who reputedly was a talented left-handed hitter. The high school kid played semi-pro baseball, and the team owner brought him to McGraw's attention. In 1925, after watching the kid spray balls all over the Polo Grounds and over the fence, McGraw predicted he would become one of the greatest hitters in National League history. McGraw decided to get him off the field quickly, and to keep him under wraps.

Less than a year later, with contract in hand, 17-year-old Melvin Thomas Ott became a member of the New York Giants. McGraw did not send the teenager to the minors for seasoning, opting to keep him with the club so he could personally oversee his training. There was no way he would allow the youngster to pick up bad habits from older players in the minors. Young Ott was not even allowed to fraternize with the players on the big league roster, at least not yet. Eventually, the older guys embraced him and for 22 years, "Master Melvin" was one of the most dynamic players in the game. The soft-spoken Ott became the Giants right fielder in 1928 and went on to lead the National League in home runs on six different occasions. Wildly popular with fans, Ott was a 12-time All-Star, was the first National League player to register eight consecutive 100-RBI seasons, the first NL player to hit 500 home runs, and was superior defensively. He played in three World Series (1933, 1936, 1937) and batted

14   THE MOST WANTED

Master Melvin

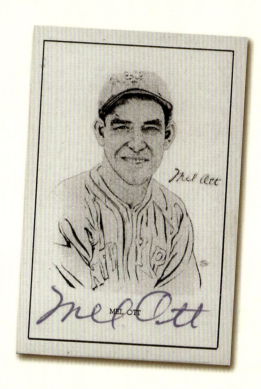

.389 in the 1933 Series to help his team win the title. Ott was so beloved that he was voted the most popular sports figure of all time in a 1944 nationwide vote by those who bought war bonds.

When all was said and done, Mel Ott finished in 1947 with a career .304 batting average, 511 home runs, 1,860 RBI and 2,876 hits. He was the Giants player-manager from 1942 through 1947, manager in 1948, and continued working with Giants farm teams until 1950. Ott was elected to the Hall of Fame in 1951 while managing in the Pacific Coast League. He then became the broadcasting voice of the Detroit Tigers from 1956 until his untimely death at age 49. On November 14, 1958, Mel Ott and his wife, Mildred, were in a head-on collision while driving through dense fog in Mississippi and he died a week later from his injuries.

" *I never knew a baseball player who was so universally loved. Why even when he was playing against the Dodgers at Ebbets Field, he would be cheered and there are no more rabid fans than in Brooklyn.*"

– Leo Durocher, Hall of Famer

PSA/DNA Authentication Services Says:

Often referred to as one of the most simplistic-looking autographs in the hobby, Ott's signature remains the toughest of all the 500 Home Run Club members in this exclusive and desirable group. From his early career until about 1933, Ott often signed his full name "Melvin Ott," later shortening the first name in his signature to "Mel." Like many top sluggers, Ott had power in his pen, not just his bat, and his signature possessed an authority that is clear to the naked eye. Because single-signed baseballs are very tough to locate, they sell for noticeable premiums. Ott usually signed the side panel instead of the sweet spot, often adding a personalization. Despite being considered a relatively accommodating in-person and mail signer, Ott signatures remain in high demand today.

THE MOST WANTED 15

Ty Cobb

The meat of Ty Cobb's career is defined by mind-boggling statistics, equaled or surpassed by very few ballplayers in the history of the game. Surrounding these statistics are two questions: Would Ty Cobb have been as great a baseball player in the modern era of the game, and does Cobb's notorious personality diminish him as a ballplayer?

Question 1 is not as simple as it seems. Certainly, Cobb's style and stats say that he could have flourished in any era: 4,189 hits, .366 lifetime batting average, 12 batting titles, a .400-plus average three times, 897 steals, 9 seasons of 200-plus hits, a career OPS of .945, and only 681 Ks in 11,434 at-bats. Tyrus Raymond Cobb was not a "product of his era." The Hall of Famer's speed, defense, hitting prowess, and run-generating style would make him a top five player in any era, including today. The problem Cobb would have as a player today would be staying on the field. Modern baseball, like society, has become ultra-sensitive. Players are suspended, fined, or ejected for brushback pitches, umpire rhubarbs, and even minor fisticuffs. This stuff was the essence of Cobb's game. Clearly, he would have had to bottle some of his famed acid to remain active.

16   THE MOST WANTED

The Georgia Peach

Can you imagine "The Georgia Peach" participating in anger management classes sponsored by Major League Baseball? Some counselor surely would have ended up with the imprint of a Louisville Slugger on his forehead.

Question 2 is equally ponderous. Was Ty Cobb an evil man? A surface analysis would answer in the affirmative. He was selfish, arrogant, mean, ornery, racist, sadistic, and sullen. All of these traits played into his success. At only 18 years of age, Cobb endured the pain of his mother fatally shooting his beloved father, the result of domestic unrest. Perhaps from this experience, he was driven to beating his opponent no matter what. Some would say that Cobb played the game the way it was supposed to be played, using any motivation, dark or otherwise, to get an edge on the opposition. Others condemn him as a diamond devil, spikes-high Satan, or baseball's Beelzebub, but is this the real truth? More than one baseball historian has noted that the elderly Cobb regretted not making more friends in the game. At 74 years old, Cobb succumbed to cancer in 1961. The 1936 Hall of Fame inductee may have been the greatest baseball player ever, and the most difficult to figure. A singular player and personality, Ty Cobb was inscrutable to the last.

PSA/DNA Authentication Services Says:

On the field, Cobb had a menacing presence and fierce competitive nature that helped make him one of the most intimidating players in the game. Cobb's signing persona couldn't have been more different than his alter ego between the lines. One of the most active signers of his generation, Cobb was perhaps only surpassed by Babe Ruth in that regard. A prolific signer throughout his lifetime, Cobb's autograph can be found on virtually all major mediums. In fact, he enjoyed writing so much that he often sent full, handwritten letters back to fans. Even single-signed baseballs can often be found with dates inscribed. The two most common variations of his signature are simply "Ty Cobb" and the less frequently seen "Tyrus R. Cobb." Despite the large number of Cobb autographs, the great Hall of Famer is still a popular target for forgers. While you may encounter an occasional clubhouse version of Cobb's signature, the majority of the non-authentic autographs in the marketplace were done with malice.

Eddie Plank

The age-old phrase "Walk the plank" certainly does not apply to Hall of Fame pitcher, Eddie Plank. For him, walks were few and far between. In a terrific career, chiefly with the Philadelphia Athletics from 1901 to 1914, Plank walked just 1,072 batters in nearly 4,500 innings pitched. The reliable workhorse of Connie Mack's pitching stable, Plank completed 410 of the 529 games he started, which is still the all-time record for most complete games by a left-hander. Plank took consistency to an absurd level, winning 14 or more games every year between 1901 and 1916. He won 20 or more games eight times, with a phenomenal career ERA of 2.35. He was nicknamed "Gettysburg Eddie" after his beloved home city in Pennsylvania, but his Gettysburg Address preferred no score to fourscore. Plank posted 69 career shutouts, still an all-time record for left-handers, leading the American League in that category in both 1907 and 1911.

Plank was stalwart on some legendary A's teams sandwiching World Series victories in 1911 and 1913 between pennants in 1905 and 1914. That 1914 team was one of baseball's greatest ever, winning 99 games. In the World Series, however, the mighty A's fell to the Miracle Boston Braves in a four-game sweep. Plank lost 1–0 in Game Two, his final postseason appearance.

Known for his endless pre-pitch fidgets, Plank orchestrated a series of gyrations and motions before tossing each pitch. His time-consuming antics frustrated batters and were probably responsible for most of his 2,246 career strikeouts. The truth is that

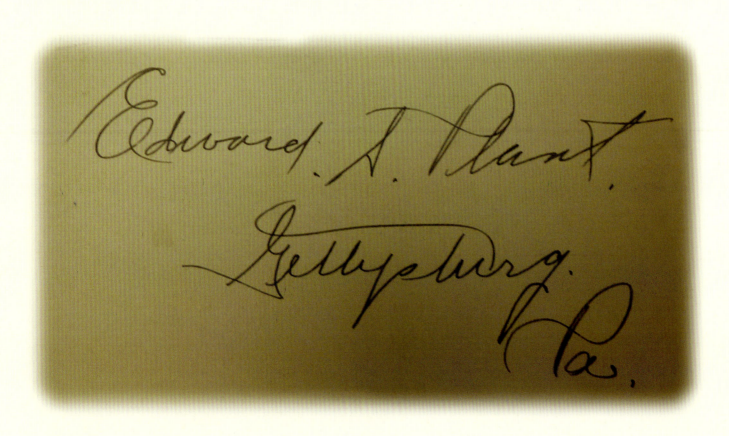

Gettysburg Eddie

> "*Eddie was one of the smartest left-handed pitchers in baseball. He was master of the cross-fire delivery and that was one of his big assets.*"
>
> - Connie Mack

Plank relied more on mind than muscle. He did not possess a lightning fastball or Bunyanesque strong arm. Instead, he painted corners and plied his craft with a level of intelligence befitting a Gettysburg Academy prep school student. Plank's sly and sidewinding style was often overshadowed by fireballers Walter Johnson and Smokey Joe Wood, but the skillful southpaw racked up 326 wins, the most by a left-hander until 1963, when Warren Spahn shattered the mark. In 1915, Plank jumped to the Federal League's St. Louis Terriers and won 21 games at the age of 39. He returned to the AL to pitch for the Browns in 1916 and 1917, and posted 21 more wins before retiring at 41 years old.

Plank returned to his Gettysburg farm, owned a Buick dealership, and sometimes gave tours of the historic battlefield. Edward Stewart Plank died of a stroke in 1926 at the age of 50. He was inducted into the Hall of Fame in 1947.

PSA/DNA Authentication Services Says:

Since Plank was a part of several World Series teams with the Philadelphia Athletics, a fairly decent number of authentic autographs are available in the marketplace. The Athletics organization was known for putting together reunions and Plank was a noted attendee, which gave the Hall of Fame pitcher ample opportunity to sign for fans. Most of these autographs were placed on team or multi-signed items, which means that single-signed baseballs remain very tough to locate. Plank's autograph was often "E. S. Plank," using initials for his first and middle name, which was a typical style used by players of the era. However, Plank's autograph remains challenging since he passed away at the age of 50 in 1926.

> "*I hated to see Plank out there on the mound as much as anyone! He was just a smart, smart pitcher.*"
>
> - Ty Cobb

10 Mickey Mantle

Just how great was the legendary Mickey Mantle? A close look at his accomplishments and contributions shows a player as great as any that ever donned a Major League uniform. Mickey Mantle played in 20 All-Star games and won the Triple Crown in 1956, batting .353 with 52 home runs and 130 RBI. He was named the American League's Most Valuable Player three times, won a Gold Glove, and led the league in home runs four times. He appeared in 12 World Series and won seven World Series titles. Mantle still holds the record for most home runs, walks, runs, extra base hits, total bases, and most RBI in the history of the World Series.

Was the Mick larger than life? No doubt. With 536 career home runs, 2,415 hits, a .298 lifetime batting average, and 1,509 RBI, his numbers are good, but nowhere near the top. Did other players put up better numbers? Without a doubt. Nevertheless, when you look at the entire body of his work, his contributions, and the effect he had on the game as a professional, a couple of words come to mind...complete, even perfect.

His personal life was a different story. The demons that dogged Mickey Mantle are well documented. In the end, when all was said and done, Mantle acknowledged he could have done things differently as a man.

As a player though, he was exceptional. Volumes could be written about all of Mantle's accomplishments. Considered the greatest switch-hitter of all time, the Mick used the entire outfield to his advantage. The prototypical power hitter, Mantle was known for his tape measure shots. In 1961, Mantle and Yankees teammate Roger Maris battled each other to break the single-season home run record held by the great Babe Ruth with his 60 home runs. An injury and illness late in the season short-circuited Mantle's quest and he finished with 54 homers, leaving Maris to break the record with 61.

A Yankee for his entire 18-year career, Mickey Charles Mantle played his last game in pinstripes when he was 36 years old. A variety of injuries hampered his play in the late 1960s, causing Mantle to retire in March of 1969. He was a first ballot choice for the Hall of Fame in 1974. After his playing days, Mantle tried several business ventures and later embraced the autograph hobby boom. After years of alcohol abuse and a liver transplant, Mickey Mantle passed away in 1995 at 63 years old.

PSA/DNA Authentication Services Says:

Babe Ruth may be the king of the autograph world, but Mantle is a close second in terms of popularity. Even though Mantle signed enough autographs to fill an abyss, his autograph remains one of the most heavily-

The Mick

forged signatures of all time. Due to the number of requests, Mantle used a clubhouse attendant to help meet demand, especially on team-signed items during his playing days. If an autograph could tell a story, Mantle's could. From a small-town prospect to the most idolized player in the Big Apple, his autograph started simple and evolved into one of the most distinctive and stylish on our "Top 100" list. From a simplistic, almost child-like signature, it evolved from the late 1940s to about 1955, a period when Mantle's style went through a metamorphosis. Around 1956, Mantle settled on a general style that he perfected over the course of his life. Mantle also helped revolutionize the business of autographs. He became a fixture on the autograph circuit and was one of the faces of mega-companies such as Upper Deck Authenticated during their launch. Mantle was known for adding some of the most colorful inscriptions you will see, often in a joking manner. While many of these are real, some are not, as forgers often add inscriptions of this nature to enhance the appeal of the piece. While Mantle was very cordial to fans, mail requests were often answered with stamps or secretarial signatures to meet the massive demand. One important note to keep in mind is that Mantle died in 1995, the year the new Gene Budig stamp was introduced on official American League baseballs, so the iconic Yankee was only alive for a short period of time while these were released. There are some authentic-signed examples, but they are very scarce.

Jackie Robinson

One of the most influential figures in the history of baseball, Jack Roosevelt Robinson broke the Major League color barrier when he was handpicked by Branch Rickey to join the Brooklyn Dodgers in 1947. A multi-sport star at UCLA, Robinson understood his role in changing the game and opening the door for future African-American players. Born in Cairo, Georgia, Robinson was raised in Pasadena, California, by his hardworking mother, and likely learned athletic skills from his older brother, Mack, who finished second to Jesse Owens in the 200-yard dash at the 1936 Olympics. After a stint in the Army, Robinson joined the Kansas City Monarchs of the Negro American League in 1945 and quickly rose to Rickey's attention.

Signed by the Dodgers, he was sent to the Montreal Royals for the 1946 season. On April 15, 1947, Robinson came up to the Dodgers to break baseball's long-held color barrier. The 28-year-old rookie batted .297, led the league with 29 stolen bases, and won the Rookie of the Year award, while withstanding the barbed attacks of racist teammates and foes with courage and dignity. In 1949, Robinson won the batting title, stroked 203 hits, and was named NL MVP. A versatile second baseman, he made the All-Star Team six times in his 10-year MLB career. Robinson posted a .311 career batting average and belted a career 137 dingers, but intelligent speed was his stock in trade. He tortured fielders and pitchers alike with non-stop motion on the basepaths. His signature hop while taking a lead is part of the visual fabric of the game. He led the league in stolen bases twice, and was legendary for his 19 career steals of home. He led his beloved Brooklyn "bums" to six pennants and one joyous World Series title in 1955.

However, Robinson's on-field exploits are not the whole story. Before he changed baseball, Robinson stood up to the United States Army, refusing to sit in the back of a segregated bus while in the military. After his playing days, he returned to his vocation of fighting prejudice and supporting rights of all minorities. He retired in 1957 and became the first African-American inductee to the Baseball Hall of Fame in 1962. Ten years later, he succumbed to diabetes at age 53, but his legacy lives on to this day. Robinson's number 42 was retired throughout baseball in 1997, but all players in MLB wear that number every year on April 15, Jackie Robinson Day, as a tribute to his courage.

Jackie

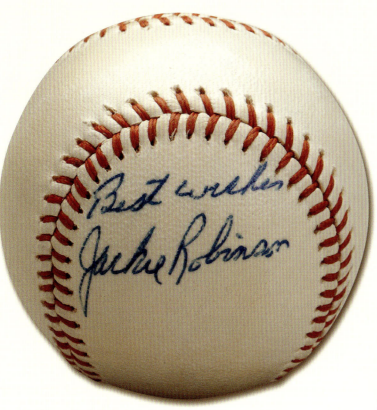

PSA/DNA Authentication Services Says:

With the adversity and turbulent times that Jackie Robinson endured, it would be understandable if the baseball icon was reclusive. Instead, the affable Robinson was extremely responsive to fans and collectors until his early death in 1972. Robinson regularly answered mail requests and was even a good signer as a collegiate athlete at UCLA, and as a Minor Leaguer. As Robinson became popular at the big league level, he did use a ghost signer from time to time and, like other players during the era, a clubhouse attendant would often add his name to team balls. Finding an authentic Robinson signature on a 1950s Brooklyn Dodger team ball can be challenging. After his career was over, Robinson stayed active and even attended many baseball games. Later in life, his declining health didn't stop Robinson from continuing to accommodate fans in public settings.

THE MOST WANTED

12 Cy Young

> "One of the fellows called me Cyclone, but finally shortened it to 'Cy' and it's been that ever since."
>
> – Cy Young

William Shakespeare penned the line, "What's in a name?" Well, let's examine the name Denton True "Cy" Young. Certainly, when he pitched, not too many batters were "Denton" the outfield walls. As for True, was there a more accurate hurler in baseball during the prime of his career? Cy was short for Cyclone, which is what occurred each time his 6-foot, 2-inch and 210 pound frame unleashed a pitch. And finally, Young, what he seemed to forever be, pitching effectively well into his 40s.

Name aside, Cy Young opens any discussion of the best pitchers ever. He was born in Gilmore, Ohio, in 1867. A quarter century later, he won 36 games with a 1.93 ERA for the National League's Cleveland Spiders. It was the first of Young's five 30-win seasons. He won 241 games in nine seasons for Cleveland, and then was assigned to the St. Louis Perfectos in 1899 and 1900. He would eventually jump to the AL's Boston Americans, where he won another 192 games over eight seasons. Along the way to immortality and a certain coveted pitching award that bears his name, Young compiled brain-crushing stats. He still holds the all-time record for wins (511), complete games (749), and innings pitched (7,356), and finished his career with a 2.63 ERA, and a .618 winning percentage. Young only pitched in the postseason twice. His 1892 Spiders lost the Championship Series to the Boston Beaneaters, and his 1903 Boston Americans beat Pittsburgh to win the first modern-day World Series. In 1901, the American League's inaugural season, Young won the pitching Triple Crown, leading the Junior Circuit in wins, strikeouts, and ERA. He tossed three no-hitters in his career and, according to the Baseball Hall of Fame, notched the first perfect game of the 20th century on May 4, 1904.

Cyclone

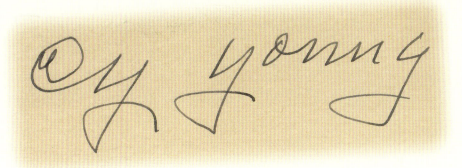

PSA/DNA Authentication Services Says:

Much like early 20th century icons Ty Cobb and Babe Ruth, Cy Young was a very willing signer and one of the first big stars to embrace the demand from the collecting public. By the 1930s and during his post-playing days, Young was on the receiving end of many autograph requests through the mail. To the delight of baseball fans across the country, Young managed to respond to a large number of them, which means that a reasonable number of surviving Young examples are available today for autograph collectors. Over time and by the 1950s, Young's large, confident signature became more labored in appearance, but he continued to answer the call as a signer until he passed away.

The trailblazing does not stop there, as Young is credited with introducing the changeup to Major League Baseball. Young led his league in shutouts seven times, but did not necessarily blow hitters away. In fact, he led the National League in hits-allowed in 1896 with 477, and surrendered more hits than innings-pitched 11 times in his 22-year career. Still, when an out was needed, Cy usually got it. Young ended his career in familiar cities, but different leagues, playing for the AL's Cleveland Naps and the NL's Boston Rustlers. He was elected to the Hall of Fame in 1937 and died in 1955, at age 88. What's in a name? Well, a player by any other name than Denton True "Cy" Young has never pitched as sweet.

> *"All us Youngs could throw. I used to kill squirrels with a stone when I was a kid, and my granddad once killed a turkey buzzard on the fly with a rock."*
>
> - Cy Young

Jimmie Foxx

With his majestic home runs and magnificent play, James Emory "Jimmie" Foxx rose to the top of the baseball world but, in the end, could not fight the demons that haunted him.

The kid from Sudlersville, Maryland, excelled at just about every sport he played. He made his Major League debut with the Athletics as a 17-year-old in 1925. Foxx was to be the next great catcher in the league, but the A's also had a catcher who had Hall of Fame talent—Mickey Cochrane. Manager Connie Mack's solution was to move Foxx over to first base because his bat was just too valuable.

Foxx had a very good year in 1928, but he exploded onto the scene in 1929, batting .354 with 33 home runs

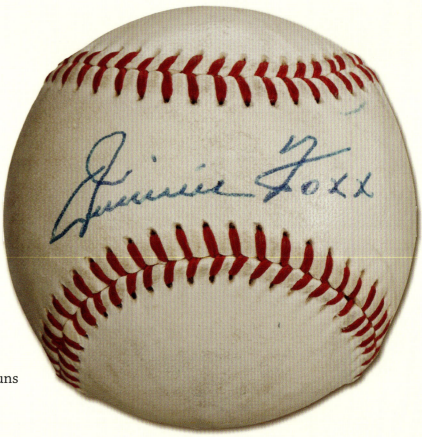

and 118 RBI. The 1929 A's with Foxx, Lefty Grove, Al Simmons, Rube Walberg, and Howard Ehmke went on to win 104 games and the World Series.

The Athletics repeated in 1930 with a 102 win season and another world championship. Again, Foxx led the charge with a .335 average to go along with 37 homers. That was the last Series win for the A's for 42 years.

Also known as "The Beast" for his powerful swing, Foxx continued to flourish. His best year, arguably, was in 1932 when he hit an amazing 58 home runs and batted .364. Along with Ruth and Gehrig, Jimmie Foxx became one of the most feared hitters in baseball. Once the A's began to lose money during the Great Depression, Connie Mack dismantled the team. Foxx moved to the Boston Red Sox where he continued to dominate the league, averaging 36 home runs over the next six years. After a two-year stint with the Cubs, his amazing career finally came to an end in 1945 with the Phillies of the National League. Jimmie Foxx racked up 3 MVPs, 9

Double-X

All-Star appearances, 2 batting titles, 4 home run titles, a Triple Crown, and 534 home runs over his 20-year career.

The affable, popular slugger suffered a beaning in exhibition play in 1934, after which he began drinking to dull the pain. By the 1940s Foxx was drinking heavily, which affected his play. After retiring, he initially dabbled in managing and coaching. Inducted to the Hall of Fame in 1951, Foxx was down on his luck by the late-1950s due to bad business investments and drinking. Sadly, the end came in 1967 when the 59-year-old Foxx choked on a piece of meat while at a restaurant.

PSA/DNA Authentication Services Says:

Jimmie Foxx was an accessible autograph signer and his autograph style changed dramatically over the course of his lifetime. In addition to changes in shape and style, especially the J in his first name, Foxx would spell his first name differently from "Jim" to "Jimmy" to "Jimmie." Every so often, Foxx allegedly used his brother to sign in his place, but the legendary slugger signed most of his own autograph requests. Along with Mel Ott, Foxx is one of the toughest 500 Home Run Club autographs to acquire, especially on single-signed baseballs. While Foxx was known as "The Beast" on the field, this Hall of Famer was one of the most affable and obliging signers of his era.

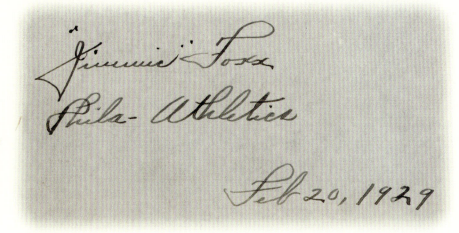

14 Walter Johnson

Washington Senators hurler extraordinaire Walter "Big Train" Johnson was the gold standard for pitchers in Major League Baseball for two decades. His kindly face and steely eyes masked the assassin within. Walter Perry Johnson was death to hitters, an unstoppable force on the hill who used intimidation to pile up some mind-boggling statistics: 417 wins, a miniscule career ERA of 2.17, and 3,509 strikeouts. However, that just scratches the surface.

Johnson led the American League in wins six times, but just as amazing were his win totals in years he *did not* lead the league. Among those totals are 25 twice, 33 and 23. Johnson's nickname could just as easily have been "K." He led his league in strikeouts a total of 12 times, eight of those being consecutive years between 1912 and 1919. Johnson did not post an ERA higher than 3.00 until his 14th season in the majors, at age 32. An incredible workhorse, he led the American League in innings pitched five times, including a baffling 370 IP in 1910 and 371 in 1914. Choosing Johnson's best season is nearly impossible. How about 1913 when he went 36–7 with a 1.14 ERA, 243 Ks, 29 complete games, 11 shutouts, and 346 innings pitched—all league-bests. Don't like that one? Let's try 1912 when he was 33–12 and struck out 303 batters in 369 innings.

Johnson was consistent. He won 25 games at the wet-behind-the-ears age of 22 and won 23 games at the over-the-hill age of 36. In between, he redefined the word "greatness" when it came to pitchers. Johnson's fearsome fortitude on the hill was in stark contrast to his off-field demeanor. Known as one of the game's true gentlemen, Johnson grew up in the lush fields of Kansas, but as a teenager moved with his family to southern California. The year-round baseball out West helped hone his game and he developed his famous sidearm delivery fastball. Johnson led the Senators to a World Series title in 1924, retired in 1927, managed the

The Big Train

> "*His fastball looked about the size of a watermelon seed and it hissed at you as it passed.*"
> – Ty Cobb

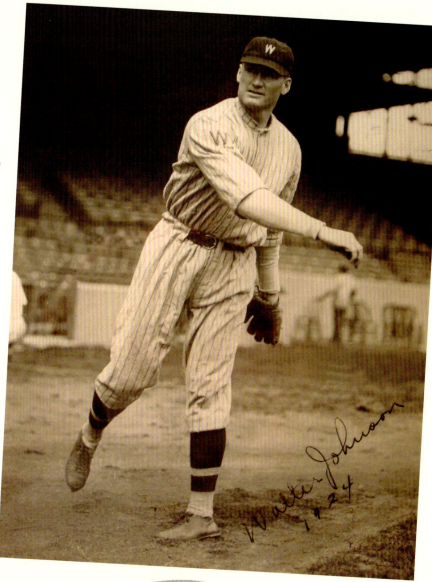

Senators and Indians, and later was a broadcaster for the Senators. A member of the inaugural Hall of Fame class in 1936, Johnson passed away in 1946, at age 59. Walter "Big Train" Johnson blazed a power pitching trail that, to this day, only a scant few have been able to follow.

PSA/DNA Authentication Services Says:

A truly intimidating presence on the mound, Johnson could deliver an overpowering fastball with a whip-like delivery. Despite his reputation as a fierce competitor, Johnson was considered one of the most courteous and respectful players in the game, and was one of the more accommodating signers of his time. Most mediums can be found, but Johnson single-signed baseballs are very difficult to locate in high-grade. While he was a responsive signer, his early passing limits the number of authentic examples found in the hobby today. Most of the signatures available in the marketplace were signed after Johnson's playing days, when autograph collecting became more popular. Johnson possessed an extremely legible signature, one where you can decipher every letter in his name. It was both neat and consistent. He remained an active signer until the year of his passing. In fact, there are some known dated examples from that year, 1946.

Napoleon Lajoie

One of the greatest hitters in baseball history specializing in base hits, doubles, and triples, Nap Lajoie had a keen eye at the plate, striking out just 347 times in

9,589 at-bats. Lajoie had over 200 hits four times, and was a base-swiping, run-scoring machine. A versatile performer with speed, smarts, and attitude, Lajoie primarily played second base, leading the league in fielding percentage six times at that position. Despite this excellence, Lajoie never saw the light of baseball's shining event, the World Series.

After just three months in the minors, the Woonsocket, Rhode Island, native came up to Philadelphia's National League Phillies, batting .326 in 1896. The likeable young superstar jumped to the newly formed American League Philadelphia Athletics in 1901 and posted a banner season. That year, Lajoie led the American League with his career best .426 batting average and 145 runs scored, and also led the new league in hits, doubles, home runs, RBI, and slugging. He started the 1902 season with Connie Mack's A's, but was forced to leave the team when the Phillies secured a Pennsylvania Supreme Court injunction banning Lajoie from playing in the state for any team but the Phillies. Lajoie signed with the American League Bronchos and would spend the next 13 seasons in Cleveland, even managing them from 1905 to 1909.

How popular was Lajoie in Cleveland? The team actually changed its name to the "Naps" in honor of Lajoie after the 1902 season. The 6-foot, 1-inch and 195 pound Lajoie hit over .300 eleven of his thirteen seasons with the Naps, and is recognized as one of the stars who brought credibility to the junior circuit American League. Lajoie also changed the game when the blue

Nap

dye in his game socks infected a spike wound causing blood poisoning. Because of this, teams began wearing sanitary white socks for games. Known for his umpire rhubarbs and a controversial battle with Ty Cobb for the 1910 AL batting crown, in which 35-year-old Lajoie hit .384 and finished a contested second place to the 23-year-old Georgia Peach, Lajoie ended his career back with the A's in 1915 and 1916. He finished his 21-year MLB career with a .338 batting average, and led the league five times in that category. Lajoie went on to play and manage in the minors for two seasons. He later worked in the rubber business and became active in local Ohio politics. He was inducted into the Hall of Fame in 1937. Napoleon Lajoie passed away in 1959 at age 85.

PSA/DNA Authentication Services Says:

Lajoie was one of the more responsive signers, especially via the mail, during a period when a small percentage of players were very active. Earlier in his career and up until the mid-to-late 1930s, Lajoie would often use his full first name "Napoleon" when signing. After that point, Lajoie started signing items as "Larry" much more frequently. The stellar hitter would often add a date to his autographs as well. This became an even more common practice after his retirement as a player. For those collectors seeking single-signed baseballs, while some do exist, they are still very scarce. This is mainly a result of Lajoie's death in 1959, before the idea of making baseballs the preferred medium became extremely popular in the following decades.

Derek Jeter

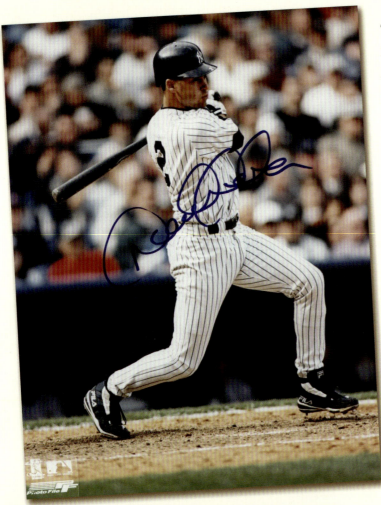

The Yankees starting shortstop for 20 seasons (1995–2014), Jeter batted a career .310. He eclipsed the 200 hit plateau eight times and led the league in that category with 219 in 1999. The 14-time All-Star was a run-scoring machine, topping 100 runs 13 times. He played for some of the greatest teams in baseball history and, along with Bernie Williams, Mariano Rivera, and Jorge Posada, formed the foundation of a Yankees dynasty that would win four World Series in five seasons from 1996–2000. In 2001, the Yankees lost one of the most memorable Fall Classics in seven games to the Arizona Diamondbacks, but that series took a backseat to the 9/11 aftermath that permeated New York and the nation. Jeter, the Yankees captain, was front and center, visiting families and local public safety personnel, and helping to ease the wounds of a city and a country. This was the essence of Derek Jeter.

He added another championship crown in 2009, batting .308 in his 33 postseason series. In 158 postseason games, basically a season, he smacked

New Jersey-born and Michigan-bred, Derek Sanderson Jeter is on that short list of truly legendary Yankees greats. His career is less about statistics and more about style. Unfazed by the New York spotlight, Jeter was equally adept in the arena of play as he was among the Big Apple glitterati. Make no mistake, however, Derek Jeter was toughness and hustle incarnate. Who could forget his unfathomable relay flip throw that saved the Yankees from elimination in Game Three of the 2001 ALDS vs. Oakland, or his valiant head-first dive into the third-base bleachers in Yankee Stadium in the heat of a 2004 pennant race vs. Boston? Even in his very last at-bat at Yankee Stadium, Jeter shined, knocking in the game-winning run vs. Baltimore in 2014.

Mr. November

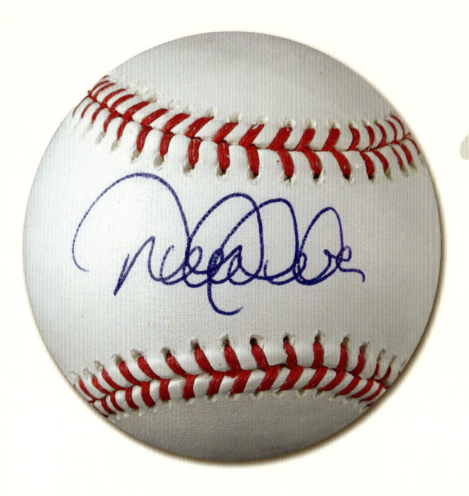

"*For those who say today's game can't produce legendary players, I have two words: Derek Jeter.*"

– George Steinbrenner, Yankees Owner

20 home runs and knocked in 61 runs. He hit over .400 in a series nine times, reaching .500 in both the 2002 and 2006 ALDS. His after-midnight home run to win Game Four of the 2001 World Series earned him the Mr. November moniker. Derek Jeter deserves his place alongside Ruth, Gehrig, DiMaggio, Mantle, and other Yankees legends. In fact, these icons should be proud to share pinstriped immortality with Jeter.

PSA/DNA Authentication Services Says:

In terms of popularity, Derek Jeter was the Michael Jordan of baseball during his era. Early in his career, Jeter signed with the noted collectibles company Steiner Sports, which provided authentic Jeter autographs to the hobby. Even though he became popular with fans almost instantaneously, Jeter remained a good signer at the ballpark and very cordial with the public. Since his rise to stardom came so quickly and large numbers of autographs were produced by the legendary Yankee, early signatures such as those signed in high school through his first year at the Major League level, tend to sell for a premium. While some baseball players tend to change the appearance of their autograph over time, sometimes dramatically, Jeter has remained relatively consistent since 1995. Despite the large number of authentic Jeter autographs in the marketplace, he remains one of the most heavily-forged athletes of the modern era.

17 Addie Joss

While some MLB stars shine brightly in the baseball galaxy for an eternity, Addie Joss was a comet, one that streaked through the game and disappeared quickly,

and tragically. He broke in with the Cleveland Bronchos in 1902 and won an impressive 17 games with an ERA of 2.77 and a league-leading five shutouts. In 1903, with his team renamed the Naps, he proved to be no fluke, winning 18 games and lowering his ERA to a paltry 2.19. Joss began a streak of four consecutive seasons with 20+ wins in 1905, highlighted by a 27–11 mark in 1907. Along the way, he baffled batters with ERA's under 2.00 in 1904 and 1906 through 1909. A lanky, long-armed, 6-foot, 3-inch, and 185 pound Wisconsin boy, Adrian Joss made minced meat of batters with his sidearm delivery and twirling, twisting off-speed junk. Of his 160 career victories, 45 were shutouts, proof positive of his diamond dominance.

In a memorable first career start, on April 26, 1902, Joss held a no-hitter vs. the St. Louis Browns through five innings. A bloop single by the Browns Jesse Burkett killed the no-no in the sixth, but Joss posted a one-hit, 3–0 shutout, and added a double at the plate for good measure. A fine righty, Joss was a fine writer as well. In 1906 he began an off-season career as a popular sports scribe for the *Toledo News Bee*, penning columns and commentaries on baseball. On October 2, 1908, with his

The Human Hairpin

Naps in the thick of the American League pennant race, Joss fashioned his best game as a pro, a perfect game, with a 1–0 victory over the White Sox. Joss won 24 games that season, walking just 30 men in 325 innings pitched. Alas, Cleveland fell short of its World Series dreams and Joss would never again get a sniff of the postseason.

The 1910 season began well for Joss with an April no-hitter against the White Sox, but his baseball career began to unravel when a torn ligament in his right elbow curtailed his season in July. On April 3, 1911, Joss fainted before an exhibition game. Diagnosed with pleurisy, the baseball world was rocked when Joss died suddenly on April 14 of tubercular meningitis at 31 years old. In July of that year, stars from the American League came together to play in an exhibition game to raise more than $12,000 for Joss's widow and two children. In 1978, the Veterans Committee elected Joss to the Hall of Fame, a fitting tribute to this star-crossed star.

"*Joss sort of hid the ball on you. One moment, you'd be squinting at a long, graceful windup and the next instant, out of nowhere, the ball was hopping across the plate – and a lot of us standing flat-footed with our bat glued to our shoulders.*"

– Bobby Wallace, Hall of Famer

PSA/DNA Authentication Services Says:

Of all the great rarities on our "Top 100" list, Joss may be the one autograph deserving of the throne. While there is very little known about his personal signing habits, Joss played during a time when signing autographs simply wasn't part of the baseball culture. In the off-season, Joss worked as a sportswriter, which would lead many to believe that at least some documents would have survived the test of time. Remarkably, his writing experience did not lead to any additional examples of his signature. To complicate matters further, Joss passed away at the age of 31, while arguably at the height of his popularity. At this time, no single-signed baseballs are known of Joss, leaving many collectors frustrated. The autograph image featured on the facing page is a facsimile.

18 Sandy Koufax

When it comes to missing the proverbial boat, both the New York Giants and Pittsburgh Pirates are right up there, failing to sign one of the most prolific pitchers in the history of the game. Both teams had the opportunity to sign the skinny Jewish kid from Brooklyn but did not pull the trigger fast enough. The Brooklyn Dodgers signed the 19-year-old, left-handed pitcher in 1954 and reaped the benefits.

During the early years of his career, Sanford "Sandy" Koufax played sparingly. He got so frustrated at his own wildness that he almost decided to throw in the towel. Then, with the help of catcher Norm Sherry, who made the suggestion that Koufax take a few miles off his fastball, it all fell into place. Koufax was actually very good in 1961 and 1962, after he figured out how to get the ball over the plate, and from 1963 through 1966, Koufax threw BBs. We would be hard pressed to find a pitcher who, for four straight years, was as dominant as Sandy Koufax.

Over his relatively brief 12-year career, Koufax was a six-time All-Star and pitched four no-hitters, including a perfect game against the Cubs on September 9, 1965. The three-time Cy Young award winner was named National League MVP in 1963, and MLB Player of the Year in 1963 and 1965. A three-time NL Triple Crown winner, he led the league in ERA for five consecutive seasons (1962–1966). Koufax pitched in four World Series, leading the Dodgers to three Series wins (1959, 1963, 1965), and was named World Series MVP in both 1963 and 1965. The four-time league leader in strikeouts, Koufax simply dominated batters.

Many people don't realize that for much of his career, Koufax pitched in great pain. Between wrist, elbow, and various hand injuries, he was wrapped in ice pretty much every day. At the top of his game, Koufax cut his career short in 1966

The Left Arm Of God

after he developed traumatic arthritis in his elbow. With a 27–9 record, a 1.73 ERA, and a World Series start that year, Sandy Koufax called it quits, no longer able to put up with the pain. Some say that Koufax had rheumatoid arthritis, a crippling disease, and that makes his story even more remarkable. Following his career, Koufax became a broadcaster for NBC, and has worked for the Dodgers in various capacities. He was elected to the Hall of Fame in 1972.

PSA/DNA Authentication Services Says:

Koufax has always been known for living a very private life and that nature carried over into the hobby for a long time, leaving collectors without nearly enough autographs to meet the demand. That changed to some degree in recent years as the legendary lefty has signed a little more frequently in private settings in response to increasing demand. Koufax's signature has stayed fairly consistent over the years, with slight variations to the S in "Sandy." His autograph has also remained attractive and legible. While you don't tend to see many clubhouse versions of his signature, collectors might encounter a secretarial signature from time to time, especially when it comes to autographs that were obtained through the mail in the 1980s.

Roger Maris

In a magical 1961 Yankees season, Roger Maris went head-to-head with teammate Mickey Mantle to challenge and break Babe Ruth's 1927 single-season record of 60 home runs. The battle was intense and, incredibly, the New York fans and press actually wanted Maris to fail. After all, if the Babe's record had to be broken, it should be by Mantle, not some kid from Fargo, North Dakota. Injured in September, Mantle finished with 54 homers. Maris kept going, and on October 1, 1961, the final day of the season, he hit a shot off Boston's Tracy Stallard for home run number 61. Maris held the record three years longer than Ruth, but in 1998 Sammy Sosa and Mark McGuire claimed it, and Barry Bonds captured it in 2001. With those names come the controversy of steroids and performance enhancing drugs, and many feel Maris still owns the record.

A solid team player both offensively and defensively, Roger Eugene Maris never hit for high averages but always contributed to winning pennants and championships. Whether it was with Cleveland, Kansas City, the Yankees, or the Cardinals, Maris put the team first. Considered a hot prospect with Kansas City, Maris was acquired by the Yankees in December of 1959. He came through with AL MVP seasons in both 1960 and 1961. The 1960 Gold Glove winner and four-time All-Star went about his business quietly and efficiently. He twice led the league in RBI (1960, 1961) and, as right fielder, he led the league in fielding percentage in 1960, 1964, and 1967. Maris played in seven World Series over his career, with title wins in 1961, 1962, and 1967.

The shy left-handed slugger hated the big city media spotlight and was happy to move on to the Cardinals following the 1966 season. Maris helped St. Louis beat the Red Sox in the 1967 World Series, and contributed to their pennant win in 1968. Often overshadowed by famous teammates, Maris more than held his own as a contributor on some star-studded teams. After an injury-plagued 1968 season, Maris left baseball to own a successful Anheuser-Busch beer distributorship in Florida. He was diagnosed with lymphoma in 1984 and passed away in 1985 at the young age of 51. Roger Maris is right up there on the list of very good players overlooked by the Hall of Fame. With a .260 lifetime batting average, 275 home runs and 850 RBI the experts are probably right. However, Roger Maris was a special player. Just look back at that wonderful 1961 season.

Maris

PSA/DNA Authentication Services Says:

One of the few non-Hall of Famers in our "Top 100," Roger Maris' signature will always have a place in most serious collections. Beyond his epic home run chase in 1961 and his back-to-back MVP awards, Maris was a real fan-favorite. By the time Maris arrived in New York, his early signature style had virtually disappeared. He began signing with more authority and pressure, which was often evident when signing a piece with Mantle. Maris was very accommodating to fans, both in person and via the mail. There was, however, a period during the 1960s when a clubhouse attendant would regularly sign Maris' name on team balls and a secretary would often handle his mail requests. While Maris was not a regular on the show circuit, he did occasionally attend a show prior to his death in 1985.

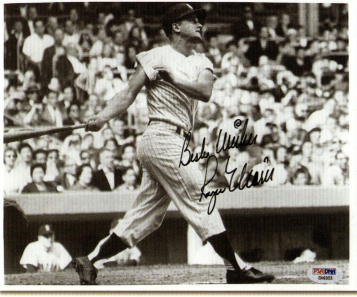

" *Roger Maris was as good a man and as good a ballplayer as there ever was.*"

— Mickey Mantle

Ted Williams

The Splendid Splinter, Teddy Ballgame, The Kid, call him what you like, Ted Williams was one of the greatest hitters of all time. A four-time home run champ and six-time AL batting champ, Williams won two Triple Crowns, was the American League MVP twice, and a 19-time All-Star. As a 20-year-old rookie outfielder for the Red Sox in 1939, Williams had 145 RBI, a rookie record that still stands to this day. Over his 19-year career with Boston, he was OBP leader 12 times. He still holds the record for highest career on-base percentage with .482, and let's not forget his .344 lifetime batting average and 521 career home runs. Along the way, he batted .406 in 1941, and is the last player to hit that rarified milestone. Think how great his numbers would have been had he not missed most of five seasons in his prime to serve as a Marine Corps flight instructor in World War II and a decorated combat pilot in the Korean War.

A true enigma, Ted Williams had a love-hate relationship with the Boston media and the fans. Because he was unfiltered in his comments, Williams was sometimes cheered and many times booed. Once booed, he vowed never to tip his cap and sometimes even got into shouting matches with fans. On the other hand, he was generous with the needy and spent countless hours with Jimmy Fund children who were battling cancer at the Dana-Farber Cancer Institute in Boston. Williams' last career at-bat in 1960 pretty much tells the whole story. After going yard one last time, he refused to come out of the dugout to be acknowledged by the fans. That was Ted being Ted.

After his retirement, Williams managed the Washington Senators several seasons and was named AL Manager of the Year in 1969. His ticket to Cooperstown was punched on the first ballot in 1966. He developed heart problems later in life and succumbed in 2002, at age 83, after suffering a stroke and a series of heart attacks. Even in death, controversy surrounded Theodore Samuel Williams. His children decided to have him cryogenically

The Splendid Splinter

items on the Hall of Famer's behalf. The Boston Red Sox were also known to occasionally use a stamp during the same time period. While playing and long after his career, Williams utilized a secretary to help sign some fan mail and occasionally employed a stamp. Williams possessed a beautiful autograph, but after suffering a series of strokes in the mid-1990s, the great slugger struggled to sign items, such as baseballs, with the same precision. That said, Williams continued to sign large numbers of autographs up until the time of his death. One of the most forged figures in the hobby, huge volumes of Williams counterfeits were seized as part of the late-1990s FBI sting referred to as Operation Bullpen.

frozen in the event that science could develop a way to bring him back to life. So there you have it. Ted Williams was loved by some and disliked by others. He was a philanthropist, a war hero, and a great ballplayer. Today he sits in a laboratory waiting to rise again to become one of the greatest hitters of all time. Don't bet against him. Ted usually got his way.

PSA/DNA Authentication Services Says:

Along with DiMaggio and Mantle, Ted Williams was one of the baseball legends that became part of the hobby boom in the 1980s and beyond. He worked with industry powerhouse Upper Deck Authenticated around their launch in the early 1990s, and later created his own brand by signing thousands of items for his family business. From the beginning, Williams showcased a confident-looking autograph, which coincided with his personality. During the 1940s and 1950s, a clubhouse attendant would often add Williams to team-signed

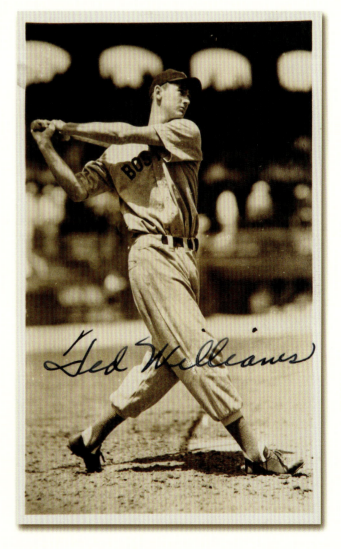

Baseball's Hall of Fame

WALTER JOHNSON'S FIRST MAJOR LEAGUE GAME

Back in 1907, a travelling salesman "sat in" at a sand lot ball game out in Weiser, Idaho, watching a tall, angular youngster whizzing the ball over the plate with the speed of a rifle bullet, and muttered:

"A wonder—a wonder."

So the salesman, who was a friend of Joe Cantillion, the Washington manager, wired to the chieftain of the Senator club:

"Come out and grab the greatest pitcher in baseball today."

Cantillion didn't answer the wire. He received too many invitations each to grab sand-lot phenoms to get excited about the advice of his friend, even though he had a lot of faith in that salesman's baseball judgment. But when Cantillion's friend continued sending along telegrams, Pango Joe sent Cliff Blankenship out to the Idaho team to look over the phenomenal pitcher in question.

A few days later, Cantillion received a telegram from Blankenship:

"Advise signing the pitcher. He looks great."

So Cantillion wired back:

"All right; sign him."

And that was how Walter Johnson became a member of the Washington Senators, and got his chance to star so creditably in Baseball's Hall of Fame. Later that same year, 1907, he pitched his first game in fast company, winning his debut.

Washington vs. Detroit, at Washington, August 2. Detroit won both games, and went into first place in the race. In the first game, Johnson, the Idaho wonder, made his debut with Washington and pitched a good game. Siever's effectiveness, however, enabled Detroit to win. The score:

WASHINGTON (AL)

	AB	R	H	PO	A	E
Otis Clymer, LF	4	0	0	2	0	0
Bob Ganley, RF	3	1	0	1	0	0
Jim Delehanty, 1B	3	0	1	10	1	0
Charles Jones, CF	4	0	1	2	0	0
George Nill, 2B	4	0	1	3	2	1
Dave Altizer, SS	4	0	0	5	1	1
Bill Shipke, 3B	3	0	0	1	6	0
Mike Hayden, C	2	0	0	3	0	0
WALTER JOHNSON, P	2	1	0	0	3	0
*Cliff Blankenship	1	0	0	0	0	0
†Harry Gehring	1	0	0	0	0	0
Totals	29	2	5	27	13	2

*Batted for JOHNSON in the eighth inning.
†Batted for Hayden in the ninth inning.

DETROIT (AL)

	AB	R	H	PO	A	E
Davey Jones, LF	4	0	0	3	0	0
Bill Coughlin, 3B	4	0	1	1	3	0
Sam Crawford, CF	4	1	1	3	0	0
Ty Cobb, RF	4	1	1	3	0	0
Claude Roseman, 1B	4	0	2	9	0	0
Tom Downs, 2B	4	1	1	3	1	0
Charley Schmidt, C	3	0	0	3	1	0
Charley O'Leary, SS	3	0	1	2	2	0
Ed Siever, P	3	0	0	0	2	0

2

The Early Years (1800s–1920)

★ ★ ★ ★ ★ ★ ★ ★ ★ ★ ★ ★ ★

The men who developed the rules of the game, the field generals who implemented the rules and devised the strategies, as well as the players who blazed the trail for future generations make up this group of interesting individuals. Alexander Cartwright, Mike "King" Kelly, John McGraw, and Albert Spalding are just a few of the baseball trailblazers from the early years of our National Pastime who are featured here along with their very desirable autographs that are, in some cases, exceptionally rare.

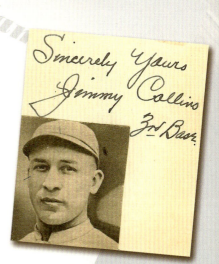

Grover Cleveland Alexander

The man they called Old Pete was actually quite young when he first made his mark in the big leagues in 1911 with the Phillies. As a 24-year-old rookie, Alexander enjoyed one of the great MLB debuts of all time with 28 wins, 31 complete games, 7 shutouts, and 367 innings pitched—all league highs. Over the next nine seasons, Alexander would establish himself as one of the game's all-time greats.

In his first 10 seasons, he led the National League in innings pitched seven times and complete games six times. He was also the senior circuit's top strikeout artist between 1911 and 1920. In 1915, Alexander led the Phillies to the World Series, posting a 31–10 record and a 1.22 ERA. Philly lost to the Red Sox, but Alexander registered a 1.53 ERA in two starts. In 1916, Alexander again won more than 30 games and set the Major League record for shutouts in a season with 16, but it would be 10 seasons before he would get another shot at a world title. This time, he made good, going 2–0 with a 1.33 ERA as the 1926 Cardinals defeated the Yanks in seven games.

While Alexander remained a viable pitcher into his 40s, there is a clear demarcation between

Old Pete

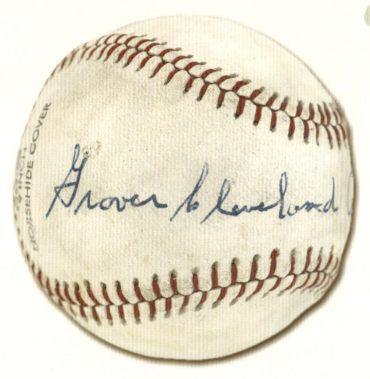

"He [Grover Alexander] could pitch into a tin can. His control was always remarkable – the finest I have ever seen."

– Grantland Rice, Sportswriter

the first and second halves of his career, largely due to his service in World War I, where he injured his right arm, developed epilepsy, and became an alcoholic. After 27 wins in 1920, he would win 20 or more games only twice: 22 with the 1923 Cubbies, and 21 with the 1927 Cards.

In addition to hitters, Alexander battled the scars of a brutal life. Four of his twelve siblings died as youngsters. When the game he helped build abandoned him after the 1930 season, he endured horrific physical, mental, marital, and financial woes that would last through his Hall of Fame induction in 1938 and continue until his death in 1950, at age 63. Grover Cleveland Alexander's father named his son after a United States President and dreamed of his boy becoming a lawyer. Old Pete may not have earned a diploma, but on the hill, he had strong closing arguments and laid down the law to opposing batters for two decades.

PSA/DNA Authentication Services Says:

Grover Cleveland Alexander had his share of off-the-field troubles, but that didn't stop the legendary pitcher from altering the formation of his signature in a significant way during his lifetime. That said, Alexander would vary how much of his name he would sign at times. You will see everything from Alexander's full name to only "Grover Cleveland" to just a simple "GC" in the hobby today. When Alexander did sign his full name, it was one of the more appealing and flowing signatures of the era. If you could catch Alexander in person, he was often an accommodating signer, but tracking him down to begin with could be a real obstacle. Alexander was fairly consistent about responding to mail requests as well, but as a result of his passing in 1950, Alexander autographs remain challenging for the collector today.

Adrian Anson

Considered by many to be the greatest superstar of 19th century baseball, Adrian Constantine Anson made his mark on our National Pastime during a career that spanned 27 years. The first player to achieve 3,000 hits, Anson was a force with his stick, batting over .300 in all but three seasons.

As a 19-year-old rookie with the Rockford Forest Citys of the National Association, Anson batted .325 in 1871, firmly establishing himself as a budding megastar. After one season, Anson hooked up with the Philadelphia Athletics where he averaged .363 over the next four years. He was signed by the White Stockings of the newly formed National League in 1876 and was named captain/manager in 1879. Now known as "Cap," Anson led Chicago to five pennants between 1880 and 1886. He was instrumental in modernizing the game and increasing its popularity with the public. A stickler on conditioning, he implemented infield drills and spring training. Anson developed innovative, aggressive baseball techniques like base stealing, refined infield play, use of the hit and run, and pitching rotation.

After Anson became part-owner of the team in 1890, they became known as "Anson's Colts." The "Colts" moniker lasted until Cap Anson's retirement in 1897 when the team became known as the "Orphans" as their leader of 19 years had left them behind after compiling a 1282–932 won-loss record. Eventually, the team name evolved to the Chicago Cubs. Playing at first base for his entire time in Chicago, the 45-year-old Anson retired holding several MLB records, and still holds the Chicago franchise record for hits, runs scored, doubles, and RBI.

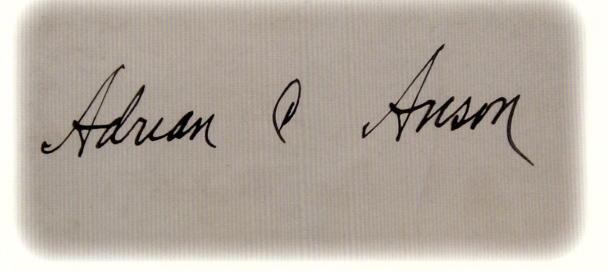

Cap

Sometimes referred to as "The Father of Baseball Segregation," Anson was a factor in keeping African-American players out of the Big Leagues. He refused to play in games if Black players were on the opposing roster. He was playing during the era when segregation became legal throughout the country, not just in baseball. After his playing days, Anson dabbled in politics and owned a semi-pro baseball team among other business ventures. He even tried his hand in Vaudeville later on in life. Adrian "Cap" Anson died at the age of 69 in Chicago in 1922. He was elected to the Hall of Fame in 1939.

PSA/DNA Authentication Services Says:

Cap Anson's signature is one of the most elusive on our "Top 100" list. As one of the first true superstars in baseball, Anson did sign his fair share of autographs during the period. The problem is the period Anson played in was over 100 years ago. Most of what remains in the marketplace was signed post-1900. Anson's autograph can vary in appearance, from the more common "A.C. Anson" to the seldom seen "Adrian C. Anson" version. After his playing days and while working at the Chicago City Clerk office in 1905 and 1906, Anson did utilize a secretarial signature on occasion. Anson was frequently required to sign off on numerous documents, so this helped satisfy the demand. Anson passed away in 1922, which contributes to the scarcity of his signature. A small number of letters, signature cuts, and calling cards are mostly what collectors have access to today.

"*For years he stood at first base for Chicago like a mighty oak, sturdy, blunt, and honest, the captain who was always kicking at decisions, the one prominent player who was loyal to the National League at the time of the Brotherhood crisis, the symbol of all that was strong and good in Baseball.*"

- Lee Allen, Historian, National Baseball Hall of Fame and Museum

THE EARLY YEARS

Charles "Charlie" Albert Bender

Chief Bender's pitching mastery was a mystery to most batters, but not as grand a mystery as Bender himself. His birthdate, based on the Indian Censuses, is uncertain, as is his place of birth. It is believed that Bender's family settled in Minnesota's White Earth Reservation.

According to most accounts, Charles Albert Bender's father was a white farmer and his mother was a member of the Ojibwe tribe. Because reservation life was harsh, as a young child Bender was sent to boarding school in Philadelphia. He graduated from the Carlisle Indian School where his baseball coach was the iconic football mentor Pop Warner. Pop's impact changed Bender's life and the young man who had endured childhood hardships and the sting of racial prejudice began his Hall of Fame career with Connie Mack's Philadelphia Athletics in 1903.

As a 19-year-old rookie, Bender went 17–14 with 29 complete games and 3.07 ERA. Arguably, his best season was 1910 when he went 23–5 with an ERA of 1.58. Over his 12 seasons with the Athletics, Bender won 5 pennants and 3 World Series, posting a 6–4 postseason record with an ERA of 2.44. He won 193 games highlighted by two 20-win seasons and led the American League in winning percentage three times. In 1913, he was 21–10 with an ERA of 2.21, and he led the AL in games finished (24) and in saves (13). Bender was clutch to say the least. His strength was his mind. A true student of pitching, he studied tendencies and relied on guile as much as grit.

In 1915, Bender jumped to the new Federal League's Baltimore Terrapins. He returned to the

Chief

> *"If everything depended on one game, I just used Albert—the greatest money pitcher of all time."*
>
> – Connie Mack

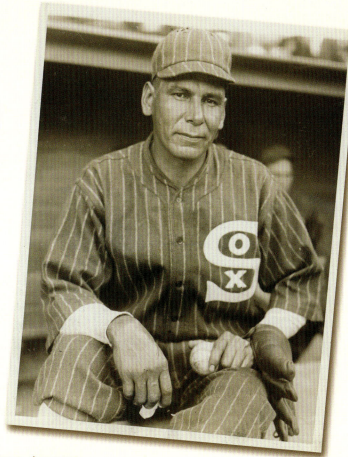

City of Brotherly Love with the Phillies in 1916 but left in 1918 to work in the shipyards during World War I. He then managed in the minors before coaching for the White Sox, pitching one last MLB game in 1925. Bender also coached for the U.S. Naval Academy and scouted for several MLB teams, including the A's. He was elected to the Hall of Fame in 1953, but the 70-year-old Bender died a few weeks before the induction ceremony in 1954. A proud Native American, Bender wished to be noted for his pitching, not his heritage. He preferred to be called Charlie or Charles, not Chief, and bristled at the ethnic slurs he endured throughout his career. Perhaps more than any other player in baseball history, the story of Chief Bender truly is the story of America.

PSA/DNA Authentication Services Says:

Bender played during a time when autographs weren't sought out with the frequency seen just one or two generations later. For that reason, autographs from his playing days are scarce, like they are for most other period players. Starting in the 1930s, after his career was over, Bender was very responsive to mail requests, which is why you see a fair number of authentic autographs in the hobby today. Often times, the Hall of Fame pitcher would sign "Chief" Bender for autograph seekers. Later on, he would occasionally sign "Chief" CA Bender as a variation, or you may encounter signatures such as "Chas. A. Bender" as well. Bender remained an active signer until his passing in 1954.

THE EARLY YEARS

Dan Brouthers

In a career that spanned 19 years (1879–1896, 1904), Dan Brouthers played for teams named the Trojans, Bisons, Wolverines, Beaneaters, Grooms, Orioles, Colonels, Phillies, and Giants. With stops in Troy, Buffalo, Detroit, Boston, Brooklyn, Baltimore, Louisville, Philadelphia, and New York City, it is amazing that Brouthers had time to unpack, let alone hit a career .342 with 2,296 hits, 1,523 runs scored and a slugging percentage of .519. Brouthers probably spent more time in train stations than he did patrolling first base.

Despite his travel travails, Dennis Joseph Brouthers could hit. After a slow start with the Troy Trojans, he blossomed with the Buffalo Bisons, beginning a mind-boggling run of 16 consecutive seasons hitting .300 or higher, with an emphasis on higher. Brouthers won five batting crowns and reached or surpassed the .350 mark six times. He was an all-around offensive threat with speed, power, the ability to drive in runs, work the basepaths, and score. He was consistently among the league leaders in runs, hits, doubles, and RBI.

Born in Sylvan Lake, New York, the 21-year-old Brouthers broke into the National League with a pitiful Troy Trojans team that won fewer games (19) than Brouthers had years on the planet. Eventually recognized as one of baseball's first true power hitters, the 6-foot, 2-inch, and 207 pound "Big Dan" Brouthers led the National League in home runs twice and smashed double-figures

in homers three times, a rare feat in the Deadball Era. Brouthers' 106 career blasts rank fourth among players who were active in the 19th century. While with Detroit, he helped the Wolverines to the National League Championship in 1887.

After leaving the Phillies in 1896, Brouthers played and managed in the minors for several years. A teammate of Brouthers with the 1894 Orioles, John McGraw brought the 46-year old slugger back up to the majors in 1904 to finish out his career with the Giants. He later scouted for McGraw's Giants and worked at the Polo Grounds. Brouthers died in 1932 at the age of 74. The Baseball Hall of Fame, which inducted Brouthers in 1945, quotes John McGraw as stating, "Brouthers was a great hitter, one of the most powerful batters of all time. Big Dan in his prime, against modern pitching and the modern lively ball, would have hit as many home runs as anybody."

> "*Brouthers was a great hitter, one of the most powerful batters of all time.*"
>
> – John McGraw, New York Giants

Big Dan

> "Dan Brouthers was one of the greatest batsmen in the history of baseball. From the beginning of his career until he retired he was noted as a slugger and as an all-round player he was the Ty Cobb of his day."
>
> – *The New York Times*, August 3, 1932

PSA/DNA Authentication Services Says:

Dan Brouthers played during an era that basically pre-dated the advent of the autograph seeker. As a result, most of the authentic Brouthers signatures that exist today are in the form of a signed document rather than a signed ball, photo, or album page. Even within our exclusive "Top 100" list, Brouthers ranks in the very top handful of autographs when it comes to sheer scarcity. This is perplexing as Brouthers remained a part of baseball for about two decades after his playing days, and lived into the early 1930s—a period when autograph signing became more popular. While extremely rare, a high percentage of the known Brouthers autographs remain archived at the Baseball Hall of Fame.

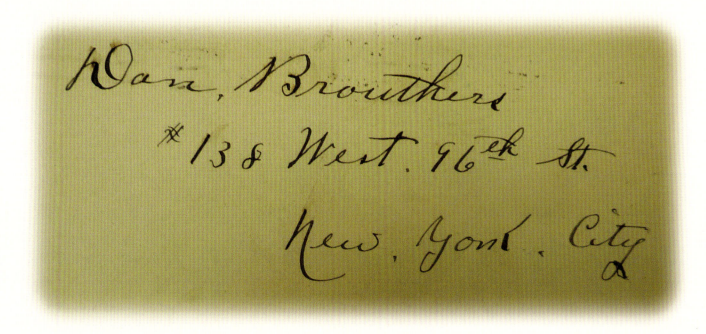

THE EARLY YEARS

Mordecai Brown

Any discussion of Mordecai Brown must start with that nickname. According to legend, Brown got the moniker "Three Finger" thanks to childhood confrontations with farm equipment, a rabbit, and a tree stump. The curve-balling righty fared much better against opposing batters during his 14-year career. An Indiana farm boy who cut his teeth in the mining towns and hard-scrabble leagues of the Hoosier State, Mordecai Peter Centennial Brown brought a workmanlike ethic to the mound.

In the annals of baseball trades, the 1964 Cubs-Cardinals deal that sent Lou Brock to St. Louis for Ernie Broglio and Doug Clemens is viewed as total folly for the Cubs, but 60 years earlier, it was the Cardinals who played the fool, trading Brown to the Cubbies for Larry McLean and Jack Taylor. Brown would thrive on the North Side, blowing away batters in a manner befitting the Windy City. He won more than 20 games in six straight seasons (1906–1911), highlighted by the 1909 campaign in which he registered 27 wins, 50 games, 32 complete games, and 342.2 innings pitched—all league-bests.

From 1906 to 1910, he posted ERA's under 2.00 and rivaled fellow Hall of Famer Christy Mathewson for National League pitching supremacy. That personal rivalry would crest as the Cubs and Giants met in a playoff game to decide the National League pennant in 1908. That game followed Fred Merkle's legendary bonehead play that forced a winner-take-all showdown. In what Brown later called his best game ever, he relieved Jack Pfiester early in the contest and led Chicago to a victory over Mathewson. The Cubbies would go on to defeat Detroit and win their second straight World Series.

The man who drew praise from the ornery Ty Cobb would see his career dip after 1911. After a brief stop with the Reds, he jumped to the Federal League for two seasons before ending his career back with the Cubs in 1916 when he was 39 years old. Like the farm equipment, rabbit, and stump, fate eventually defeated Brown as he passed away in 1948, at age 71, just one year shy of his Hall of Fame election. Needless to say, the man who was short on fingers was truly long on talent.

Three Finger

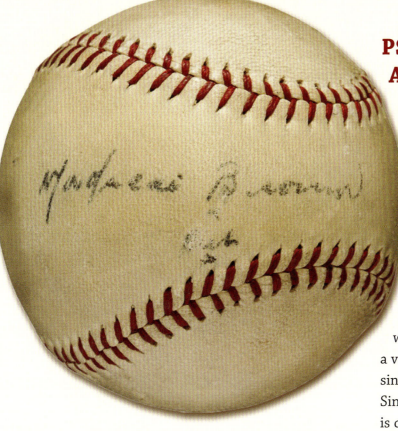

PSA/DNA Authentication Services Says:

Brown had one of the more popular nicknames in baseball history, but it clearly wasn't something the Hall of Fame pitcher was comfortable adding to his autograph over the course of his life. That said, Brown would often add "A Cub" as an inscription to many of his autographs, particularly through the mail. Brown's wife would occasionally respond to mail requests on his behalf, and there are even examples of his wife endorsing the back of checks made out to him. A frequent guest at Cubs Old Timers games, Brown was known for being an obliging signer. He possessed a very legible signature, which is most coveted on single-signed baseballs due to their tremendous scarcity. Since Brown passed away in 1948, finding his signature is considerably tougher than signatures of players who lived during the next few decades, as autograph signing became increasingly popular through the years.

> "*Brown is my idea of the almost perfect pitcher…It will usually be found at the end of a season, that he has taken part in more key games than any other pitcher in baseball.*"
> – Christy Mathewson

THE EARLY YEARS

Jesse Burkett

Jesse Cail Burkett was an ornery, dirt-kicking, foul-mouthed competitor who would take an opponent out at the knees to stretch a single to a double. Nicknamed "The Crab," he was an awesome force at the plate, capable of hitting the ball with immense drive and power. That, however, was not his game. Burkett smacked the ball all over the field, ran the bases with a fiery furor, and believed in moving runners over and scoring runs. Burkett was a pure pest; fouling off numerous pitches, working the count, and drawing walks. He was also recognized as one of the most skilled bunters of his generation.

In both 1895 and 1896, Burkett eclipsed the .400 mark in batting average, putting him in the rarified air of guys named Cobb and Hornsby. Burkett's 1896 season is a statistical landmark with 160 runs, 240 hits, a .410 average, and 317 total bases—all league highs. He was seemingly omnipresent with 133 games played, 647 plate appearances, and 586 at-bats. Five years later, in 1901 with the St. Louis Cardinals, Burkett again led the league in those categories setting the pace in batting (.376), runs (142), and hits (226).

Burkett broke into the National League in 1890 with the Giants and became a star with the Cleveland Spiders from 1891 to 1898. Between 1893 and 1901, his lowest batting average was .341. In the 1892 Championship Series versus the Boston Beaneaters, Burkett hit .320, but his Spiders lost the title. That Cleveland club featured a 25-year-old pitcher with a record of 36–12 and a 1.93 ERA. Cy Young and Burkett would remain teammates in Cleveland until 1898. Before he became a feared hitter, Burkett was a Minor League pitching phenom, going 39–6 for an Atlantic Association club in Worcester, Massachusetts. Alas, his big-league pitching slate is less impressive with a career 3–11 record and 5.56 ERA in short stints with the Giants, Spiders, and St. Louis Browns.

Burkett finished his playing career in 1905 with the Boston Americans when he was 36 years old. A shrewd salary-saver, he purchased a New England League team in 1906 and moved it to his hometown of Worcester, Massachusetts. Burkett's hitting led his club to several league titles. Later, to the dismay of collegiate and professional umpires, he would coach at Holy Cross and alongside John McGraw with the Giants. In 1946, still as crotchety and curmudgeonly as ever, Jesse Burkett was inducted into the Baseball Hall of Fame. He passed away in 1953 at the age of 84.

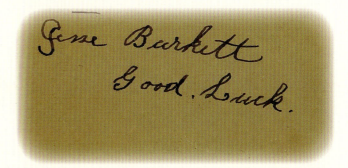

54   THE EARLY YEARS

The Crab

PSA/DNA Authentication Services Says:

Burkett falls into the same category as Brouthers and other players from their generation, at least as it relates to finding signatures that date to their playing days. This includes an obvious lack of team-signed items as well. While he lived until 1953 and was by all accounts a responsive signer, Burkett passed away before sending mail requests to players became a more universally accepted practice just one decade later. While single-signed baseballs are extremely rare and desirable, so are Burkett signatures on other mediums, such as Black and White Hall of Fame postcards. At this time, there are less than 10 of these postcards signed by Burkett known in the hobby.

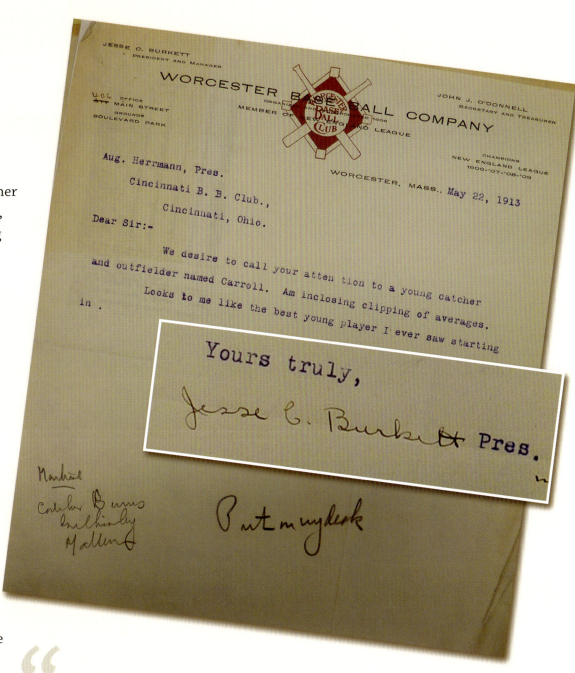

"*In the days before the foul strike rule came in [Burkett] was one of the most feared men in the game because he could stand up and foul them off until pitchers would fairly gnash their teeth in frenzy. In short, Burkett was one of the few men who have been able to make batting a science.*"

– Baseball Magazine, 1911

THE EARLY YEARS

Alexander Cartwright

> "The bases shall be from "home" to second base, forty-two paces; from first to third base, forty-two paces, equidistant."
>
> – Alexander Cartwright, *Knickerbocker Rules*

When the Baseball Hall of Fame calls you, "The Father of Modern Baseball," you must have done something special. In the case of Alexander Joy Cartwright Jr., it was more than just one thing. Cartwright helped establish the first organized baseball club ever, the Knickerbocker Base Ball Club of New York City. He is also credited with creating many of the game's rules that are still in existence today. Cartwright's Hall of Fame plaque says it best: "Set bases 90 feet apart. Established 9 innings as game and 9 players as team...Carried baseball to Pacific Coast and Hawaii." Pretty impressive.

Cartwright's vision of an organized baseball league took root in stickball games on the streets of New York City. Eventually, his club moved to the famous Elysian Fields of New Jersey. Cartwright is credited with developing the concepts of batting orders, three outs per inning, and foul territory. Baserunners of all eras are also thankful that he outlawed throwing the baseball at runners to retire them. Ever the baseball explorer, Cartwright brought his newly-found game to western territories in the mid-1800s. Major Leaguers who hail from California and Hawaii owe a debt of gratitude to Cartwright for sure. He so loved the Hawaiian Islands that Cartwright made the region his home and became both a Honolulu fire chief and faithful aide to Queen Emma of Hawaii.

With all of these firsts and accomplishments, why is Cartwright not more well-known to casual fans of the game? Well, he suffers from the same myth vs. reality battle that plagues another would-be baseball founder, Abner Doubleday. Many baseball historians, and even some of Cartwright's peers, have questioned the many innovations for which he is credited. Due to a lack of recorded evidence and gaps in the timeline of his travels, there are some loose strings in the webbing of Cartwright's grandeur. Many argue that he headed west not to establish baseball in the territories, but to seek his fortune in the California Gold Rush of 1849. Moreover, diaries and documents confirm that Cartwright aligned himself with Hawaiian royalty, but contain no mention of baseball at all. Was Cartwright more interested in mining than managing, more focused on ingratiating than innovating? The answers,

The Father of Modern Baseball

like a good team defense, are most likely somewhere up the middle. Cartwright took those answers to his grave when he passed away in 1892, at the age of 72. In 1938, he was elected to the Baseball Hall of Fame.

PSA/DNA Authentication Services Says:

While Cartwright is credited with helping form the game many fans know and love today, finding his signature on baseball-related mediums has been a futile endeavor for collectors. On rare occasions, you will encounter correspondence accompanied by his signature, including various types of signed documents and checks. When it comes to the aesthetic appeal of his signature, Cartwright possessed one of the most attractive autographs in baseball history. His beautiful, flowing signature is one that stands out, even amongst the top signatures on our "Top 100" list. One important note to be aware of is that Cartwright was known for making carbon copies of documents so, while some of these have been offered in the hobby as originals, they are simply holographic in nature.

Henry Chadwick

> "Americans do not care to dawdle over a sleep-inspiring game, all through the heat of a June or July day. What they do they want to do in a hurry. In baseball all is lightning. Thus the reason for the American antipathy to cricket can readily be understood."
>
> – Henry Chadwick

If you are a baseball geek looking for a founding father, Henry Chadwick might just be your guy. While he never played baseball at any high level, he developed many aspects that make following baseball a little more fun. The 1938 Baseball Hall of Famer is credited as a pioneer in sportswriting. He chronicled the game with great aplomb for half a century, but his legacy does not stop there. Chadwick invented the box score that baseball fans still examine on a daily basis to recount the exploits of the day's games. He also developed the modern method of scoring a game. Chadwick chaired the rules committee of the first-ever national baseball organization and, in 1858, created baseball's first rule book. He is one of those rare personalities whose contributions to the game are still quite tangible today.

Born in Exeter, England, in 1824, Chadwick took his love of baseballesque games such as cricket and rounders to the United States at age 13. Legend has it that Chadwick became smitten with baseball when he witnessed it as a reporter for *The New York Times*. While writing for the *New York Clipper* and *Sunday Mercury*, Chadwick's "newfangled" box score included the new symbol for a strikeout, the letter "K." Little did Chadwick know that his demarcation would one day be pasted in bright red letters on stadium placards throughout the country. He also became a sentinel of baseball, championing good sportsmanship and criticizing players who gambled, caroused, and abused alcohol.

Chadwick eventually teamed with another titan of baseball, as the editor of A. G. Spalding's Official Base Ball Guide. He locked horns, however, with Spalding's belief that baseball was discovered by Abner Doubleday. Chadwick argued that the game was, in fact, a descendent of his beloved cricket and rounders. A precursor to today's sabermetricians, Chadwick viewed the game from a statistical and scientific standpoint. He also marveled at baseball's artistry, perhaps stemming from his love of music and days as a piano teacher and composer. Among the other publications for which Chadwick wrote or edited were the *Brooklyn Long Island Star*, *Beadle's Dime Base-Ball Player*, *Sporting Life,* and the *Brooklyn Eagle*. He died in 1908 at the age of 83. Known

The Father of Baseball

to many as the "Father of Baseball," Henry Chadwick is on that short list of true pioneers, an Englishman who came to the colonies and helped construct this most American of games.

PSA/DNA Authentication Services Says:

Chadwick is one of the great rarities in the baseball autograph world. While genuine examples are seldom seen, Chadwick has been the target of forgers for years as the market has been inundated with counterfeits. Even though Chadwick's autograph is hard to locate, handwritten letters have been discovered. Some of that rare, yet authentic correspondence contains baseball content, which is always desirable to collectors. As a result of Chadwick's relatively early death, compared to so many other figures on our "Top 100" list, he wasn't a big target for autograph seekers. Chadwick died in 1908, which was long before the concept of autograph chasing became a somewhat common practice. When it comes to appearance, Chadwick's autograph was the antithesis of Alexander Cartwright's, having a very basic, printed look.

"*My Dear Chadwick: I congratulate you on your eightieth year and your fiftieth year in journalism . . . and you are entitled to the good wishes of all for that part you have taken in behalf of decent sport.*"

– Theodore Roosevelt

THE EARLY YEARS

Jack Chesbro

Jack Chesbro is the last Major League pitcher to win more than 40 games in one season. In 1904, he went 41–12, a modern era record for wins. Four years later, Ed Walsh of the White Sox would go 40–15, but Chesbro's 41 still stands as a lasting monument to a time when pitchers took the ball and finished what they started. In that remarkable 1904 season, John Dwight Chesbro, a 30-year-old native of North Adams, Massachusetts, started 51 games and completed 48 of them. His 1.82 ERA and 454 innings pitched led the American League. The New York Highlanders won 92 games that season led by Chesbro and Jack Powell, who went 23–19. They had just one .300 hitter in the lineup: 32-year-old Willie Keeler hit .343 and led the club with 186 hits.

Nicknamed "Happy Jack," Chesbro was the antithesis to many of the hardscrabble and just plain angry ballplayers of his era. He played semi-pro ball in Cooperstown, New York, and would come full circle as a Baseball Hall of Fame inductee in 1946. Chesbro won 198 games in 11 seasons with the Pirates, Highlanders, and Red Sox. He won 20 games or more five times, and his career ERA is 2.68. He fanned 239 batters in that landmark 1904 season and finished with over 1250 Ks for his career. While Chesbro's Hall of Fame credentials are cut and dry, the baseballs he used were anything but. The spitball was a legal pitch in Chesbro's day and he took full advantage of the wet and wild time.

Chesbro never pitched in a World Series and the spitter may have been the reason why. On the final day of that 1904 season, New York and Boston played a doubleheader to decide the pennant. The Boston Americans held a one-and-a-half game lead over the Highlanders as Chesbro started the first game. Tied 2–2 in the ninth inning with two outs and Boston's Lou Criger on third, Chesbro threw a wild pitch to Freddy Parent scoring Criger. New York lost that game and the next one. Boston took the AL Championship, and 1904 is remembered more for Chesbro's pennant-losing wild pitch than his 41 wins. Ironically, Chesbro's career ended in 1909 with that same Boston team, now known as the Red Sox. He coached at what is now the University of Massachusetts and died of a heart attack in 1931, at age 57. In 1904, Chesbro threw one ill-fated wild pitch, but he had 41 unforgettable wins, a legacy and a number that most likely will never again be approached.

JACK CHESBRO WINS 41ST GAME

Happy Jack

PSA/DNA Authentication Services Says:

Since his playing career ended in 1909, Chesbro retired prior to the autograph seeker revolution. Furthermore, Chesbro was not really considered one of the elite pitchers in the game while he was playing, and he was not inducted into the Hall of Fame until 1946, long after he passed away in 1931. Despite having a few very good seasons, including a remarkable 1904 campaign when he won 41 games, not many people believed he would be enshrined with the other greats of the game. As a result, Chesbro was not pursued in aggressive fashion. Chesbro often signed "Jack" instead of his legal name, but he did use "John" when signing legal documents. While multi-signed baseballs have been discovered with Chesbro's name, authentic single-signed examples have remained a White Whale for many advanced collectors.

" *Broad-shouldered with a sandy complexion, Chesbro normally carried 180 pounds on his 5'9" frame. Before mastering the spitball, he relied on an excellent fastball, which he delivered with a straight-over-the-top motion.*"

— Wayne McElreavey, SABR

John Clarkson

One of baseball's first pitching superstars, John Clarkson was one of the most successful pitchers in the early years of the game, setting standards that few have matched. John Gibson Clarkson, of Cambridge, Massachusetts, was 20 years old when he broke into the National League with the Worcester Ruby Legs in 1882. He moved to the Chicago White Stockings in 1884 and began a Hall of Fame career with unfathomable numbers. Clarkson won 53 games in 1885, followed by win totals of 36, 38, 33,

> "*In knowing exactly what kind of a ball a batter could not hit and in his ability to serve up just that kind of ball, I don't think I have ever seen the equal of Clarkson.*"
>
> – Cap Anson

and 49 the next four seasons. A veritable innings-eating machine, he eclipsed the 600 innings-pitched plateau in both 1885 and 1889, and he led the National League in that category four times.

During that epic 1885 season, he added 308 strikeouts and finished 68 of the 70 games he started. All stats are relative, but the case could be made that Clarkson's 1885 season was the best ever with 53 wins, 308 Ks, 68 complete games, 10 shutouts, a 1.85 ERA, and a no-hitter versus the Providence Grays. Less than a quarter of the batters he faced that season reached base via a hit or a walk. That was dominance, and it was worth dollars. Clarkson was sold to the Boston Beaneaters in 1888 for $10,000, an astounding sum at the time.

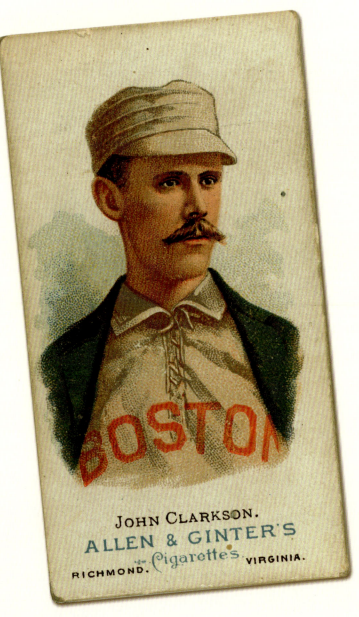

Clarkson was no stranger to money. His father was a successful jeweler and young John worked in the family business while attending business school. He used this financial aptitude to negotiate salary raises and engineer profitable trades for himself. Clarkson was a leader in the Brotherhood that formed the renegade Players League, but shrewdly worked both sides of that battle between players and owners. Business acumen aside, Clarkson's chief career path was pitching, and it was a curvy path at that. He was a side-winding savant, and his immense breaking ball arrived at home plate by way of Toledo. At 5-foot, 10-inches, and 155 pounds, he was not a menacing figure on the hill, but his arm struck terror in hearts of hitters and struck out 1,978

62   THE EARLY YEARS

The Pitcher

career batters. Clarkson retired in 1894 after winning an amazing 328 games in just 12 Big League seasons. In addition to pitching, he coached baseball at Dartmouth and was a boxing referee. Clarkson later owned a cigar business and managed in the minors but by 1905 he was delusional from drinking and was hospitalized during his final years. In 1909, at 47 years old, Clarkson died from pneumonia. He was inducted into the Baseball Hall of Fame by the Veterans Committee in 1963.

PSA/DNA Authentication Services Says:

If you are seeking an authentic autograph of John Clarkson, please take a number and wait in line. Not only did he play during an era when autograph signing wasn't a common practice, Clarkson spent the last several years of his life in various sanitariums and psychiatric hospitals, making his autograph almost impossible to obtain during that tragic time. Clarkson would die while admitted in 1909 at the age of 47. After a family visit that same year, Clarkson suddenly fell ill and passed away a short time later. As a result, Clarkson's autograph is, arguably, the toughest of any player of the Deadball Era, no matter the medium. As of this writing, PSA has not certified a Clarkson autograph.

" *Clarkson fields his position better than any other League pitcher.*"

– *Sporting Life*

Eddie Collins

Best wishes from Eddie Collins

In a career that spanned 25 years, Eddie Collins was a second sacker extraordinaire and became a key figure in the game's growth and history. A man defined by championships, Collins won World Series titles in 1910, 1911, and 1913 with Connie Mack's Philadelphia A's and in 1917 with the White Sox. He also lost two World Series, in 1914 with Philly to the "Miracle" Boston Braves, and in 1919 with a White Sox team now known as the Black Sox. However, it should be noted that Collins was not involved in the Black Sox 1919 World Series fixing scandal.

Collins' game was predicated on smarts and speed. He attended Irving Prep School and Columbia University where he quarterbacked the football team and started at shortstop. While still at Columbia, Edward Trowbridge Collins Sr. was signed by the astute Connie Mack and played briefly for the A's in 1906 and 1907. Once he established himself as a bona fide big leaguer in 1908, Collins worked pitchers over, consistently drawing walks and getting on base. He eclipsed the century mark in walks with 101 in 1912, and led the American League in 1915 with 119 walks. Collins had a lifetime OBP of .424 and an OPS of .853. Once he was allowed to reach base, the fun really began. He topped the league in steals four times, swiping 81 in 1910. Collins led the AL in runs scored

Cocky

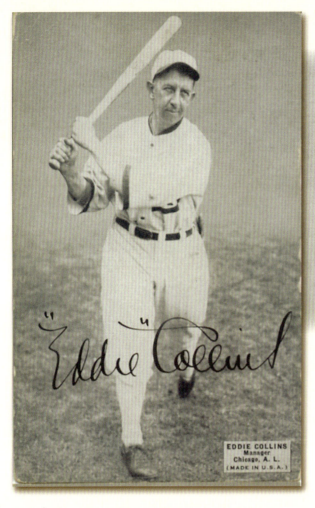

three consecutive seasons between 1912 and 1914, and he tallied over 100 runs four other times.

In 1911, Collins was part of the Athletics' famous $100,000 infield along with Home Run Baker, Jack Barry, and Stuffy McInnis. Although named the AL MVP in 1914, Collins was sold to Chicago when Connie Mack dismantled his team after their World Series loss to the Braves. Collins helped turn around the perennial losing White Sox when he joined the team in 1915. As player-manager for Chicago from 1924 to 1926, Collins did not enjoy great success. He returned to the A's to finish out his playing days, retiring in 1930 with a career .333 BA and 3,315 hits. When fellow Irving Prep alum Tom Yawkey bought the Red Sox in 1933, Collins became the team's Vice President and General Manager, and he remained with the club until his death in 1951 at 63 years old. Eddie Collins was part of the Hall of Fame class of 1939. He was known as "Cocky" and had ample reason to be just that.

PSA/DNA Authentication Services Says:

Within our "Top 100" list are a host of signers who possessed autographs that range from aesthetically pleasing to indiscernibly scribbled. If we define autograph signing as an art form, then Eddie Collins autographs would rank near the very top of the list in terms of sheer visual appeal. His large, flowing signature exhibits fantastic style and it remained consistent for most of his life. Up until the late-1910s, Collins often signed his name "Edward Collins," but that changed consistently to "Eddie Collins" as the decade came to a close. Considered a responsive signer through the mail, Collins continued to be accessible as an executive for the Boston Red Sox. A collector will rarely see a clubhouse or proxy version of his signature as a result of Collin's accommodating nature. While his autograph is not nearly as tough as some of the true rarities of his generation, the beauty of his autograph and his membership in the 3,000 hit club propels Collins into our exclusive list—with ease.

THE EARLY YEARS 65

Jimmy Collins

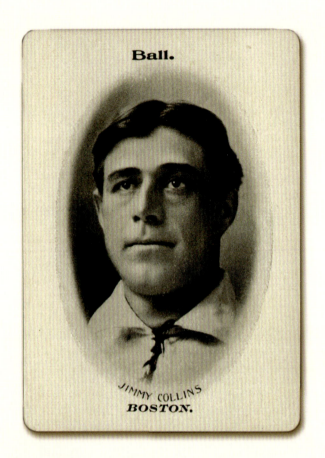

When Jimmy Collins passed away some of the old "Royal Rooters" fans from Boston traveled to Buffalo, New York, for his wake. According to legend, they placed the 1903 Championship Cup in his arms, and toasted him while standing around the casket. This legend is immortalized by the Dropkick Murphys' song "Jimmy Collins' Wake" penned by Dick Johnson, Curator of The Sports Museum in Boston.

Arguably the best defensive third baseman of his era, James Joseph Collins was a star in Boston, playing most of his 14-year career there. With the Beaneaters from 1895 to 1900, Collins hit .300 or better three times, helping his team win the National League pennant in 1897 and 1898. When he joined the new Boston Americans as player-manager in 1901, his star power gave the upstart American League and the team credibility. As the first manager for the team that later became the Red Sox, Collins hit .332 that year, leading his team to a second place finish. In 1902 he hit .322, but 1903 was the pinnacle of his great career. That year, Collins and crew won the AL pennant and went on to win the first modern-day World Series Championship, beating the Pittsburgh Pirates five games to three. 1904 saw a second AL pennant win, but there was no World Series contest that year.

A good hitter with a .294 career BA, Collins was better known for his stellar third-base play. As five-time league-leader in putouts at that position, he innovated fielding bunts barehanded, and developed how to properly plant on the throw. Collins was a fiery competitor who was not afraid to mix it up on the field or with management, but he was the cornerstone of his teams and a favorite with fans. He was elected to the Hall of Fame in 1945. Irish Jimmy Collins died in 1943 at the age of 73 with his loyal fans in attendance to give him a proper sendoff.

We've gathered here to bid adieu
Us Boston Boys, alas are few
Some from crosstown, some from the coast
To give our skipper one last toast…

…Let's raise a glass and lift it up
Then sip from Jimmy Collins' cup
And hail the lads that won the crown
While turning baseball upside down…

Irish Jimmy

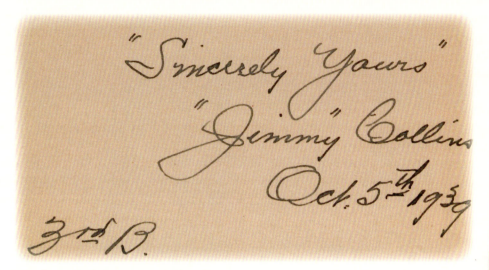

...Our days with you
Indeed were great
And now that you have crossed the plate
And scored that final run of life...

...We'll lift our heads
With one loud voice
Pay homage
To 'The People's Choice'
– Dropkick Murphys, "Jimmy Collins' Wake"

PSA/DNA Authentication Services Says:

While still very difficult to find, authentic Collins autographs are actually considered slightly easier to locate than several of the Deadball Era figures on our "Top 100" list. Collins remained close to the game throughout his lifetime, in various capacities at the Minor-League and Major-League level once his playing career came to an end. Collins possessed one of the more visually-appealing autographs you will find in the hobby and he often placed quotation marks around his first name "Jimmy" while signing. Collins was also known for adding salutations to his signature such as "Sincerely Yours" or "Very Truly Yours" in letters or other mediums. While finding Collins' signature on baseballs is quite challenging, you will occasionally encounter his autograph on multi-signed balls.

THE EARLY YEARS

Charles Comiskey

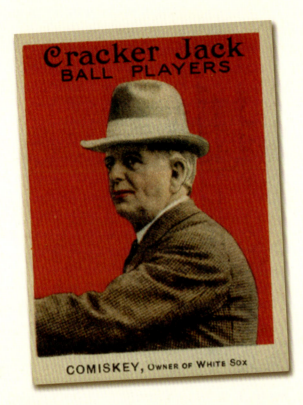

Mention the name Comiskey and two things come to mind: the old ball yard in Chicago where the White Sox played their home games from 1910–1990, and the Black Sox scandal in which eight members of the Chicago White Sox threw the 1919 World Series against the Reds. A park and a scandal, it is indeed one of baseball's sad legacies that the name Comiskey is associated with these two simple concepts. The truth is that Charles Albert Comiskey was anything but simple. In fact, the game and the landscape of baseball, as we know it today, would not exist if not for the man they called "The Old Roman."

Comiskey's first foray into baseball was with the American Association's St. Louis Brown Stockings in 1882. The dashing young star advanced rapidly to become player-manager from 1883 to 1889, leading St. Louis to four pennants (1885–1888). As a player, his game was predicated on speed. Comiskey stole 416 bases in his 13-year playing career, 117 in 1887 alone. He was also a terrific first baseman. Giants manager, John McGraw, once said of Comiskey, "He taught first basemen how to play the position. He furnished the rest of the infielders with new strategy." During his career, Comiskey was a league-hopper, playing in the American Association, the renegade Players League, and the National League.

In 1895, 35-year-old Charles Comiskey saw opportunity for baseball in the western part of the country, and set about forming the Western League with Ban Johnson. Comiskey became owner of the Sioux City Cornhuskers and moved them to St. Paul where he managed the team for five seasons before moving them again to Chicago as the White Sox. The Western League soon became the American League, and the White Sox soon became one of the most profitable franchises in the nation. In 1910, Comiskey opened his namesake park, a model baseball stadium at the time. Nine years later, the Black Sox scandal hit and "The Old Roman" was never the same. He continued on as owner of the White Sox until his death in 1931, at age 72, and his family carried on his legacy as owners until 1959. This great architect of the game was inducted into the Baseball Hall of Fame in 1939. How great was Charles Comiskey? Let's yield once again to John McGraw who stated, "He gave you the impression, wherever you happened to meet him, that he was always thinking." Enough said.

> *The fellow who can pay only twenty-five cents to see a ball game always will be just as welcome at Comiskey Park as the box seat holder."*
>
> - Charles Comiskey

The Old Roman

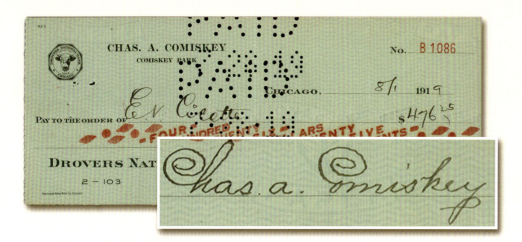

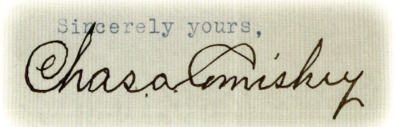

"*Baseball is the greatest sport in the world. It is the cleanest, besides affording more people the right kind of amusement than any other. I do not say that because I have made my living at it. I say it from the heart.*"

– Charles Comiskey

PSA/DNA Authentication Services Says:

Charles Comiskey, one of the most recognizable names from the baseball executive world, signed his fair share of items during his lifetime. This is primarily a result of the number of documents, including letters, relating to his role in the Chicago White Sox organization and not really attributed to signing autographs for the public. Most of the dated Comiskey autographs a collector will encounter are from the pre-Black Sox scandal era. Shortly after the scandal broke, Comiskey distanced himself from the game. His secretary, Harry Grabiner, also signed items on Comiskey's behalf during the 1910s and 1920s, often when the owner was on the road. In terms of appearance, a number of authentic signatures possess Comiskey's distinctive C, which resembles a pinwheel and was often used in his first name only. This ornate C has almost a drawn appearance and it often differs from his second and more traditional-looking C. That said, there were instances where Comiskey would employ the pinwheel style to both his first and last name while signing.

THE EARLY YEARS

Roger Connor

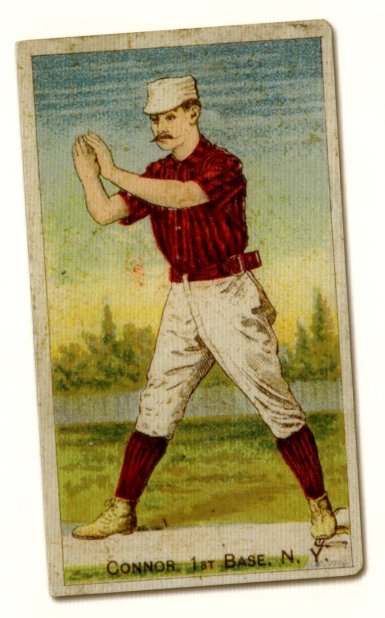

Known as the "Babe Ruth of the 1880s," Roger Connor retired from baseball in 1897 with 138 career home runs. That number stood as the career standard until Babe Ruth eclipsed the mark in 1921. At 6-foot, 3-inches, and 220 pounds, Connor more resembled the husky sluggers of the 1980s than the fleet afoot, diminutive ballplayers of his own era. He spent a decade of his 18-year career in New York. Truly a Gentle Giant, his calm demeanor and friendly personality were in stark contrast to the violent manner in which he treated a baseball.

From 1887 to 1890, he registered season home run totals of 17, 14, 13, and 14, truly impressive Deadball Era power numbers. He also hit for average, posting a .316 career mark and 12 seasons of .300-plus batting averages. Strangely enough, Connor's best overall season was his worst in terms of home runs. In 1885, he had 169 hits, 225 total bases, and batted .371 with an OBP of .435—all league highs. His home run total that season? One. A more typical season was 1889 when he hit 13 home runs and led the league with 130 runs and a .528 slugging percentage. Power and patience personified, he drew over 1,000 career walks and regularly walked two or even three times more often than he struck out. Connor's vicious cuts at the plate were the stuff of legend. In 1881, he swatted MLB's first-ever grand slam home run. Five years later, he hit a blast that sailed out of New York City's vast Polo Grounds right onto 112th Street.

Born in 1857 to Irish Catholic immigrants in Waterbury, Connecticut, young Roger took many a whipping from his hard-working father for his foolish pursuit of baseball. After his father's death, Connor immersed himself in the sport and broke into the Bigs with Troy in 1880. He joined the New York Gothams in 1883. Legend has it that his prodigious size was the inspiration for changing the team's name to the Giants in 1885. He helped New York to two championships (1888, 1889) and later played for the National League's Phillies and Browns. Back home in Waterbury, Connor continued to play baseball well into his 40s. He was player-manager and owner of Waterbury's Minor League team from 1897 to 1901, and the Springfield team from 1902 to 1903. Forgotten by the sport he loved, Connor died without fanfare in 1931, at age 73. When he was inducted into the Hall of Fame in 1976, baseball's first home run king finally received a proper crown.

Dear Old Roger

PSA/DNA Authentication Services Says:

Connor falls into an elite group of those who made a serious impact on the game in its early stages, but that impact came long before the pursuit of autographs emerged as a real hobby. Just a small group of authentic Connor signatures are known at this time. Some of the authentic examples discovered have come in the form of team sheets from the late 1800s. Connor lived until 1931 and remained close to the game and active in the community as a school inspector. One would assume that a larger number of genuine Connor autographs would have been found by now, but he remains a hole on many autograph collector lists.

> "Connor's honorable and straightforward conduct and affable and courteous demeanor towards all with whom he is brought into contact have won him deserved popularity both on and off the ball field."
>
> – The New York Clipper

George Davis

A truly great shortstop, George Davis could bring it both offensively and defensively. His great 20-year career began with the Cleveland Spiders in 1890, at age 19. The young switch-hitting infielder moved on to New York to play for the Giants from 1893 to 1901, managing them for parts of three seasons. Davis found his home at shortstop position in 1896 and was usually at or near the top of fielding stats. Considered a top echelon player, Davis led the league in fielding percentage four times and hit over .300 nine consecutive seasons (1893–1901). In 1897, he batted .353, and led the league with 135 RBI.

Davis, along with Giants teammates Kid Gleason and Mike Grady, were credited with saving lives in a horrific tenement fire in 1900. They helped carry women and children from the burning building, but the soft-spoken Davis would not take credit for his heroic feat, deferring to his two teammates. When he moved on to the Chicago White Sox in the upstart American League in 1902, Davis was caught in the war between the leagues. He ended up bouncing between the Sox and the Giants for a season until the Sox prevailed. A key player for Chicago, Davis helped the 1906 "Hitless Wonders" to a World Series Championship, and played for the Sox until he retired in 1909. The fleet-footed Davis swiped a career 619 bases, ranked 17th in baseball history, and retired at age 38 with a career .295 batting average.

> *How is it possible for a man to play big league baseball for twenty seasons, manage the New York Giants twice, start a war between the National and American Leagues and then utterly vanish, without leaving a trace?"*
>
> – Lee Allen, Historian, *The Sporting News*, August 7, 1968

After his retirement, Davis managed Des Moines in the Western League in 1910, coached for Amherst College, and scouted for the Yankees and Browns, but by 1919 he was all but forgotten by baseball. He managed a bowling alley and worked in automotive sales for a brief time. After Davis was diagnosed in 1934 with paresis, a brain infection caused by syphilis, he lived out his life in a psychiatric hospital, dying in 1940 at age 70. Forgotten by baseball for many years, historians and sportswriters ramped up a campaign to induct him into the Hall of Fame in the 1990s. Finally elected by the Veterans Committee in 1998, George Stacey Davis is now acknowledged as one of baseball's top shortstops. No longer "his era's most forgotten best player," George Davis is simply another great player whose recognition was long overdue.

Gorgeous George

PSA/DNA Authentication Services Says:

Autographs of George Davis rank near the very top of the most difficult Deadball Era players in baseball history. Some would argue that Davis might very well be *the* toughest Hall of Fame autograph to locate in the entire hobby. Elected by the Veterans Committee in 1998, Davis was not a shoe-in like most other stars of the day, which meant autograph seekers didn't pursue him or save autographs like they may have of other big names. Davis did stay around the game long after he ceased playing. He even acted as the Amherst College baseball coach until 1918, which seemingly offered continued opportunities to obtain his autograph. However, the practice of signing autographs was not commonplace during his playing days or lifetime, resulting in the limited number of genuine examples today.

"*George Stacey Davis has been his era's most forgotten best player.*"

– Dave Andersen, *New York Times*

THE EARLY YEARS 73

Ed Delahanty

E. J. DELAHANTY.

One of the all-time great Philadelphia Phillies, Ed Delahanty was a power hitter extraordinaire during his 16-year big league career (1888–1903). "Big Ed" was just that. Standing 6-foot, one-inch, and weighing in at a slight, but sturdy, 170 pounds, Delahanty could really turn his wiry frame on a baseball, smacking 101 home runs in his career, and leading the league with 19 homers in 1893 and 13 in 1896. Moreover, he is one of the scant few ballplayers who eclipsed the .400 mark multiple times. In both 1894 and 1895, Delahanty hit .404 with 200 and 194 hits respectively. He topped that in 1899 with a league-leading .410 batting average, 238 hits, 55 doubles, and 137 RBI. His RBI totals are staggering. Delahanty drove in 146 runs in 1893 and 126 in 1896, leading the NL both years. For his career, he drove in an impressive 1,466 runners, and his 58 stolen bases in 1898 were also best in the league.

Surrounded by great hitters in the Phillies lineups, like Jack Clements, Joe Sullivan, Sam Thompson, and Billy Hamilton, Big Ed became a run-scoring machine, crossing the plate 1600 times in 16 seasons. Despite having multiple .300 hitters on the roster, there were no title wins during Delahanty's 13 years with the Phillies.

The eldest of five brothers who played in the majors, Edward James Delahanty was a five-tool player who patrolled the outfield with graceful aplomb and could pick it around every infield position. He was inducted into the Baseball Hall of Fame in 1945, and his plaque details that he twice went 6–6 in games and once hit four homers in one contest. While a Phillie at heart, Delahanty did go for the cash with Cleveland of the Players League in 1890, and again with Washington of the new American League in 1902 and 1903. His attempt to sign a lucrative deal with the Giants in 1903 was blocked and, as his personal life unraveled, he became angry, depressed, and subject to drinking binges, the

Big Ed

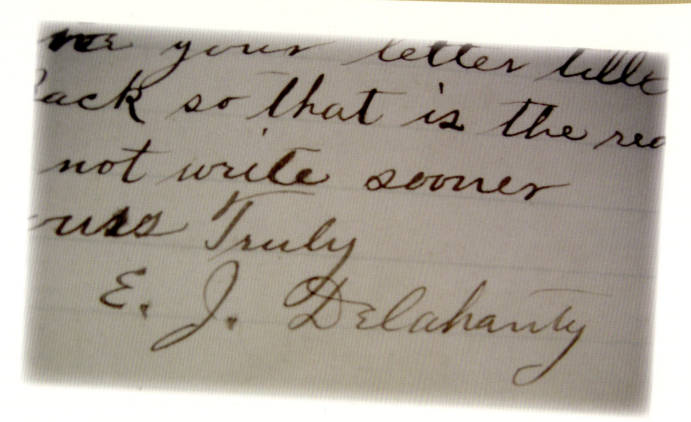

last of which cost him his life. The stories are cloudy, but reports say that on July 2, 1903, after a scuffle on a train, a drunk and disoriented Delahanty was either pushed, stumbled, or jumped off the International Railway Bridge at Niagara Falls in the thick of the Ontario night. The 35-year-old Delahanty's body was found down river at Horseshoe Falls. His luck as one of baseball's premiere sluggers had run its course.

PSA/DNA Authentication Services Says:

An Ed Delahanty autograph is one of the most challenging in the collecting world, and he easily makes our "Top 100" on that factor alone. During the Deadball Era, autograph collecting had yet to become a noticeable cultural practice. As a result, very few authentic specimens exist today for any players of that period. Autographs simply weren't requested with any frequency at the time. While authenticating his signature can prove more difficult than most, there are a handful of known examples, and most are signed in similar fashion "E. J. Delahanty." All of the baseball autographs on our list are often forged by unscrupulous individuals. However, those seeking a Delahanty signature should be on heightened alert with so few authentic autographs known.

THE EARLY YEARS

William Ewing

William "Buck" Ewing's first five years as a Major Leaguer was a study in incremental improvement. In that quintuplet of seasons, he showed a steady upswing in his stats, never dominant, but always getting better. The Hoagland, Ohio, native broke in with the National League's Troy Trojans in 1880 and promptly hit an unimpressive .178. From there, it was .250 in 1881, .271 in 1882, and .303 in 1883. After a slight dip to .277 in 1884, Ewing would begin a streak of nine consecutive seasons in which he batted over .300. His best season was in 1893 with the Cleveland Spiders when he knocked in 122 runs, batted .344, and stole 47 bases. Ewing won two championship titles with the New York Giants in 1888 and 1889, batting .290 in postseason play with 13 RBI.

The versatile Ewing played every position on the field, including pitcher, although his lifetime 2–3 record with a 3.45 ERA was not the reason for his induction into the Baseball Hall of Fame in 1939. Neither was his pedestrian managerial record of 489–395 with the Giants and Reds. No, it was Ewing's prowess behind the plate that puts him in the company of baseball's immortals. Many of the greatest baseball minds of several eras used superlatives in describing Buck's talents. The Baseball Hall of Fame quotes the *1940 Official Baseball Guide* as saying, "Ewing is considered by many to have been the greatest all-around player who ever lived...He could run, bat, and how he could throw! When he was catching he would squat down behind the plate and seemingly hand the ball to whoever was playing second base."

Ewing was a born leader, a team captain, and field general behind the plate. Moreover, with a makeshift mask and no chest protector or shin guards, he was as tough as they come. Today's catchers resemble knights clad in suits of armor. Ewing had no such protection in his 636 career games behind the dish. At five-foot, ten-inches, and 188 pounds, he was both sturdy and speedy. An athletic catcher, Ewing was usually among the league leaders in double plays turned by a catcher and range factor. You could say he was a precursor to the mobile catchers of the modern era. There is no doubt that Buck Ewing was truly a backstop for the ages. In 1906, just six years after his stint as Giants manager, Ewing died of diabetes and Bright's disease at age 47.

PSA/DNA Authentication Services Says:

Ewing was one of the greatest players from the 19th century and, like most of his contemporaries, his signature is extremely scarce. Adding to the high level of difficulty is the fact that Ewing passed away in 1906, which represents one of the earliest deaths in our "Top 100" list. Of the scant few examples that are known at this time, Ewing signed his name "WM Ewing." With Ewing and some of the other true rarities in the hobby, being selective about the autograph medium will only lead to frustration for the collector. For example, at the time of this writing, no signed baseballs from Ewing's playing days are known. Finding an authentic autograph of any kind is challenging enough. The autograph image featured on the facing page is a facsimile.

Buck

Wm Ewing

" *His throwing to bases was deadly, while at the bat he was a sort of terror to all of the best pitchers in the league. He was also an admirable base runner, not overly speedy, but his excellent judgment in starting enabled him to steal a majority of bases in safety. Ewing was a natural baseball player, for besides catching, he was able to play any other place on the team.*"

— The New York Times, October 21, 1906

Billy Hamilton

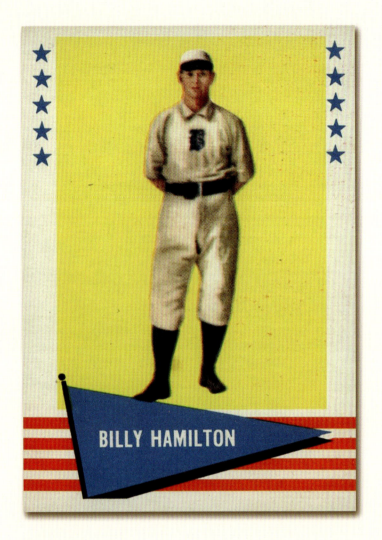

When you look at the careers of Rickey Henderson, Ty Cobb, Lou Brock, Tim Raines, and other great base stealers, there is one individual who always seems to slip through the cracks. "Sliding" Billy Hamilton, not only ranks third all-time for most career stolen bases in the history of the game, he was also a tremendous offensive force. Incredibly, in 1894, Hamilton scored 192 runs in 129 games, still the all-time record. To this day, Hamilton is the Philadelphia Phillies career leader in batting average with .361 compiled over his six seasons with the team.

How would Hamilton compare to today's base stealing leaders? Before the turn of the century, base stealing rules were certainly much different. Moving up on a throw to another base, for instance, was considered a stolen base, as was moving up on a throwing error. By today's rules, Hamilton is credited with 914 to 937 stolen bases, which was the all-time record until Lou Brock bested it in 1978.

A high school sprinter from Newark, New Jersey, Hamilton broke into the pros with the Kansas City Cowboys of the American Association in 1888 at the age of 22. The 5-foot, 6-inch, and 165 pound center fielder became an impact player almost immediately. While with the Phillies from 1890 to 1895 and the Boston Beaneaters from 1896 to 1901, Hamilton tore up the National League. He led the league in stolen bases, walks, and on-base percentage five times, runs and singles four times, and batting average two times. He hit .300 or better 12 of his 14 seasons, including .403 in 1894. Known for his head-first slides, Hamilton had four seasons with 100 or more stolen bases.

He retired from the majors when he was 35 years old in 1901 with a .344 batting average and .455 on-base percentage. Hamilton then played and managed in the minors through 1910, served as a scout for the Boston Braves, and was part-owner and manager of Worcester in the Eastern League in 1916. He died in Worcester, Massachusetts, in 1940, at the age of 74. After his playing days, Hamilton was not credited as the stolen base record holder. That title was erroneously given to Ty Cobb. Because of that, Sliding Billy Hamilton was overlooked for many years. However, if you look at his full body of work offensively, he certainly deserves accolades, not only for swiping bases, but also for his remarkable hitting. William Robert Hamilton was elected to the Hall of Fame in 1961.

Sliding Billy

PSA/DNA Authentication Services Says:

Hamilton's autograph is one of the most challenging on our "Top 100" list. While there are a small number of handwritten letters that have surfaced over the years, Hamilton's autograph remains difficult to find on virtually any medium. Early versions of his autograph, from the pre-1900 era, were often signed "WR Hamilton." This differs from his full name signature "William Robert Hamilton," a version Hamilton employed later and nearly up until his passing in 1940. Despite staying around the game after he played, which included serving as a scout for the Boston Braves at one point, and for being known as a responsive signer through the mail, Hamilton's autograph remains a hole in many advanced autograph collections.

> "Hamilton is now playing the finest game of his career, and that means he is the most valuable center fielder, all things considered, today in the game."
>
> – T.H. Murname, *Boston Daily Globe,* June 13, 1898

THE EARLY YEARS

Miller Huggins

At 5-foot, 6-inches, and 140 pounds, Miller James Huggins looked more like a batboy than a future Hall of Famer, but the man they called Mighty Mite became a giant in the history of baseball. As second baseman for the Cincinnati Reds (1904–1909) and the St. Louis Cardinals (1910–1916), Huggins' main claim to fame was his uncanny ability to draw walks. He led the National League in walks four times, eclipsing the 100 walk plateau on three occasions. Huggins was a good hitter and excellent base stealer who used guile and intelligence to forge a solid big league career. In short, he got on base to the tune of a career .382 OBP. The quintessential Huggins day at the ballpark was June 1, 1910, when, according to the Baseball Hall of Fame, he drew four walks and got two sacrifice flies, setting a Major League record with six plate appearances and no official at-bats. While Huggins would never reach the postseason as a player, his second career in baseball would more than compensate for that.

> *"We had a few battles, but there was no man I liked better in baseball. Whatever he said to me was for my own good."*
>
> \- Babe Ruth

Huggins became player-manager of the Cardinals in 1913, but never finished higher than third in five seasons at the helm. Still, Yankees owner Jacob Ruppert saw a glimpse of hope in Huggins and hired him to manage the floundering Yanks in 1918. After one fourth-place and two third-place finishes, Huggins ripped off three straight pennants and brought home the Yankees first World Series title in 1923. That roster featured names like Babe Ruth, Bob Meusel, Lou Gehrig, Waite Hoyt, Sad Sam Jones, Bullet Joe Bush, and Herb Pennock. After reloading in 1924 and 1925, Huggins won three more pennants and two World Series from 1926 to 1928 featuring some of the best players and teams in baseball history. The 1927 "Murderers' Row" Yankees remain standard bearers for team greatness. They finished 110–44 and swept the Pittsburgh Pirates in the World Series. Joining Ruth and Gehrig in

Mighty Mite

Huggins' clubhouse were players like Tony Lazzeri, Earle Combs, Urban Shocker, and Wilcy Moore. Huggins, who won over 1,400 games as a manager, should not be dismissed as merely benefitting from great players. He had a keen eye for young talent and deftly handled the petulant Ruth while sculpting a winner. Tragically, the 51-year-old Yankees manager died suddenly from a blood infection on September 25, 1929. Miller Huggins was inducted into the Baseball Hall of Fame in 1964 and will be remembered as the skipper who built baseball's greatest dynasty.

> "There seemed to me to be an impression here and there that anybody could manage so great a team. That's wrong. It took Huggins to make those fellows fight and hustle."
>
> – Connie Mack

PSA/DNA Authentication Services Says:

Since Miller Huggins is tied to some of the greatest New York Yankees teams in baseball history, the most successful franchise in the sport, the demand for his autograph ranks near the top of all great managers. While you will encounter Huggins' autograph on mediums such as team-signed baseballs and documents, it is more difficult to find his signature on items such as photos or album pages. The legendary manager would usually sign his name "M. J. Huggins" instead of spelling out his first name. There is evidence that Huggins used a clubhouse attendant to add his name to different items as far back as the early 1920s. What is, perhaps, more shocking is that Huggins would occasionally have someone sign official documents on his behalf, but that was a very rarely the case. Huggins' early death in 1929 at the age of 51 also contributes to the relative difficulty in locating authentic examples.

THE EARLY YEARS

Hughie Jennings

Hughie Jennings broke into the big leagues with the Louisville Colonels in 1891 and eventually became baseball's all-time leader in hits—but not the kind where the bat hits the ball, the kind where the ball hits the batter. Two hundred and eighty-seven times that Jennings stepped to the plate, he got thumped by a variety of pitches. He led the National League in HBP five straight seasons (1894–1898) as a member of the Baltimore Orioles. In addition to his penchant for being plunked, Jennings was a slick shortstop and a solid hitter, batting .312 over his 18-year career and eclipsing the 200-hit plateau in both 1895 and 1896. He used speed on the basepaths, regularly stretching singles to doubles and doubles to triples. He was also a terrific RBI man, recording an OBP of .400-plus seven times.

After a stellar run in Baltimore, including three straight NL titles between 1894 and 1896, Jennings helped the Brooklyn Superbas to the 1899 NL pennant, played for the Phillies, and managed the Eastern League Orioles for several seasons before landing with the sixth-place Detroit Tigers as player-manager in 1907. Jennings leadership brought the Tigers to three straight American League pennants (1907–1909). All three trips to the Fall Classic resulted in losses: to the Chicago Cubs in 1907 and 1908, and to the Pittsburgh Pirates in 1909. Yes, Hughie Jennings was the last Major League manager to lose a World Series to the Cubs. Jennings' years as Tigers manager coincided with the best years of Ty Cobb's career. Under Jennings, Cobb won all of his 12 batting crowns, and led the AL in hits eight times, stolen bases six times, and RBI four times. Known as "Ee-yah" for the unmistakable sound he made cheering on his players from the coaches' box, Jennings remained as the skipper in Detroit until 1920, but never again captured the flag. He coached for John McGraw's Giants during four pennant-winning seasons (1921–1924) and managed them for parts of the 1924 and 1925 seasons while McGraw was ill. Under Jennings' watch, the club went 32–12 in 1924.

While with the Superbas, Jennings studied law at Cornell and he developed a second career as a renowned trial lawyer during the off-seasons in Scranton, Pennsylvania. Jennings achieved success from humble beginnings. He was born in Pittston, Pennsylvania, and worked the coal mines at age 12. Sadly, Jennings was diagnosed with tuberculosis after the 1925 season and

Ee-Yah

his health failed rapidly. Hugh Ambrose Jennings passed away in 1928, at age 58. He was elected to the Baseball Hall of Fame in 1945.

PSA/DNA Authentication Services Says:

Like many early baseball figures on our "Top 100" list, Jennings stayed around the game for a good portion of his adult life, managing both the Detroit Tigers and the New York Giants after his playing career was over. In fact, he continued managing until just a few years before he passed away in 1928. Since Jennings was considered one of the premier players in baseball during his playing career, early signatures can occasionally be found as a result of his popularity. That said, you will more frequently see autographs signed during his coaching and managing career, although some of those were signed by a clubhouse attendant in Jennings' place. Typically, Jennings would sign his name "Hugh Jennings," but would occasionally vary his first name by signing "Hughie Jennings" instead.

> "There was nothing sedate about Hughie [Jennings]. He once survived a running dive into a concrete swimming pool - after the pool had been unexpectedly drained."
>
> - Ty Cobb

THE EARLY YEARS 83

Tim Keefe

Thought by many to be the pitcher in Ernest Thayer's poem "Casey at the Bat," Tim Keefe was dominant during baseball's formative years. He performed at the top of his game through many early baseball rule changes. As a 23-year-old rookie with the National League's Troy Trojans, Keefe pitched from a distance of 45 feet and posted a 0.86 ERA in 1880. For the next 12 years, he pitched from 50 feet, and it was not until 1893, his final season, that Keefe pitched from the current 60-foot, 6-inch distance.

The 5-foot, 10-inch, and 185 pound right-handed twirler posted some astounding numbers as his career progressed. In his prime, Keefe pitched when a two-man rotation was the norm. While pitching every other day, "Sir Timothy" used his head, choosing to baffle batters with a confusing array of pitches, and he is considered one of the first to use the change-up. In 1883, with the American Association's New York Metropolitans, Keefe went 41–27 with a 2.41 ERA. That was the first of six consecutive 30-win seasons, including his career-high of 42 wins in 1886. All totaled, Keefe won 342 games over his stellar career.

The son of a carpenter, Timothy John Keefe worked in carpentry before baseball. During his playing days, he studied accounting and shorthand to better himself, and he invested in real estate and a sporting goods firm. Known as "Sir Timothy" for his unflappable manner and cerebral approach to the game, Keefe was also one of the first to use holdouts as a salary negotiation ploy.

With the New York Giants from 1885 to 1889, Keefe won the Triple Crown in 1888 and led the Giants to the pennant and postseason exhibition wins in both 1888 and 1889. Because the reserve clause rankled him, Keefe helped start a rival league called the Players League, which only lasted one year. He was also involved with the Brotherhood of Professional Base Ball Players, which fought for the welfare of Major League players. Keefe finished his career with the Philadelphia

> *I never saw a better pitcher. True, he did his best work from 50 feet, but he still would have had no superior at 60 feet, six inches."*
>
> – Mickey Welch, Hall of Famer

Sir Timothy

PSA/DNA Authentication Services Says:

Even though it is widely known that Tim Keefe spent most of his adult life around the game and attended Boston Red Sox games regularly into the late-1920s, his autographs remain scarce to this day. One of the handful of authentic examples known can be found on a signed team sheet, but it is one of the few Keefe signatures that survived through the decades. Even though he passed away in 1933, which is still long before autograph collecting became more commonplace, one would imagine that some people would have pursued Keefe's signature prior to his death. His stature in the game and accessibility later in life would have seemingly produced more autographs for collectors today, yet it was not to be. The autograph image featured on the facing page is a facsimile.

Phillies from 1891 to 1893, retiring when he was 36 years old. His many accomplishments over his 14-year career include leading the league in wins twice, ERA three times, and strikeouts twice. In retirement, Keefe coached for Harvard University, was a MLB umpire, and managed his Cambridge, Massachusetts, real estate investments. He died in 1933 at the age of 76. The Veterans Committee elected Keefe to the Hall of Fame in 1964.

> *Keefe is said to be one of the most scientific pitchers in the country – that is, he uses his head as well as his hands while in the box."*
>
> – *Boston Globe*, October 14, 1885

Willie Keeler

"**W**ee Willie" Keeler stood 5-foot, 4-inches, and weighed a slight 140 pounds, but he was a behemoth of a hitter in his 19-year Hall of Fame career. He played for Baltimore from 1894 to 1898 but, except for those

> "*He may have been small in size but he was huge with the bat.*"
> – Ted Williams

five seasons, the Brooklyn native stayed close to home playing for the New York Giants, Brooklyn Grooms/Superbas, and New York Highlanders. What William Henry Keeler really loved to do was hit a baseball. In 8,591 career at-bats, he struck out just 136 times and walked just 524 times. For Keeler, it was all about making contact, and his motto was, "Hit 'em where they ain't." He sprayed the baseball all over the field, using his speed to navigate the basepaths to score a career 1,719 runs.

Truly one of the greatest pure hitters of all-time, Keeler batted a career .341, good for 14th on the all-time list. He had over 200 hits eight years in a row from 1894 to 1901, a record that stood for a century until Ichiro Suzuki topped it in 2009. In both 1897 and 1898, Keeler led the National League in hitting, batting .424 and .385 respectively. In addition to the lofty batting average in 1897, the highest for a left-handed hitter in baseball history, Keeler led the league with 239 hits, had 27 doubles, 19 triples, stole 64 bases, and had a gaudy 1.003 OPS. Keeler began that watershed season with a 44-game hitting streak that stood as the MLB single-season record until Joe DiMaggio's 56 in 1941.

A smart ballplayer, terrific bunter, and classic leadoff table-setter, Keeler helped his teams win five pennants. The son of Irish immigrants, Keeler honed his toughness as a lad by boxing, but baseball quickly became his true sport's calling. He broke in with the Giants in 1892, hitting .321, but soon joined the skilled likes of John McGraw, Hughie Jennings, and Wilbert Robinson in Baltimore to build a National League dynasty. The Orioles were known for feuds and

Wee Willie

clubhouse scuffles, but on the field, they were serious and sublime. Keeler and McGraw battled, but there was a respect there as well. In 1910, Keeler finished his big league career with McGraw's Giants when he was 38 years old. After retiring, he coached and scouted for a brief time before getting involved in real estate and other business ventures. Sadly, Keeler died of heart disease in 1923 at the young age of 50. He was inducted into the Baseball Hall of Fame in 1939.

PSA/DNA Authentication Services Says:

The practice of signing autographs was simply not part of the culture during the time Keeler played, which is true for several other entries on our "Top 100" list. While Keeler did live until 1923, he didn't stay around the game long after retirement, unlike many other baseball figures. Even though Keeler did become active in the real estate market, not many documents bearing his signature have survived from that period in his life. While not quite in the same league as Addie Joss when it comes to scarcity, Keeler autographs still rank high on our overall list.

> "Keep your eye clear and hit 'em where they ain't; that's all."
>
> – Willie Keeler

THE EARLY YEARS

Mike Kelly

Mike "King" Kelly to baseball was like Rudolph Valentino to movies. Undoubtedly the reigning idol of baseball during the 1880s, Kelly is credited with innovations that helped shape our National Pastime, like the hook slide, the hit-and-run, and backing up first base as a catcher. Michael Joseph Kelly could play every position with gusto, even pitcher, and he became an instant fan-favorite for his on-the-field heroics. Primarily an outfielder and catcher, the flamboyant Kelly was known to use a little trickery to gain the upper hand on his opponents. It is said the handsome outfielder sometimes kept a ball in his pocket that he pulled out if the actual hit ball was over his head. Kelly made it look like he made the catch without fans or umpires realizing what actually happened. As a catcher, he sometimes dropped his catcher's mask on home plate, so the advancing runner could not touch the plate.

The most popular player of his day, Kelly became the "King of Baseball" soon after he came up to the Cincinnati Reds in 1878. The two-time National League batting champ had eight .300 or better seasons, hit a lofty .388 for the Chicago White Stockings in 1886, and led the league in runs scored three times. Over his 16-year career played mostly with the Chicago White Stockings and the Boston Beaneaters, he batted .308 and is credited with 368 steals from 1886 to 1893. Kelly was the highest paid player on the circuit, and justifiably so, as he drew packed houses wherever he played. Famous for his hustle on the basepaths, fans called out "Slide, Kelly, Slide" during games. Because of his immense popularity, outgoing personality, and penchant for booze, gambling, and carousing, Kelly became a national celebrity. In 1889, the song "Slide Kelly Slide" was a Vaudeville hit and later became the first hit record in American history in 1892. During the off-season, Kelly appeared in Vaudeville and acted in theatrical productions, delighting fans when he stood center stage and recited the newly released poem "Casey at the Bat" with his typical King Kelly flair. He played his last game for the New York Giants in 1893 and died just one year later, four days after contracting pneumonia while traveling by boat from New York to Boston in November of 1894. He was only 36 years old. The entire country was in shock, and reportedly over 7,000 people attended his wake in Boston. The King was elected to the Hall of Fame in 1945.

> "That most idolized ballplayer, Mike Kelly, was one of the most fascinating figures ever to dig a cleated shoe into the diamond. He was a slashing, dashing, devil-may-care athlete, good-natured, big-hearted, sincere. He had perhaps the keenest brain that baseball ever knew."
>
> - Frank Menke, *Encyclopedia of Sports*, 1944

King

PSA/DNA Authentication Services Says:

Along with the likes of Cap Anson, Kelly was one of the first superstars of the sport during the late 1800s. Because Kelly was such an important baseball figure, coupled with the extreme rarity of his autograph, the only known signed image of Kelly sold for a record $214,936 in 2011. The signature appeared on an 1887 banquet photo and it remains the only one known of its kind. Of the small number of authentic Kelly autographs that still exist, most of them come in the form of documents or cuts that originated from full documents. What you will mostly see are autographs signed "M. J. Kelly," which was a common style of the time, using initials for the first and middle names. At the time of publication, no signed baseballs were known, including multi-signed or team-signed examples.

THE EARLY YEARS

Connie Mack

The 1893 scouting report for Connie Mack might have looked like this: A so-so hitting catcher from East Brookfield, Massachusetts, the kid is basically a pipe cleaner with a mitt, all 6-foot, 1-inch, and 150 pounds of him. A fastball from even the most rag-arm pitcher might

> *"After all my years, there are two things I've never got used to – haggling with a player over his contract and telling a boy he's got to go back."*
>
> *– Connie Mack*

knock him to the backstop. The kid has a decent grasp of the game and broke in big time with the Washington Nationals in 1886 batting .361 in 10 games, but he has been inconsistent, hitting .187 in 1888, .293 in 1889, .214 in 1891, and .286 in 1893, for Washington, Buffalo, and Pittsburgh. The kid has no power, but can steal a few bases and has a knack for handling decent pitchers. Might make a better manager than player. End of report.

In fact, Mack did become player-manager for the Pirates in 1894, but never finished higher than 6th in his three seasons. Despite this, he became part-owner and manager of the Philadelphia Athletics of the fledgling American League in 1901, and the rest is truly baseball history. Mack set the standard for future managers, and not just in haberdashery with his sharp suits and trademark hats. With pitchers like Eddie Plank and Rube Waddell and a lineup that included seven .300-plus hitters, the Athletics won the 1902 American League pennant. Mack managed the A's for an unprecedented and unmatched 50 years, winning nine pennants and five World Series titles. His Athletics were the AL's first regal franchise, winning six of the league's first 14 flags, four of them in a dynastic run between 1910 and 1914. Mack periodically jettisoned his high priced talent to rebuild and reload for future and continued success. This philosophy made him baseball's all-time leading manager in both wins (3,731) and losses (3,948). His clubs finished first or second 16 times, and seventh or eighth 22 times.

The Tall Tactician

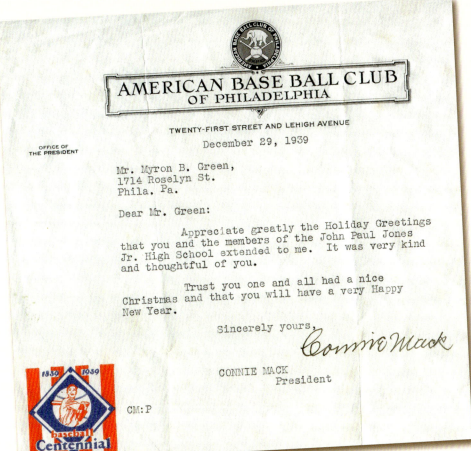

Over the years, Mack managed many baseball legends, including: Al Simmons, Jimmie Foxx, Mickey Cochrane, Lefty Grove, Tris Speaker, Eddie Collins, Nap Lajoie, and Ty Cobb. The man they called "The Tall Tactician" was also a true gentleman who managed his players with dignity and respect. Cornelius Alexander Mack was elected to the Hall of Fame in 1937, and continued on as manager and president of the A's until 1950, retiring at age 87. He passed away several years later in 1956. The Baseball Hall of Fame quotes Connie Mack as saying, "Humanity is the keystone that holds nations and men together. When that collapses, the whole structure crumbles."

PSA/DNA Authentication Services Says:

Mack spent virtually his entire life in the game as a player, manager, and, eventually, an owner. His signature is defined by extreme pressure and a bold appearance, which is a clue to his personality. It was almost like Mack wanted you to know that he was in charge. Most items were signed "Connie," but you will find some correspondence from him signed "Cornelius" from time to time. While Mack was known for signing frequently throughout his life, collectors will encounter the occasional clubhouse autograph on team-signed items or secretarial signature on various types of correspondence. Although he passed away in 1956, finding an authentic Mack signature is relatively easy. As an important note, a facsimile signature appears in Connie Mack's Baseball Book (1950) that some sellers offer as actually signed by the Hall of Famer.

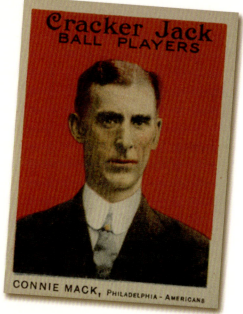

Joe McGinnity

Joseph Jerome McGinnity had a brief but memorable Hall of Fame career highlighted by a 1904 season with the New York Giants in which he went 35–8 with a 1.61 ERA in over 400 innings pitched. Known as the "Iron Man" for his work in the family foundry business and his durability on the hill, McGinnity led the National League in innings pitched four times. After six seasons of Minor League and semi-pro ball, the 28-year-old rookie came up to the NL's Baltimore Orioles in 1899 and led the league with 28 wins. In 1900, he moved to the Brooklyn Superbas and again posted a league-leading 28 victories.

After a brief return to Baltimore on the American League side, McGinnity settled in with the Giants and enjoyed his greatest success, winning 114 games from 1903 to 1906. The ultimate workhorse, McGinnity finished 314 of 381 games started in his 10-year MLB career and was famous for pitching both ends of doubleheaders. He won a career 246 games with 2.66 ERA in nearly 3,500 innings pitched. In 1905, McGinnity went 21–15, dominating the league with teammate Christy Mathewson's 31–9, and the Giants won the World Series.

McGinnity was the Giants third-base coach during baseball's infamous Merkle "Bonehead" game on September 23, 1908. With the Giants battling the Cubs in a pennant race, New York's Fred Merkle lined a two-out, bottom-of-the-ninth single to right field sending teammate Moose McCormick to third. Al Bridwell then hit one up the middle, scoring McCormick with what seemed to be the winning run. Thinking the game was done, Merkle stopped short of second base and headed to the dugout. Cubs center fielder Solly Hofman had fielded Bridwell's hit and tossed it to second baseman Johnny Evers. Somehow McGinnity got hold of the ball and tossed it into the crowd in celebration. Evers found another baseball  and argued that Merkle was out on a force play because he had not touched second. That claim was upheld, and the game ended in a 1–1 tie, eventually costing New York the 1908 pennant.

The Giants released the 37-year-old McGinnity after that season, but the durable hurler went on to pitch, manage, and own in the Minor Leagues, posting 207 more wins in 13 seasons, pitching his last game at the age of 54 in 1925. Joe McGinnity, truly an Iron Man at all levels of the game, died in 1929 and was inducted into the Baseball Hall of Fame in 1946.

Iron Man

> "McGinnity was a magician in the box. It was difficult for a batter to get his measure... He knew all the tricks for putting a batter on the spot."
>
> – Connie Mack

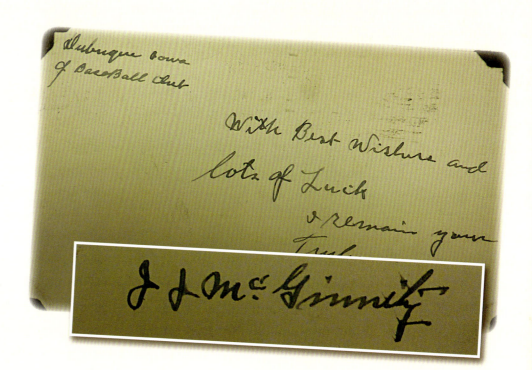

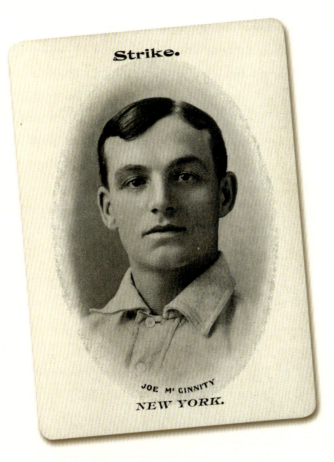

PSA/DNA Authentication Services Says:

McGinnity falls into a select group of early baseball figures whose autographs are scarce by nature. When you add to that the fact that he passed away in 1929, the difficulty is taken to a new level. Like many players of the period, the Hall of Fame pitcher would use initials for his first and middle name when signing, "J. J. McGinnity." While his autograph remains very tough, some quantity of signed letters and single-signed baseballs have been discovered. Some dated examples have also surfaced, but most of them originate from the last few years of his life in the mid-to-late 1920s.

John McGraw

In 1902, New York Giants manager Horace Fogel had a 21-year-old pitcher with 20–20 record over the previous two seasons. Fogel quit on the kid, moving him to first base and outfield. The Giants finished 40 games under .500 but when John McGraw took over as manager in July, he immediately put that young pitcher back on the mound. The kid's name was Christy Mathewson and he would win 14 games in 1902, and 339 more over the rest of his career. Creating the legend known as Christy Mathewson would be a fine feather in any baseball man's cap, but John McGraw's career cannot be defined by one masterful maneuver.

Fiery does not begin to describe the internal inferno that was John Joseph McGraw. The flames were fanned in a childhood of heartache. McGraw was born in Truxton, New York, in 1873 and, by 1885, had lost his mother and three of his seven siblings to diphtheria. McGraw's father was alcoholic and abusive, and young John had to work and struggle for every coin and morsel of food. His eventual nickname "Little Napoleon" fit. McGraw stood just 5-foot, 7-inches, and weighed 155 pounds. What he lacked in girth, he made up for in guile. As a player, McGraw was as cunning as he was confounding. In his 17 seasons with the Orioles, Cardinals, and Giants, McGraw was a fly that the opposition could not swat, drawing walks, stealing bases, and scoring runs in frenetic fashion. In 1898 and 1899, he led the National League in both runs scored and walks. He had a career OBP of .466 and batting average of .334.

McGraw parlayed his knowledge of the game's finer points into an extraordinary managerial career, first in Baltimore (1899, 1901–1902) and for an incredible 31 years with the Giants (1902–1932). Along the way, he tiptoed

Little Napoleon

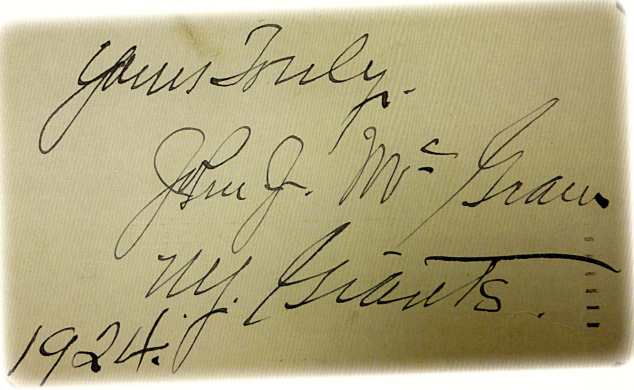

the line between celebrity and sanctimony, dabbling in some questionable business dealings in politics, entertainment, and gambling. He was also instrumental in booting the Yankees from the Polo Grounds, upset by Babe Ruth's home run prowess that was in stark contrast to McGraw's "small ball" style. While few opposing managers got the best of McGraw, prostate cancer and uremic poisoning eventually did, and Little Napoleon died in 1934, at age 60. As a manager, the 1937 Hall of Famer won 10 pennants, three World Series, and is second all-time to Connie Mack in wins with 2,736. If you are keeping score, that is some 2,698 more than Horace Fogel.

PSA/DNA Authentication Services Says:

John J. McGraw possessed one of the more beautiful signatures on our "Top 100" list. Flowing and graceful, McGraw would often sign his full name to various pieces. During his managerial career, McGraw was known for signing most of the requests that came his way, avoiding the use of a proxy in his place. While McGraw did sign a fair number of autographs, most of his activity pre-dated the mail signing boom, which is why we see a smaller selection of signed GPCs and index cards in the marketplace today compared to other figures of the pre-1950 era. That said, McGraw's wife was known for sending along signed checks and check cuts to seekers of his autograph through the mail to help satisfy the demand.

THE EARLY YEARS

Amos Rusie

Born in Mooresville, Indiana, Amos Wilson Rusie was known as "The Hoosier Thunderbolt" and the moniker fit—batters never knew when or where Rusie's fastball would strike. He fanned 1,950 batters in just over 3,778 innings pitched, but also led the National League in walks for five straight seasons (1890–1894). Between 1890 and 1895, he led the NL in Ks five out of six seasons, topping 300 strikeouts in 1890, 1891, and 1892. Rusie

> *"Words fail to describe the speed with which Rusie sent the ball. . . . It was like a white streak tearing past you."*
>
> – Jimmy Ryan, Chicago Colts outfielder, 1894

regularly surpassed the 400 or 500 innings-pitched plateau and was among the perennial league-leaders in games, games started, and games finished. He won more than 30 games in four consecutive seasons, topping out at 36 in 1894. That season, he won the pitching Triple Crown, leading the NL in wins, strikeouts, and ERA. The Giants won the inaugural Temple Cup Series in 1894, beating second place Baltimore in a four-game sweep.

Rusie broke into the Bigs in 1889 with his hometown Indianapolis Hoosiers. When that club folded, he was assigned to New York where he enjoyed a superb run with the Giants from 1890 to 1898. At 6-foot, 1-inch, and 200 pounds, the fireballing right-hander was a truly menacing figure on the hill, even more so before 1893 when the mound was just 50 feet from home plate. Rusie was known to plaster many a foe with a wild pitch and famously plunked Hughie Jennings, rendering the future Hall of Famer unconscious for four days. Wildly popular with New York fans, Rusie believed his immense talent warranted immense dollars, and he often clashed with frugal Giants management. The Giants actually released Rusie in 1892 to save a month's salary. When the Cubs swooped in and signed the hurler, New York had to buy him back for a larger sum. One of the first players to challenge baseball's reserve clause, which bound players to one team, Rusie held out of spring training and the regular season, but his economic leverage ended in 1898 when he developed

The Hoosier Thunderbolt

Amos Rusie

arm woes. The Giants traded him to Cincinnati in December of 1900 for a 19-year old kid named Christy Mathewson. The 30-year-old Rusie played only three games for Cincinnati before retiring in 1901. He ended up working as night watchman at the Polo Grounds, owned a chicken farm, and when the 71-year-old Rusie passed away in 1942, he was seemingly forgotten by baseball. Amos Rusie, the most powerful pitcher of his time and players' rights pioneer, finally became a Baseball Hall of Famer in 1977.

PSA/DNA Authentication Services Says:

Rusie is another early baseball figure who played during the 19th century and while his autograph is still tougher than most on our "Top 100" list, the number of available examples is greater than many of his contemporaries. This is primarily a result of his relatively long lifespan, at least for the era. Rusie passed away at the age of 71 in 1942, which means he lived through a period where autograph collecting became slightly more popular than the pre-1920 era. In addition, since he ended up working at the Polo Grounds for a time after his playing days were over, fans still had public access to Rusie. Most of the autographs that have survived were signed in similar fashion, "Amos W. Rusie."

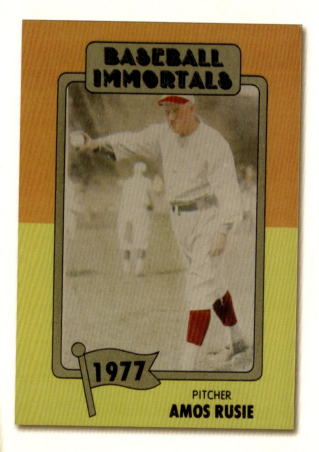

Amos W. Rusie

THE EARLY YEARS 97

Albert Spalding

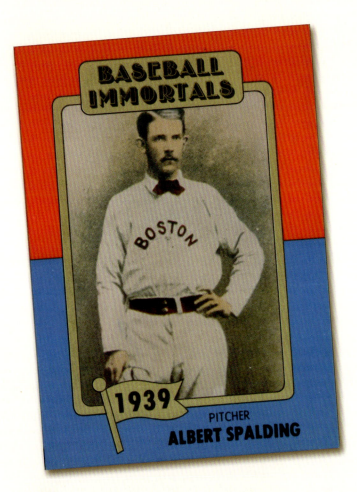

An outstanding pitcher, innovator, and businessman, Spalding's contributions to the game still resonate to this day. As an innovator, Spalding organized the National League, wrote the first set of baseball rules, was the first player to use a fielding glove on a regular basis, and is credited with developing the business aspect of our National Pastime. As a pitcher, Spalding put together an outstanding 252–65 won-loss record with the highest winning percentage of all time (.795). Although the rules of the game and distance to home plate were different than today's standards, it is still amazing that Spalding won 52 games in 1874 and 54 games in 1875.

When the 20-year-old right-handed hurler joined Harry Wright's Boston Red Stockings in 1871 he became an immediate star. He led the National Association in wins every year of the five years it was in existence, and Boston won the pennant every year from 1872 to 1875.

When the NA was folded into the new National League in 1876, Spalding went to the Chicago White Stockings as player-manager. He led the league with 47 wins that year, propelling his team to the first NL pennant. As manager, Spalding posted a 78–47 record over his two years at the helm in Chicago. Also good with a bat, Spalding retired in 1878 with a .313 batting average over his seven-year playing career.

Spalding and his brother opened up a sporting goods store in Chicago in 1876, and today the Spalding Sporting Goods name is still the benchmark for all others. To promote his company and the game, Spalding organized exhibition games all over the world. He was president of the Chicago White Stockings from 1882 to 1892, and they took five NL pennants during his tenure. As his company flourished, Spalding left the game to concentrate on his business. In addition to baseball equipment, he expanded to manufacture balls for all sports and other sporting equipment. Albert Goodwill Spalding remained active as a businessman, philanthropist, and lover of the arts. He was involved in municipal projects in San Diego, California, and helped organize the 1915 Panama-California Exposition. Spalding was 65 years old when he died in September 1915. He was elected to the Hall of Fame in 1939. So, when you take out those old Spalding Executive golf clubs, shoot some hoops with that official Spalding basketball, or play catch with that Spalding baseball, think of Albert Spalding, who touched all sports in this country in one way or another.

> *Baseball gives a growing boy self poise and self reliance."*
>
> – Al Spalding

Al

PSA/DNA Authentication Services Says:

Compared to other early baseball pioneers, whether on the field or behind the scenes, Spalding's autograph is not nearly as difficult to find compared to most who made their mark during the early days of the game. In addition to helping form the sport we know today, Spalding was a sporting goods tycoon and his great commercial success kept him in the spotlight more than the average executive. Spalding's book, *The National Game*, was very popular and collectors will encounter signed copies in decent numbers today, with many examples having been inscribed and dated by the baseball icon (often 1911). Collectors will also find a reasonable number of documents signed by Spalding, often on company letterhead. Most of the known Spalding signatures appear as "A. G. Spalding," with his first and middle names represented by initials.

> "Baseball is the exponent of American Courage, Confidence, Combativeness, American Dash, Discipline, Determination, American Energy, Eagerness, Enthusiasm, American Pluck, Persistency, Performance, American Spirit, Sagacity, Success, American Vim, Vigor, Virility."
>
> – Al Spalding

THE EARLY YEARS

Tris Speaker

The double might just be the quintessential baseball play. It has a great nickname, "a two-bagger," requires both power and speed, and epitomizes the hustling nature of the game. Not as arrogant as a home run or as flashy as a triple, and certainly not as ho-hum as a single, the double is stylish, regal, and professional. The man who is the all-time leader in doubles, with 792, can be described similarly. Although he retired in 1928, Tris Speaker, "The Grey Eagle," still holds records for doubles, as well as for assists (449) and double plays (143) by an outfielder. He patrolled the outfield for 22 seasons and his glove work has seldom been approached. One of the great hitters of his or any other time, Speaker finished with a career batting average of .345, good for 6th place on the all-time list. If defensive and offensive prowess are not enough, how about leadership? As player-manager for the Cleveland Indians from 1919 to 1926, Speaker went 617–520. He batted .388 with 107 RBI and 214 hits in 1920, capturing Cleveland's first

> *When I was a rookie, Cy Young used to hit me flies to sharpen my abilities to judge in advance the direction and distance of an outfield-hit ball.*
>
> – Tris Speaker

100 THE EARLY YEARS

The Grey Eagle

pennant, and then hit .320 in the Series against Brooklyn, leading the Tribe to their first World Series victory.

As a player, Speaker won two world championships during his nine years with the Red Sox (1912 and 1915). Winning championships for two star-crossed franchises like the Red Sox and Indians is enough to put anyone in the Hall of Fame, but Speaker did much more than that. With several standout seasons, it is difficult to choose his best. There was 1912, his MVP season, when he led the league with 53 doubles, had 222 hits, a Deadball Era power surge of 10 home runs, and a .464 OBP. How about 1923 when, at age 35, he batted .380 with 218 hits, and led the league with 59 doubles and 130 RBI? Maybe it was 1916, when Speaker hit .386 to wrest the batting title from Ty Cobb, while smacking 211 hits, 41 doubles, and slugging .502 with .470 OBP and .972 OPS—all league highs. Speaker flirted with .400, hitting over .380 five times. With his combination of style, substance, and stats, Tristram E. Speaker will be remembered as one of the greatest players of his day. The 40-year-old Hubbard, Texas, native retired in 1928 and was inducted into the Hall of Fame in 1937. Always a fan favorite, Speaker later became a broadcaster and scout for Cleveland and was an ambassador for the game until his death in 1958, at age 70.

PSA/DNA Authentication Services Says:

While somewhat overshadowed by Cobb, Speaker was one of the true greats of the game during the early 20th century and one of its best ambassadors. The personable Speaker attended many baseball-related banquets, charity functions, and Old Timers games after his playing days. His adoring fans found him to be very approachable in person and responsive to mail requests. One of the more frequently-seen Speaker autographs can be found on Cleveland Indians postcards (circa 1950s) that were autographed and sent to fans who contacted the legendary hitter through the mail. Since Speaker was such an active signer, collectors will rarely encounter a clubhouse or secretarial signature of The Grey Eagle. As with most players of the era, single-signed baseballs are one of the most elusive and desirable Speaker collectibles in the hobby.

THE EARLY YEARS

Joe Tinker, Johnny Evers, Frank Chance

The number 3 is intrinsically interwoven into the game of baseball. There are 3 outfielders, 3 outs per half-inning, and 3 bases. The number 3 is also synonymous with a triumvirate of players who were solid individually but sweetly sublime as a trio. Joseph Bert Tinker, John Joseph Evers, and Frank Leroy Chance are all enshrined in the Baseball Hall of Fame and, in fact, were inducted the same year: 1946. This legendary Cubs infield was immortalized by Franklin Pierce Adams' poem, "Baseball's Sad Lexicon."

A columnist for the *New York Evening Mail*, Adams wrote from the perspective of the Giants fans who whined and wailed every time the Chicago threesome ended an inning or turned a New York hit into an out or a double play. To be sure, shortstop Tinker, second baseman Evers, and first sacker Chance were poetry in motion. Originally entitled "That Double Play Again," Adams' poem first appeared in the *Evening Mail* in 1910. It sure took Adams long enough to pen his poem. Tinker, Evers, and Chance got together in the Cubs' infield in 1902, some eight years before Adams finally found time to rhyme.

He wrote:

These are the saddest of possible words:
'Tinker to Evers to Chance.'
Trio of bear cubs, and fleeter than birds,
Tinker and Evers and Chance.
Ruthlessly pricking our gonfalon bubble,
Making a Giant hit into a double -
Words that are heavy with nothing but
 trouble:
'Tinker to Evers to Chance.'

Gonfalon is a synonym for pennant, by the way, and Adams' lament was justified. The trio, along with players such as Harry Steinfeldt, Johnny Kling, and Hall of Famer Mordecai Brown, launched the Chicago Cubs into an early baseball dynasty, winning pennants in 1906, 1907, 1908, and 1910, and the World Series in 1907 and 1908. Joe Tinker was consistent if unspectacular, always hitting in the mid-to-high .200s with solid doubles and RBI numbers. With a keen eye, Johnny Evers was a slightly better hitter, drawing walks and rarely striking out. The best offensive player of Chicago's "Big Three," Frank Chance was a career .296 hitter, led the league in stolen bases twice, and topped the NL in slugging in 1905. Chance managed the Cubbies to

Tinker to Evers to Chance

their 1907 and 1908 titles and later held a stake in ownership with the team. So, how did these fair-to-decent ballplayers make the Hall of Fame? The answer is as easy as 1, 2, and most importantly, 3.

PSA/DNA Authentication Services Says:

Amazingly, despite the fanfare and attention this trio received during their careers, an item signed by just the three of them has yet to be certified. However, items have been found with Evers and Tinker autographs

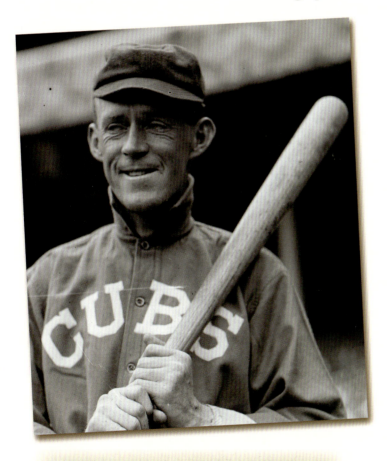

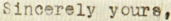

on them. All three men possessed visually-appealing autographs, but they vary in scarcity. Chance passed away in 1924, and of the three Chicago icons his autograph is the toughest to find, with a good portion of the existing examples coming in the form of personal correspondence or signed cuts clipped from larger formats. Although they both passed away before 1950, Evers and Tinker were active signers. After retiring from the game, the duo remained accessible in person and through the mail. An interesting aspect to Evers' signature is that he would occasionally add "Tinker to Evers to Chance" as an inscription. Evers suffered a stroke later in life, but continued to sign as best he could to accommodate fans.

Rube Waddell

The strikeout king of the early 20th century, George Edward "Rube" Waddell led the American League in Ks for six consecutive seasons with Connie Mack's Philadelphia Athletics from 1902 to 1907. In July of 1902, on the

way to a 24–7 record, Waddell became the first pitcher to ever strike out the side on nine pitches. In 1903, he went 21–16 with a league-high 34 complete games, a 2.44 ERA, and 302 strikeouts. Known for his crazy antics both on and off the field, Waddell had his share of demons. American League president, Ban Johnson, suspended Waddell during the 1903 season for beating up a gambler in the stands, and his irresponsible behavior often pushed Mack's patience to its limits. Still, Waddell followed up that 1903 season with an even better 1904 campaign: 25 wins, 1.62 ERA, 39 complete games and a whopping 349 Ks. Waddell anchored Mack's pitching staff as the Athletics started to develop into the American League's model franchise. In 1905, Waddell won the AL Triple Crown with 27 games, a miniscule 1.48 ERA, and 287 Ks. The A's won the AL flag that year but lost the World Series to the New York Giants in five games. Waddell would not stay in Philly long enough to enjoy the sweet taste of World Series victory. In 1908, he was purchased by the St. Louis Browns. Philadelphia would win the Series in 1910, 1911, and 1913 while Waddell would languish for the hapless Brownies.

Waddell grew up in the Pennsylvania oil fields and was highly eccentric. He wrestled alligators, was obsessed with fires, and even played pro football. At 6-foot, 1-inch, and nearly 200 pounds, Waddell cut an imposing figure on the hill, but he did not survive solely on pure power pitching. He set up his humming fastball with a bevy of breaking balls that befuddled and baffled batters. A wild colt in his early days with

104   THE EARLY YEARS

Rube

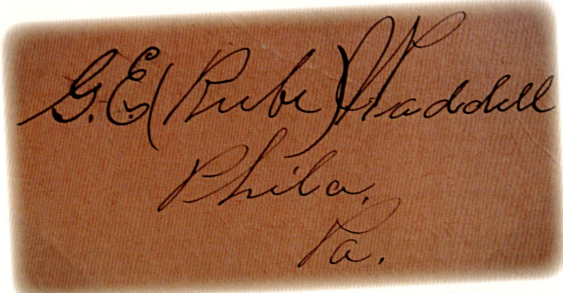

all mediums are very tough since Waddell passed away at the young age of 37 in 1914, long before autograph collecting developed into a more popular endeavor. As of this writing, no single-signed or multi-signed baseballs have ever been discovered containing the autograph of this legendary pitcher.

the Louisville Colonels, Pittsburgh Pirates, and Chicago Orphans, Waddell came into his own with the Athletics. As the colorful Waddell's popularity grew in Philly, a host of products were named for him including one that would be his downfall, liquor. For all of his success and popularity, Waddell often drowned his inner thoughts and battles in the bottle. This, no doubt, led to the premature end of his career in 1910 and his life in 1914, at age 37. One of the most prolific strikeout artists ever, Rube Waddell was inducted into the Baseball Hall of Fame in 1946.

PSA/DNA Authentication Services Says:

George Edward Waddell ranks very high on the list of extremely scarce autographs within our "Top 100" list. The miniscule number of autographs that exist today often share a similar appearance where his first and middle names are initials "G. E. Waddell." That said, you may encounter examples signed "G. E. (Rube) Waddell" or "Rube Waddell – G.E." as well, but these variations are even more scarce. Some of the existing examples come in the form of handwritten letters, but

THE EARLY YEARS

Honus Wagner

Honus Wagner managed the Pittsburgh Pirates for five games in 1917. He went 1–4 and Pittsburgh finished in eighth place that season. This ends the negative portion of Honus Wagner's baseball career. Wagner may just be the greatest baseball player who ever lived. In a 21-year career (1897–1917), Wagner set a standard for hitting and fielding that few have approached. He played outfield and every infield position except catcher, and even pitched a bit in 1900 and 1902. It was at shortstop, however, that Wagner's legend was formed. At the plate, Wagner had few peers. He hit over .320 for 14 straight seasons, winning eight batting crowns and leading the NL in hits twice, runs twice, triples three times, RBI four times, steals five times, and doubles seven times. Along the way, he was a perennial pace-setter in OBP and slugging, eclipsing the .500 mark an amazing eight times. Wagner's excellence was tempered with patience. He struck out just 735 times in over 10,000 career at-bats. With the Pirates, Wagner won pennants in 1903 and 1909. In the latter season, "The Flying Dutchman" was the quintessential Most Valuable Player, although the actual award did not yet exist. He led the NL in RBI, batting, OBP, and slugging as the Bucs won 110 games. In the World Series win over Detroit, he batted .333 with six RBI. That Series was highlighted by a legendary melee between Wagner and fellow star Ty Cobb.

A hard-nosed, large-nosed, Western Pennsylvania product, Wagner began his big league career with the NL's Louisville Colonels in 1897. He hit .322 over three seasons in

The Flying Dutchman

> "*I name Wagner first on my list, not only because he was a great batting champion and base-runner, and also baseball's foremost shortstop, but because Honus could have been first at any other position, with the possible exception of pitcher. In all my career, I never saw such a versatile player.*"
>
> – John McGraw

PSA/DNA Authentication Services Says:

One of the elite players of the early 20th century, Wagner was included in the inaugural Hall of Fame class of 1936. Like fellow greats Cobb and Ruth, Wagner was a prolific signer. Examples of his signature date from the pre-1910 era virtually up to his passing in 1955, and often include inscriptions and dates. Visually, Wagner's autograph changed dramatically over time. His early signature varied from "John H. Wagner" to "J. Honus Wagner" to "J. Hans. Wagner," and was often ornate in appearance. As time went on, the signature lost a bit of its eye-appeal and also changed in form. By the 1930s, Wagner signed his name "Hans Wagner," but changed to "Honus Wagner" by the mid-1940s, often adding inscriptions such as "Pirates Coach" under his signature.

Louisville, but was inexplicably traded to Pittsburgh with Rube Waddell and others for Jack Chesbro and a bevy of ballplayers in 1899. He is considered by many to be the greatest Pirate of them all, strong words considering the likes of Roberto Clemente and Willie Stargell also donned the Pittsburgh colors. When he retired in 1917, Wagner held several NL and MLB records. He later coached for the Pirates from 1933 until 1951. Johannes Peter Wagner was elected to baseball's inaugural Hall of Fame class in 1936, and passed away at the age of 81 in 1955. By the way, in that 1917 season, when Wagner lost four of five games as a manager, he was also a player. In 74 games, he batted .265 with 61 hits, 24 RBI, 15 runs, 5 steals and an OBP of nearly .340 – at the age of 43. Legend.

THE EARLY YEARS 107

Ed Walsh

Ed Walsh is never among the first names mentioned in a rundown of the game's all-time greatest pitchers. Other legends and even modern day heroes seem to get more credit. Such is the arbitrary nature of baseball analysis. Walsh is the last pitcher to win 40 games in a single season and is baseball's all-time leader with a career ERA of 1.82.

His 40–15 record in 1908 was adorned with additional league highs in winning percentage, games, games started, complete games, saves, innings pitched, and strikeouts. It was one of the most dominant seasons any pitcher ever delivered, but Ed Walsh was no one-year wonder. He won 24 games in 1907 and 27 games in 1911 and 1912 respectively.

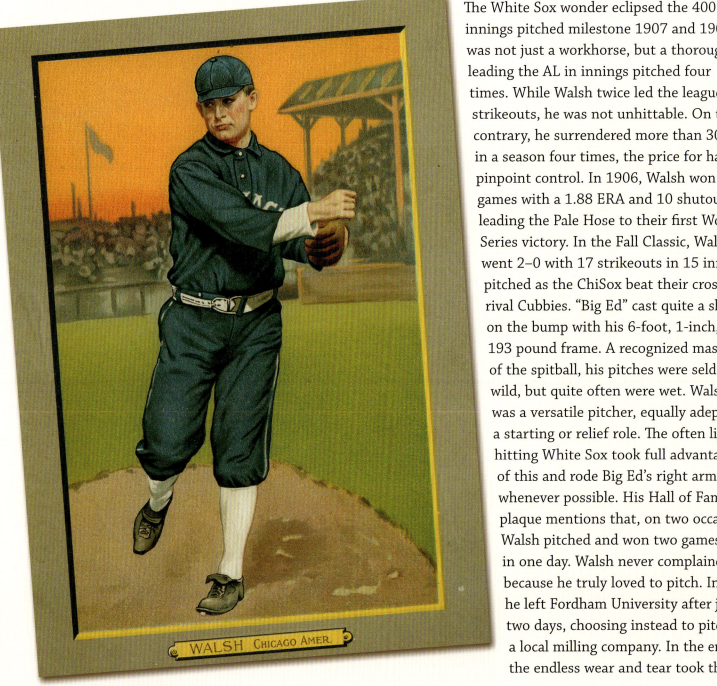

The White Sox wonder eclipsed the 400 innings pitched milestone 1907 and 1908. He was not just a workhorse, but a thoroughbred, leading the AL in innings pitched four times. While Walsh twice led the league in strikeouts, he was not unhittable. On the contrary, he surrendered more than 300 hits in a season four times, the price for having pinpoint control. In 1906, Walsh won 17 games with a 1.88 ERA and 10 shutouts, leading the Pale Hose to their first World Series victory. In the Fall Classic, Walsh went 2–0 with 17 strikeouts in 15 innings pitched as the ChiSox beat their crosstown rival Cubbies. "Big Ed" cast quite a shadow on the bump with his 6-foot, 1-inch, and 193 pound frame. A recognized master of the spitball, his pitches were seldom wild, but quite often were wet. Walsh was a versatile pitcher, equally adept in a starting or relief role. The often light-hitting White Sox took full advantage of this and rode Big Ed's right arm whenever possible. His Hall of Fame plaque mentions that, on two occasions, Walsh pitched and won two games in one day. Walsh never complained because he truly loved to pitch. In fact, he left Fordham University after just two days, choosing instead to pitch for a local milling company. In the end, the endless wear and tear took their

Big Ed

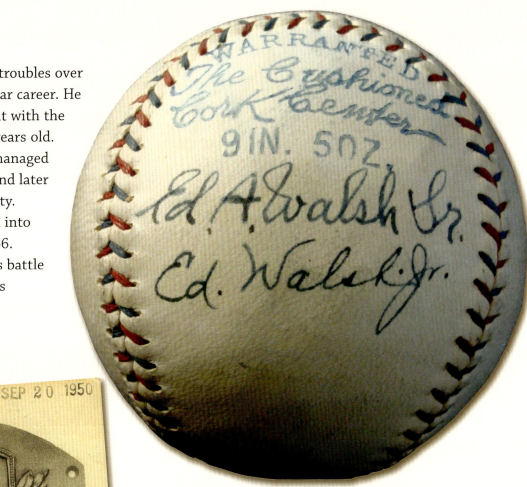

toll and Walsh experienced arm troubles over the last five seasons of his 14-year career. He retired in 1917 after a short stint with the Boston Braves when he was 36 years old. He coached for the White Sox, managed them for three games in 1924, and later coached at Notre Dame University. The spitball wizard was inducted into the Baseball Hall of Fame in 1946. Edward Augustine Walsh lost his battle with cancer in 1959 when he was 78 years old.

PSA/DNA Authentication Services Says:

Ed Walsh possessed the kind of eye-appealing autograph that people want to collect. Most of the time he employed a large, clean-looking signature "Ed. A. Walsh" and also added "White Sox" inscriptions under his name after his playing days. While considered a good signer with the public during his career, most surviving examples date to Walsh's post-career. A large percentage of those signatures can be found on mediums such as GPCs and index cards as Walsh regularly responded to mail requests. Since he passed away in 1959, single-signed baseballs are very rare as the trend to obtain them had yet to take hold. Unless you were one of the legends of the game such as Cobb, Ruth, or Foxx, requests for those were far less common in the pre-1960 era. Once in a while, Walsh's wife would sign mail requests on his behalf, but not often.

THE EARLY YEARS   109

Buck Weaver

An excellent defensive fielder and a solid, consistent hitter, Buck Weaver came up from the San Francisco Seals of the Pacific Coast League in 1912. His talent impressed, and Weaver became the starting shortstop for the Chicago White Sox as a rookie. With his slick fielding and timely hitting, "The Ginger Kid" became both a fan favorite and leader in the White Sox dugout. In 1917, he switched to third baseman, the ChiSox took the pennant, and Weaver batted .333 with seven hits in the Series to help the Sox beat the Giants for the championship. Ironically, his best season was his last. In 1920, Weaver batted an impressive .331 and banged out 208 hits, but it all came crashing down when he was implicated in the infamous 1919 Black Sox scandal. After nine years in the majors, Weaver was on the cusp of becoming a genuine star but instead he lost everything.

Buck Weaver made two major mistakes in his life. The first was not stepping forward when some of his teammates planned to throw the 1919 World Series. Weaver actually had no part in throwing the Series. As a matter of fact, he batted .324 with 11 hits in the Fall Classic, which is consistent with his 1917 Series performance. However, he knew about the plan and never reported it. As a result, Weaver was forced to go to trial with seven other teammates. Although they were all acquitted, Baseball Commissioner Kenesaw Mountain Landis banned all of them from playing in the Major Leagues for life. Weaver fought to clear his name and get reinstated, maintaining that he was not involved in the game fixing, but Landis made an example of Weaver, sending a stern warning for players to speak up if they were aware of any shenanigans.

What was Weaver's other mistake? After his Major League career ended, he played for various semi-pro teams before leaving baseball for the business world. Weaver and his brother-in-law established a chain of six successful drugstores in Chicago. They were approached by Charles Walgreen to partner with him and expand all

The Ginger Kid

George "Buck" Weaver

over the country. Buck and his brother-in-law declined the offer. Walgreen's went on to become one of the largest drug store chains in the country, but Weaver shuttered his stores during the Depression. George Daniel Weaver continued the fight to clear his name until his fatal heart attack in 1956 at age 65. Right or wrong, he paid the price.

> *No player who sits in conference with a bunch of crooked players and gamblers where the ways and means of throwing games are discussed and does not promptly tell his club about it will ever play professional baseball.*
>
> – Kenesaw Mountain Landis, Commissioner of Baseball

> *I was not certain just what men, if any, had accepted propositions, whether they accepted. I could not bring myself to tell on them, and even if I was certain, I decided to keep quiet and play my best.*
>
> – Buck Weaver

PSA/DNA Authentication Services Says:

The mystery and intrigue of the 1919 Black Sox scandal has captivated collectors over the years, with collectibles related to the banned figures often selling for big premiums. Autographs are no exception. A player who allegedly knew about the fix but didn't participate, Weaver was very popular before and after his banishment, but few of his autographs have survived. Weaver's signature varied quite a bit over time. You may encounter examples such as "Geo Buck Weaver," "George Buck Weaver," or simply "Buck Weaver," which is the common version a collector will see. Weaver also alternated between cursive writing and printing when signing his name on items. No authentic single-signed baseballs of Weaver are known at this time and while his autograph is not the toughest of the Black Sox players, he remains one of the most intriguing figures in the group.

BUCK WEAVER
3rd B.—Chicago White Sox
186

THE EARLY YEARS   111

Harry Wright

When it comes to evaluating his contributions to the game of baseball, Harry Wright is right up there with Cartwright, Spalding, and Chadwick. As founder and player-manager of the first professional, salaried team, the 1869 Cincinnati Red Stockings, Wright was responsible for the whole concept of paying players according to their talent level. He helped shape the game with a variety of innovations. Wright established various defensive techniques, helped develop the farm system, and actually brought some of his teams south to train before the start of the season to hone their skills. Wright was a very competent field manager, fostering teamwork and implementing the use of hand signals, platooning, and relief pitching, as opposed to many early managers who simply filled out lineup cards.

Born in Sheffield, England, William Henry Wright immigrated to New York City as a baby. His father was a professional cricket player, and young Harry left school at age 14 to work as a jeweler's apprentice and play professional cricket with his father's team. He also played some baseball with the NYC Knickerbockers and the Gothams. Wright moved to Cincinnati to play cricket but soon formed the Red Stockings, a team that quickly became famous for an incredible 57–0 record in 1869. The team disbanded after the 1870 season and Wright moved, with some of the team players, to Boston to play in the new National Association. As player-manager of the Boston Red Stockings, Wright led his team to four consecutive titles (1872–1875) and posted an exceptional 71–8 record in 1875. After Wright's Boston team joined the new National League in 1876 they captured two more pennants (1877, 1878). As a player, Wright only managed a .276 lifetime batting average and 224 hits over his career, and although not a standout, he filled in adequately as an outfielder and relief pitcher. He retired as player in 1877 but continued on as manager in Boston through the 1881 season. After a two-year stint managing the NL Providence Grays, Wright managed the NL Philadelphia Quakers/Phillies from 1884 to 1893, finishing his 23-year management career with a 1,225–885 record and

The Pioneer

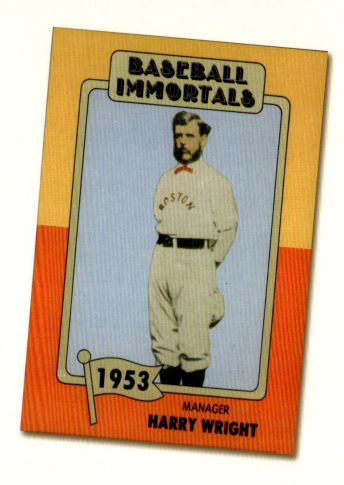

a .581 winning percentage. Known for his ethics and gentlemanly sense of fair play, Wright was appointed National League Chief of Umpires in 1893, a position he held until his death from lung disease in 1895 at age 60. He was inducted into the Hall of Fame as Pioneer-Executive by the Veterans Committee in 1953.

> "[Harry Wright was] the most widely known, best respected, and most popular of the exponents and representatives of professional baseball, of which he was virtually the founder."
>
> – Henry Chadwick

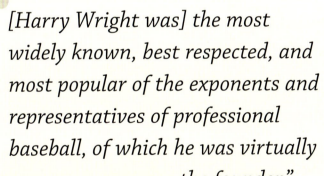

PSA/DNA Authentication Services Says:

One would think that an autograph from a man who is often described as the Father of Professional Baseball, a man who died in 1895, would be nearly impossible to find today. While Harry Wright remains a tough void to fill for many collectors, his autograph is not quite as difficult to locate as one would believe. One key reason is the fact that he and his brother George were part owners of a sporting goods company called Wright & Ditson. As part of that company, Wright signed a number of documents related to his role. Collectors may also see examples of his signature on scorecards, which come up for sale from time to time. Not only was Wright a pioneer in the game itself, he was also somewhat of a pioneer in the autograph world. Wright would often add "Compliments of" prior to signing his name on items, which was not a common practice during that early period in baseball.

3

Baseball's Golden Age (1920–1960)

★ ★ ★ ★ ★ ★ ★ ★ ★ ★ ★ ★ ★ ★ ★

From Gorgeous George Sisler, to Joltin' Joe DiMaggio, to Yogi Berra, to Stan the Man Musial, the period from 1920 to 1960 was filled with players that became household names in America. With the advent of radio and television, we were able to follow our favorite teams and players on a regular basis. These players quickly became larger than life stars, and fans sought autographs both in-person and through mail requests. DiMaggio's 56-game hitting streak and Casey Stengel's incredible run as skipper of the Yankees are just a few of the highlights from the Golden Age of baseball. Our National Pastime was flourishing, and so was the hunt for the autograph.

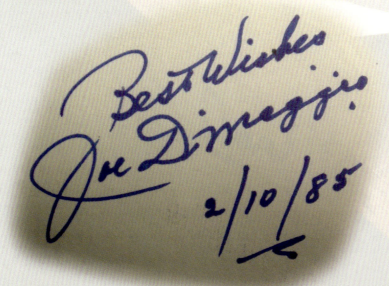

Moe Berg

How can a catcher with a lifetime batting average of .243, a grand total of six career home runs and 441 total hits be included in a list of the greatest baseball autographs? Morris "Moe" Berg never made an All-Star Team, never had more than 352 at-bats in a season, and played for five different teams over a 15-year period; not exactly Hall of Fame material. Yet, Berg is one of the most intriguing Major League players ever to wear a uniform. Moe Berg's fame did not come as a ballplayer, but as a spy.

The 21-year-old Princeton University graduate signed with the Brooklyn Robins in 1923 and moved on to the Chicago White Sox in 1925 where he was used as a journeyman until he settled in as backup catcher in 1928. Considered a decent defensive catcher, he was skilled at calling games and had extensive knowledge of hitters. Berg studied law at Columbia in the off-season, receiving his degree in 1930. As a lawyer, Berg continued to play in the majors for the Indians, Senators, and Red Sox. The brilliant but eccentric Berg developed a reputation as the smartest man in baseball, but as Casey Stengel aptly put it, he was also, "The strangest man ever to play baseball."

As Berg's baseball career wound down in 1939, his career as a spy ramped up. Because of his education and his fluency in twelve languages, Berg was recruited by the OSS, the precursor to the CIA. One of his assignments was to investigate the atomic capabilities of our enemies and, if necessary, assassinate scientists developing the atomic bomb for them. He was also sent overseas to convince Italian scientists to work in the United States rather than aid the Nazis.

After the war, Berg continued with the CIA until his contract expired in 1954. This marked the end of his undercover spy days as the CIA considered him too eccentric to continue. After investing in a business venture that failed miserably, Berg stayed

The Spy

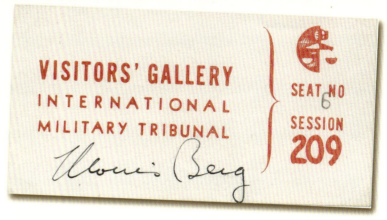

under the radar and refused interviews. He lived with siblings until his death in 1972 at age 70. Since he was a mediocre catcher, why did he play in the majors for so long? Was it his cover? Did MLB employ him at the government's request? Was Berg really a trained assassin? Was his story more fluff than substance? The answers went to the grave with him. One thing is for certain—Moe Berg was one of the most interesting characters ever to set foot on a Major League field.

PSA/DNA Authentication Services Says:

As a baseball player, Moe Berg wasn't in great demand as a signer simply because his on-the-field exploits were nothing to write home about. As a result, you rarely find single-signed baseballs in the marketplace. Most of the Berg autographs we see today are on team sheets or album pages. You may also see signed checks circulating in the hobby. In addition, during his life, Berg moved around quite a bit, rarely living in the same place for extended periods of time. While his autograph is not considered extremely rare today, pinning Berg down for autographs via mail requests proved to be challenging for collectors and fans during the period. If fans only knew sooner that Berg was a spy.

BASEBALL'S GOLDEN AGE   117

Yogi Berra

Is Yogi Berra more famous for his "Yogi-isms" or his Hall of Fame baseball career? There are those who consider Lawrence Peter Berra the greatest catcher of all time. The American League's Most Valuable Player in 1951, 1954, and 1955, Berra appeared in 14 World Series as a player, winning 10 of them. He was a 15-time All-Star and at one time or another led the league in many catching categories, including: putouts, games caught, most double plays turned, and fielding percentage.

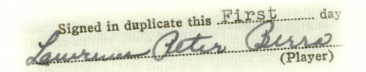

Born Lorenzo Pietro Berra in St. Louis to recent Italian immigrants in 1925, Berra quit school in eighth grade. Signed by the Yankees in 1943, he played for their Norfolk Tars affiliate for one season before serving as a Navy machine gunner in World War II.

" *When you come to a fork in the road, take it.*"
– Yogi Berra

Once Casey Stengel became Yankees manager in 1949, he mentored the young catcher. First valued as a hitter, Berra had an unusual batting style. He had a knack for swinging at and making contact with bad pitches. A pitch could be over his head or at his ankles and he could turn on it with success. Over the course of his 18 years playing for the Yankees, Berra racked up a career BA of .285 and 358 home runs.

He had lightning quick reflexes defensively. Pitchers loved him because he was both a calming influence and very consistent in his game calling. By the way, Berra was behind the plate for Don Larsen's perfect game in the 1956 World Series, one of the greatest pitching feats in baseball history.

Yogi

> *You should always go to other people's funerals, otherwise, they won't go to yours*
>
> – Yogi Berra

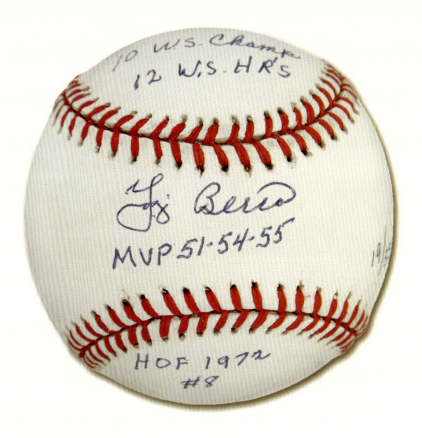

Berra managed the Yankees to the pennant in 1964 before joining the Mets in 1965 to coach for Casey Stengel. He managed the Mets from 1972 to 1975, leading them to a pennant win in 1973. Berra returned to the Yankees as coach from 1976 to 1983, and manager in 1984 and 1985. He coached the Houston Astros from 1986 until he retired in 1989. Exactly 69 years to the day after his September 22, 1946 MLB debut, Yogi Berra passed away at age 90, in 2015. He was elected to the Hall of Fame in 1972 and was voted to MLB's All-Century Team. As a ballplayer, Yogi Berra had all of the tools, or as he so succinctly put it, "Baseball is 90 percent mental. The other half is physical." You gotta love Yogi!

PSA/DNA Authentication Services Says:

Yogi Berra's signature is one of the more consistent autographs you will ever see, from his early playing days in the mid-1940s right up to his death in 2015. The one noticeable change occurred right around 1950, when Berra transitioned from signing his first name "Larry" to "Yogi" most of the time. From his days as a player to his days as manager and coach, Berra remained approachable and was considered a gracious signer in person and via the mail. Once in a while, you may encounter a secretarial, clubhouse, or stamped signature, but Berra did sign most of the requests that came his way. Long after his playing days were over, Berra formed LTD Enterprises, Inc., which provided authentic signed memorabilia to the public. The LTD stood for Larry, Tim, and Dale. Tim and Dale are Yogi's two sons who helped run the business for many years, making Berra's autograph more obtainable for collectors.

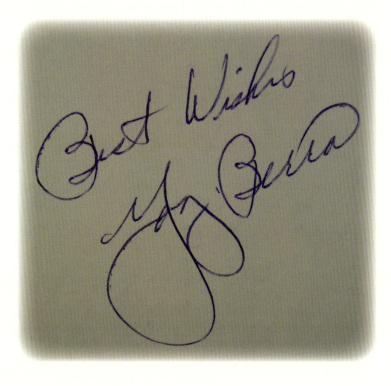

BASEBALL'S GOLDEN AGE

Roy Campanella

From the very early days of the game, many ballplayers supplemented their player salaries with off-season jobs, business interests, and product endorsements. Roy Campanella owned and operated Roy Campanella Choice Wine and Liquors, a successful business venture in New York's Harlem. On January 28, 1958, after closing the store for the night, the 37-year-old Campanella hit a patch of black ice while driving home to Long Island. Tragically, his car flipped over, leaving him paralyzed from a broken neck. In seconds, his career came to a screeching halt. The career of one of the greatest catchers of all time was over. However, Roy Campanella had already made an indelible mark on Major League Baseball.

Ranked by *Sporting News* as the third greatest catcher of all time (behind Berra and Bench), Campanella made his Major League debut one year after Jackie Robinson broke the color barrier. Signed out of the Negro National League by Branch Rickey in 1946, Campy took over as catcher for the Brooklyn Dodgers in July of 1948 and, as the saying goes, the rest is history.

One of the best-hitting catchers in baseball, the good-natured Campanella made the All-Star Team eight straight times (1949–1956). During that span the Dodgers won five pennants. The three-time National League MVP (1951, 1953, 1955) was very consistent from both the offensive and defensive side. Although his 1953 season is considered by many as his best, it was in 1955 that the 33-year-old catcher was a catalyst in the Dodgers' World Series win over the Yankees.

Although the automobile accident in 1958 ended his 10-year MLB playing

Campy

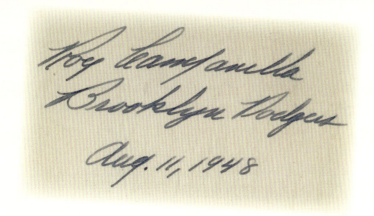

PSA/DNA Authentication Services Says:

Prior to the horrific car accident that shortened his career and left the gregarious star paralyzed from the shoulders down, Campanella had one of the most beautiful signatures of his era. Through many years of therapy, Campanella was able to regain some use of his arms and hands, but he was never the same. Campanella's affable nature was present on the field and while interacting with fans. As a result, he was a very good signer during his career. The issue for collectors today is simply that his career was so short, leaving a small window for Campy to sign. Single-signed baseballs are particularly difficult to find. You will see a fair number of post-accident Campanella autographs in the marketplace, which were generated by the Hall of Fame catcher with the help of a machine, but they sell for a fraction of the pre-accident examples since they lack the same eye appeal.

career, Campanella stayed in baseball for many years, working with the Dodgers in public relations, coaching and scouting. In 1959, a year after the Dodgers moved the franchise to California, they held an exhibition game in Los Angeles to raise money for Campy. More than 93,000 fans, the largest crowd in baseball history, showed up to watch the Yankees beat the Dodgers that day. It was a great testimonial to Campanella's popularity throughout Major League Baseball.

Roy Campanella was elected to the Baseball Hall of Fame in 1969, becoming one of the first African-American players to be so honored, and in 1972 the Dodgers retired his uniform number 39. He passed away in 1993 at 71 years old. Like Addie Joss and Lou Gherig before him, tragedy cut short Campanella's great career, but because of his great ability and popularity he had a significant impact on the game.

> *Campanella will be remembered longer than any catcher in baseball history.*
>
> – Ty Cobb

BASEBALL'S GOLDEN AGE

Oscar Charleston

One of the top Negro League players of all time, Oscar Charleston "The Hoosier Comet" is always in the "best-of-the-best" conversation along with teammates Josh Gibson and Satchel Paige. A hard-nosed athlete, Charleston played to win and was not afraid to mix it up with the competition. He was sometimes compared to Ty Cobb because of his hitting ability, his fiery competitive nature on the field, and his tendency to slide hard into bases.

Born in Indianapolis, Indiana, in 1896, Oscar McKinley Charleston was one of 11 children. He left home at the young age of 15, enlisted in the army, and served in the Philippines, where he played baseball in the Manila League in 1914. After his return, he was signed by the Indianapolis ABCs in 1915, beginning a career that would span nearly 40 years. From 1915 through 1941,

Charleston had affiliations with 14 different teams either as a player or player-manager. An exceptional power hitter and fielder, Charleston's batting average was well over .300 most seasons, but he hit a lofty .444 in 1921 with the St. Louis Giants and bested that in 1925 with his .451 BA with the Harrisburg Giants. Records disagree on his lifetime batting average. The Hall of Fame credits him with a .339 BA while other sources claim .350, .353, .357, or .376. A whiz on the basepaths, Charleston is the all-time Negro Leagues leader in stolen bases. Considered an elite player, Charleston held his own against some of the great MLB teams of his time, posting a career average of .318 in 53 exhibition games between the Negro Leagues and MLB teams between 1915 through 1936.

After his playing days, he managed the Philadelphia Stars and Branch Rickey's Brooklyn Brown Dodgers. Charleston also scouted for Branch Rickey, recommending both Jackie Robinson and Roy Campanella to integrate the Brooklyn Dodgers. The 57-year-old Charleston managed the Indianapolis Clowns to the NAL pennant in 1954, dying just one month after reaching that milestone.

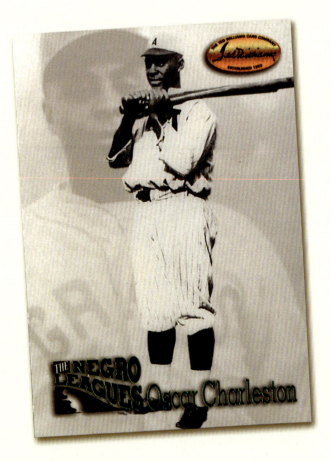

> *"Charleston could hit that ball a mile. He didn't have a weakness."*
> – Dizzy Dean

The Hoosier Comet

A favorite of fellow players and fans alike, Charleston was an outstanding teacher and mentor to young African-American players, and was very accommodating to fans. As a manager, he was considered one of the best. He was elected to the Hall of Fame in 1976 and was named to the 100 Greatest Baseball Players List by the *Sporting News* in 1998.

> "*Charleston was the greatest outfielder that ever lived…greatest of all colors. He can cover more ground than any man I have ever seen. His judging of flyballs borders on the uncanny.*"
>
> – Ben Taylor, Hall of Famer

PSA/DNA Authentication Services Says:

Like many former Negro League players, Charleston's autograph is rarely encountered. Despite being considered one of the best players of his generation and staying around the game deep into his adult life, which included working for the Dodgers organization in the 1940s, a very small number of Charleston autographs have surfaced. When you do find authentic examples of his signature, they often appear on team sheets or documents that have survived the test of time. He remains one of the more elusive components to baseball autograph collections of advanced nature.

BASEBALL'S GOLDEN AGE

Mickey Cochrane

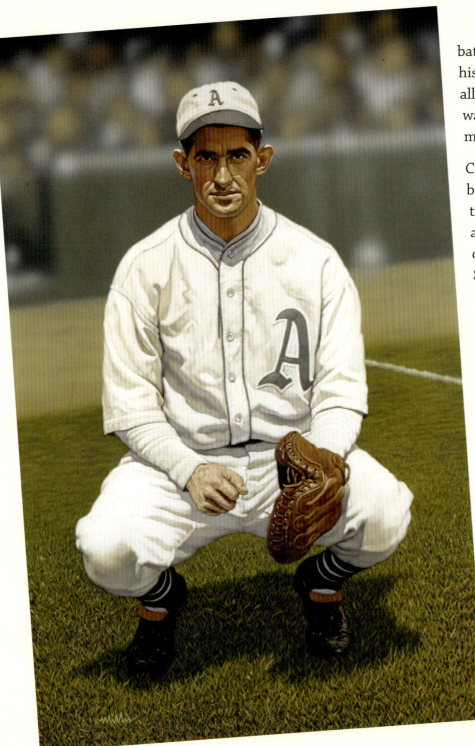

With a no-nonsense personality to go along with his lifetime .320 batting average, Mickey Cochrane was referred to as "The greatest catcher of them all" by his longtime batterymate, Hall of Famer, Lefty Grove. While history does not consider him the greatest of all time, make no mistake about it, if Cochrane was on your side, your level of play jumped more than a notch or two.

Cochrane's competitiveness was contagious, but his nickname "Black Mike" described the darker side of his personality. By all accounts, off the field he was affable, even charming. In between the baselines, Gordon Stanley Cochrane was as tough as they come. Hitting for Connie Mack's Athletics in front of Al Simmons and Jimmy Foxx, Mickey consistently got on base and hit with decent power. A good catcher defensively, he led the American League in putouts six times (1926–1930, 1932) and had a knack for handling his pitchers. A two-time All-Star, Cochrane was twice voted the American League MVP (1928, 1934). The A's had a great run, winning the World Series in 1929 and 1930, and losing in 1931. Connie Mack famously dismantled his team in 1933, selling Cochrane to the Detroit Tigers. As player-manager, Cochrane led a team that was not supposed to go anywhere, but instead won the 1934 AL pennant. In 1935, the Tigers took it all the way, winning their first ever World Series.

In 1936, things started to unravel for Cochrane when he suffered a nervous breakdown. After recovering and opening up the 1937 season, Mickey Cochrane's career came to an abrupt end when he was hit in the head with a pitch that fractured his skull. The 34-year-old manager recovered enough to take the helm at the beginning of the 1938 season, but was never the same. The

Black Mike

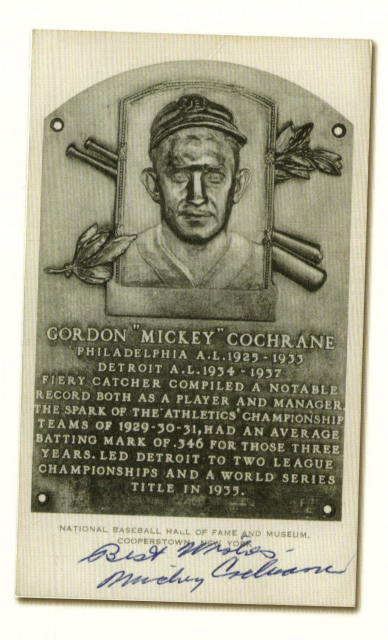

that date to the 1940s and 1950s, as the Hall of Famer was very responsive to mail requests during that time. While great vintage Cochrane signatures exist, like early Philadelphia Athletics photo albums featuring the two-time AL MVP, single-signed baseballs are rare since he passed away during the 1960s.

competitive edge was gone, and he was replaced as manager. Cochrane was later General Manager of the A's, and scouted for the Yankees and Tigers. After baseball, he owned and operated a dude ranch in Montana.

Mickey Cochrane is remembered as someone who inspired the people surrounding him, and as a result brought out their best. He has consistently been ranked in the Top 100 Greatest Players, and *Sporting News* ranks him in the Top 5 catchers of all time. Black Mike died in 1962 at the age of 59. He was inducted into the Baseball Hall of Fame in 1947.

PSA/DNA Authentication Services Says:

An active signer from his playing days until the end of his life, Mickey Cochrane's signature evolved from a more unsophisticated appearance to a flowing signature laced with confidence. It is not uncommon to find team-signed baseballs from the 1920s and 1930s with Cochrane's name stamped on it instead of a live signature. Though rare, you may also encounter secretarial Cochrane signatures from around the same period. After his career was over, Cochrane frequented special baseball events such as Old Timers games and reunions, where autographs were obtained by fans. You will also see a fair number of Cochrane autographs

Dizzy Dean

Every once in a while a team captures the fancy of the entire baseball world, not just their hometown fans. Heading up that list is the "Gashouse Gang," the 1934 St. Louis Cardinals. The leader of this ragtag collection of very good ballplayers was an Arkansas bred fireballing character who brought trash talking to a new height. However, Jay Hanna "Dizzy" Dean could pretty much back up whatever spewed out of his tobacco chewing gums.

As the leader of the Gashouse Gang, Dizzy Dean was a four-time All-Star. From 1933 to 1936, Diz was a monster, but the highlight of his career was 1934 when he won 30 games, led the Cards to a World Series Championship, and was named the NL MVP. Dizzy teamed with his brother, Paul "Daffy" Dean, for a combined 49 wins to lead the Gang to victory that year. One of the most colorful teams in baseball history, the Gashouse Gang's dirty uniforms, and unshaven, unkempt look made them popular with the public during the hardscrabble times of America's Great Depression.

After a foot injury in the 1937 All-Star Game, Dean adjusted his pitching motion to favor his recovering foot and, in the process, ruined his arm. He did have a few more decent seasons

The Great Man

but his career was never the same. He helped lead the Cubs to the pennant in 1938 and retired as a Cubby in 1941.

Dizzy Dean then became a successful broadcaster for several Major League teams. Although he left school after second grade, his country-style language and homespun tales made for great color in the broadcasting booth. While broadcasting for the Browns in 1947, Dean pitched four innings in their last game of the season as a publicity stunt. He later became the voice of the Cardinals, Yankees, and the network Game of the Week until 1965. Dizzy Dean died in Reno, Nevada, in 1974, at age 64.

Although he won just 150 games in his 12 seasons as a Major League pitcher, Dean twice led the league in wins, games played, and shutouts. He led the league in complete games three times, and strikeouts four times. Dizzy Dean was elected to the Hall of Fame in 1953. His leadership, wacky style, and competitive nature all contributed to the huge impact that he made during the height of his career. As Dizzy poignantly put it, "It ain't braggin' if you can back it up."

PSA/DNA Authentication Services Says:

Dizzy Dean, who possessed one of the more stylish and attractive signatures on our "Top 100" list, had the reputation of being very approachable. His personable nature was not only evident as an active player, it also extended into his post career as a broadcaster and beyond. Dean's willingness to be a passionate ambassador for the game added to his appeal with fans and collectors. During the 1950s, Dean used a ghost signer to help respond to autograph requests via the mail. For many years, these ghost-signed Dean autographs were sold and traded in the hobby as the real deal. In the ensuing decades, while his wife was known to handle some mail requests by signing his name, Dean did respond to a portion of these autograph requests as well.

> "When ole Diz was out there pitching it was more than just another ball game. It was a regular three-ring circus and everybody was wide awake and enjoying being alive."
>
> – Pepper Martin, Gashouse Gang teammate

BASEBALL'S GOLDEN AGE 127

Martin Dihigo

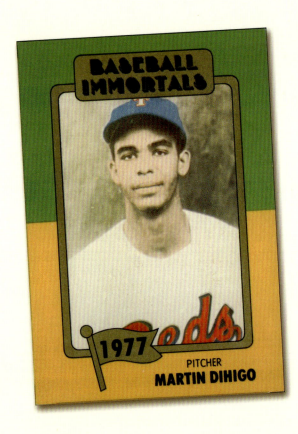

If you take a look at various lists of the greatest Cuban players of all time, you will usually see names like Luis Tiant, Tony Perez, or Tony Oliva. All of these players were outstanding talents and each left his mark on Major League Baseball. If you dig a bit deeper a talent pops up that surpasses not only these three players, but just about any other Cuban ballplayer. In the eyes of many, Martin Dihigo leaps to the top of the list. Martin Dihigo? It is likely that most American fans have no idea who Martin Dihigo was. Hall of Famer, Buck Leonard, referred to Dihigo as "the best player of all time, black or white." Pretty strong words about a guy who never got to play in the majors because of the color barrier.

Dihigo started in the Cuban League and quickly developed into an exceptional player. Dubbed "El Maestro" and "El Inmortal" in Cuba, Dihigo played year-round throughout his career, traveling between the Cuban League, Negro League, and Mexican League. Between 1922 and 1947 he played for 14 different teams in those three leagues, and was a bona fide superstar for all of them. By the way, he also played in Venezuela and the Dominican Republic. Considered a great power hitter who could hit for average, Dihigo was a talented pitcher. Overall, his documented pitching record was 288–142, although dozens of victories were never recorded. Defensively, he excelled at just about every position. He was a two-time Negro Leagues All-Star, won the Cuban MVP Award four times, and holds a variety of pitching records. For example, while pitching in the Mexican League in 1938, Dihigo went 18–2 with an amazing 0.90 ERA, and won the batting title with his .387 average.

After his playing career ended, Dihigo managed in Venezuela, worked as radio announcer for the Cuban Winter League and, after Fidel Castro took over, he became the Minister of Sports in Cuba. The very affable Dihigo died at the age of 65 in 1971. Elected to the Hall of Fame in 1977, Dihigo is also a member of both the Cuban Hall of Fame and the Mexican Hall of Fame. Cuba's National Treasure, Martin Dihigo was an exceptional talent. It's unfortunate that his career ended just as MLB's color barrier was broken. If not for that, more people would recognize his greatness.

The Immortal

PSA/DNA Authentication Services Says:

One of the most popular Cuban players during the first half of the 20th century, Dihigo played in both the Negro Leagues and Latin America Leagues, traveling to various countries and excelling at different positions. There is little doubt that Dihigo signed with some frequency as a result, but since his travels often took him outside of the United States, finding authentic autographs can be challenging, as they were often lost to time. A good percentage of the signatures you see today are found on documents and contracts. Collectors may also encounter secretarial signatures, which were most likely produced towards the end of his life when his health was failing. Dihigo did possess a very attractive, flowing signature and would occasionally inscribe items for the recipient.

"*He was the greatest all-around player I know. I'd say he was the best ballplayer of all time, black or white. He could do it all. He is my ideal ballplayer, makes no difference what race either. If he's not the greatest I don't know who is. You take your Ruths, Cobbs, and DiMaggios. Give me Dihigo and I bet I'd beat you almost every time.*"

– Buck Leonard, Hall of Famer

Joe DiMaggio

The mere mention of the year 1941 creates an historic passion play. It was a time of war, a time of change, and a significant year in the story of America's National Pastime. More than this, however, it was the year of Joltin' Joe. If one were to construct the perfect ballplayer, the resulting image would be Joseph Paul DiMaggio. With his long, lean frame, intense eyes and strong hands, DiMaggio looked the part, and then some. In 1941 he took baseball fans on a magical journey, bashing 30 home runs, knocking in 125 runs and batting .357. The latter stat is incredible for a number of reasons, chiefly, the fact that it was 49 points behind the American League's leading hitter that season. Yes, 1941 was also the year of Ted Williams, and the iconic pair staged their own Yankees-Red Sox fight to the finish. Williams batted .406, the last man to hit the fabled .400 mark, but it was DiMaggio who set a record that is still revered and chased today. From May 15 until July 17, he hit safely in 56 consecutive games. Only the lightning quick glove of Indians third sacker Ken Keltner kept DiMaggio from extending his streak.

The son of a Sicilian immigrant fisherman from San Francisco, Joe DiMaggio was the embodiment of the American Dream. With New York for his entire 13-year career, the 13-time All-Star, led his Yankees to nine World Series Championships. Also known as "The Yankee Clipper," DiMaggio could literally do it

Joltin' Joe

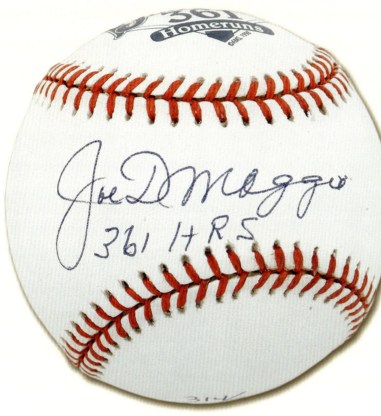

PSA/DNA Authentication Services Says:

Due to his almost immediate success with the New York Yankees, his high-profile marriage to Marilyn Monroe, and his stature in baseball history, Joe DiMaggio was always in the spotlight. One of the more prolific signers in the history of the hobby, DiMaggio was a private person but he did make time to sign autographs for fans. He became a regular on the show circuit during the hobby explosion in the 1980s and 1990s and also signed items for various memorabilia companies during that time. Despite the large number of authentic autographs in the marketplace, DiMaggio was a huge target for forgers. Collectors should be aware there are many clubhouse DiMaggio signatures on team-signed items in the marketplace. In addition, DiMaggio's sister signed fan mail for him during the 1970s and 1980s, and even signed his checks on rare occasions. It is well known that DiMaggio refused to sign anything Monroe-related after her death, but some autograph seekers tricked the legendary Yankee into autographing these items by masking their appearance.

all. Besides being the American League Most Valuable Player three times, he also led the league in batting twice, and RBI twice. As a center fielder, DiMaggio made every play look effortless. The word "class" is always associated with DiMaggio. Part of it was the manner in which he carried himself, including the way he wore his uniform with such great pride. A true baseball hero, DiMaggio was beloved and admired by fans, even as a visiting player. He hung up the pinstripes in 1951 with 2,214 hits and 1,537 RBI, 361 home runs, and a career .325 batting average. If he had not lost three seasons of his prime to military service during World War II, imagine what those numbers would be. An American icon, Joe DiMaggio was elected to the Hall of Fame in 1955, and was voted to the All-Century Team in 1999. That same year, he succumbed to lung cancer at age 84. Timeless, unforgettable, regal, that was Joe DiMaggio.

BASEBALL'S GOLDEN AGE 131

Hank Greenberg

In the eyes of fans and historians alike, "Hammerin' Hank" Greenberg is on a short list of truly great first basemen. Greenberg had to battle through anti-Semitism from many fans and opponents during the early part of his career, but never allowed it to compromise his performance. The famous umpire George Moriarty once went so far as to clear the Chicago Cubs bench during the 1935 World Series because the Cub players were peppering Greenberg with anti-Semitic remarks. Greenberg rose above it all to become a five-time All-Star and two-time American League MVP. The four-time home run champ also led his team to World Series Championships in 1935 and 1945.

The New York City native was signed by the Detroit Tigers in 1930 but wasn't brought up from the minors until 1933 when he was 22 years old. The young right-handed slugger hit .301 that year, which began a streak of eight consecutive years where he hit .300 or better. Greenburg worked first base for the Tigers through 1939 and then switched to left field for the balance of his career. Arguably, Greenberg's two greatest seasons were 1937 and 1938

132 BASEBALL'S GOLDEN AGE

Hammerin' Hank

when he dominated American League pitching. His 1937 season consisted of 40 home runs, 200 hits, a .337 average, and 184 RBI. He followed that in 1938 with 175 hits, 147 RBI, and a .315 average, while closely chasing Babe Ruth's record with an amazing 58 home runs. Over the course of his 13 Major League seasons Greenberg slammed 331 home runs.

One can only imagine what that home run number would have been if he did not lose several seasons in his prime. Greenberg served in the Army Air Corps from May of 1941 until June of 1945, attaining the rank of Captain with the 20th Bomber Command. Upon his return, he rejoined the Tigers and helped lead them to their 1945 pennant win with his ninth-inning grand slam home run on the last day of the season. In 1947 he moved on to the Pittsburgh Pirates to play his last season. After his retirement, Greenberg was part-owner of the Cleveland Indians (1950–1957) and the Chicago White Sox (1959–1961), after which he left baseball behind for Wall Street. In 1956, Hank Greenberg became the first Jewish ballplayer to be elected to the Hall of Fame. Henry Benjamin Greenberg passed away at age 75 in 1986.

PSA/DNA Authentication Services Says:

When it came to meeting the demands of fans and collectors, Greenberg was one of the most personable and kind players in baseball history. Because Greenberg lived until 1986, he was able to sign a reasonable amount of autographs during the emergence of the hobby as a full-fledged industry. That said, single-signed baseballs remain relatively tough to find considering his accommodating nature. Many forgers have made the mistake of placing counterfeit Greenberg signatures on baseballs manufactured after his death. During his career, there are examples of clubhouse attendants adding his name to team-signed items, but these are not very common. In the 1930s and 1940s, the Detroit Tigers team was known to use stamps to add signatures to various items in response to mail requests. For most of his life, Greenberg would sign "Hank" instead of his full first name "Henry," although you will encounter the full name version from time to time.

" *He was one of the truly great hitters, and when I first saw him at bat, he made my eyes pop out,*"

– Joe DiMaggio

Lefty Grove

It is fitting that Robert "Lefty" Grove's middle name is Moses. The man parted his way through batters like the Red Sea, fashioning one of the greatest pitching careers in baseball history. Although it is unfair to describe any ballplayer on mere statistics, Grove's numbers are so mind-boggling, it is inevitable. He led the American League in strikeouts his first seven seasons in the majors. That feat alone might qualify a pitcher for Hall of Fame consideration, but Grove was no mere fireballer. He also topped the Junior Circuit in ERA in 9 of his 17 seasons (1925–1941). Between 1927 and 1933, Grove never won less than 20 games, and topped out at 31 wins in 1931. That season, he won league MVP honors, adding a 2.06 ERA and 27 complete games to his stat sheet. In 1930 and 1931, Grove won what is now known as the pitching Triple Crown, setting the AL pace in wins, ERA, and strikeouts. Amazingly, in three other seasons, he missed that honor by just one category. Overall, Grove won exactly 300 games and lost just 141 for an impressive .680 winning percentage. In the postseason, Grove upped his game, playing in three consecutive World Series (1929–1931) with Connie Mack's Philadelphia Athletics. He was 4–2 with an ERA of 1.75 leading the A's to titles in 1929 and 1930.

Ironically, Grove's MLB debut came in 1925 against the Boston Red Sox. Nine years later, he joined the Red Sox at age 34 and won 105 games over the next eight seasons, highlighted by a 20–12 mark in 1935 for a mediocre Boston club managed by Joe Cronin. The son of a Maryland mining family, Grove hopped through odd jobs before he found baseball. His stats are even more impressive given that he spent 1920 through 1924 playing Minor League ball for the AA Baltimore Orioles where he won

Lefty

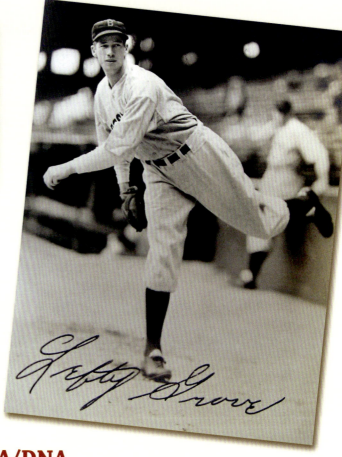

> "Just to see that big guy glaring down at you from the mound was enough to frighten the daylights out of you."
>
> – Joe Cronin, Hall of Famer

an additional 108 games. In 1925, Mack outbid several other clubs and Grove became an Athletic. He overcame his youthful lack of control on the hill and pitched in some of the most memorable games in baseball history including Game Four of the 1929 World Series in which the A's overcame an 8–0 deficit to beat the Cubs 10–8. Grove was a student of pitching and a source of wisdom for younger or less-gifted teammates. He was inducted into the Baseball Hall of Fame in 1947 and passed away in 1975, at age 75. So, while the biblical Moses offered 10 Commandments, the baseball Moses lived by just one: Thou shalt not get a hit off of Lefty Grove.

PSA/DNA Authentication Services Says:

Grove was one of the more active signers of his generation, especially after his playing days were over. His autograph is most frequently found on mediums such as album pages and government postcards, which were often sent through the mail by autograph seekers. Grove really enjoyed the interaction with fans and, over time, he became one of the most popular players at Hall of Fame weekend in Cooperstown, New York. For the most part, Grove would sign "Lefty" instead of his legal name "Robert" unless it was on a legal document or check. For a time, the Philadelphia Athletics employed the use of a stamp to apply player autographs on various items, but Grove's obliging nature ensured that a reasonable number of authentic examples still exist today.

BASEBALL'S GOLDEN AGE

Harry Heilmann

One of the premier hitters of the 1920s, Harry Edwin Heilmann was a magician with the bat. With his .342 lifetime batting average, Heilmann was not just a singles hitter but was among league leaders in doubles, triples, and hits. Defensively, Harry was another story. A mediocre fielder, Heilmann was given the nickname "Slug" because of his defensive difficulties and his lack of speed. The young right fielder was switched to first base in 1919 by Detroit Tigers manager Hughie Jennings and Heilmann proceeded to lead the league in errors two straight years. Once Ty Cobb became player-manager in 1921, he switched Heilmann back to right field and he improved to lead the league in putouts and assists in 1924 and 1925.

The 6-foot, 1-inch, and 195 pound San Francisco native may not have been fast, but he was an outstanding hitter. With the advent of the Live Ball Era of baseball in 1920 and Ty Cobb's tutelage, Heilmann's batting average soared from .309 in 1920 to .394 in 1921, and from 168 hits to 237 hits. Harry flirted with the .400 mark on two other occasions, batting .393 in 1925 and .398 in 1927. The four-time batting champ's best year was in 1923 when he batted an amazing .403, ten points higher than Babe Ruth's .393 average that year. For the entire decade of the 1920s, Heilmann was the premier hitter in the American League. He reached the 100 RBI milestone eight times, and posted 12 consecutive .300 plus seasons.

Slug

PSA/DNA Authentication Services Says:

Heilmann was considered one of the more accessible baseball figures during his playing days and post-playing career. Serving as the Detroit Tigers announcer kept Heilmann close to the game up until his death in 1951. He was considered a very responsive signer through the mail and, as a result, the commonly-seen Heilmann autographs are found on mediums such a government postcards and index cards. Based on the eye-appeal of his autograph, it is very apparent that Heilmann took great pride in his signature. It is one of the more beautiful autographs on our "Top 100" list. One of the more interesting notes about Heilmann's autograph is that forgers often forget that he was enshrined into the Hall of Fame after he passed away, making a signed Hall of Fame postcard of Heilmann impossible.

After 15 years in the Tigers outfield, Heilmann tried to extend his career with the Cincinnati Reds in 1930. He developed arthritis in both wrists causing him to miss the 1931 season. Heilmann called it a career in 1932, at age 37, retiring with the second highest batting average among right-handed hitters in American League history.

After his retirement, Heilmann became the play-by-play radio broadcaster for the Tigers. His folksy sense of humor endeared him to fans, and he worked until a year before his death. Harry Heilmann passed away from lung cancer at 56 years old, in 1951. He was elected to the Hall of Fame a year later, in 1952. The "Slug" may not have been the best fielder in baseball history, but he was certainly one of its greatest hitters.

> "*I rate Harry the greatest right-handed hitter I have ever seen. He was more than a great mechanical ballplayer. He was ideal from a manager's standpoint. A fine outfielder, he would fill in at any position if it would help the team.*"
>
> – Ty Cobb

BASEBALL'S GOLDEN AGE

Gil Hodges

Jackie Robinson broke the color barrier. Duke Snider broke records. Gil Hodges broke the mold. Of all the great Brooklyn Dodgers, no one was more emotionally attached to the Dodger faithful than Gilbert Raymond Hodges. According to the HBO documentary *The Ghosts of Flatbush*, this love was displayed during Hodges' epic 1952 World Series slump. Instead of booing the beleaguered Hodges, Brooklyn fans prayed for him to bounce back. The prayers did not work as Hodges went 0–21 in that Series and the Dodgers lost another heartbreaker to the hated Yankees. During Hodges' tenure in Brooklyn (1943–1957, minus two seasons lost to military service), the Dodgers played the Yanks in the World Series six times and beat them only once, in 1955. Despite being an eight-time All-Star, with 370 career home runs, over 1,200 RBI, and a respectable .273 career batting average, Hodges remains on the outside looking in at Cooperstown.

For seven consecutive seasons, 1949 to 1955, Hodges topped the 100 RBI plateau. For 11 straight seasons, 1949 to 1959, he topped the 20 homer mark, and clouted over 30 dingers six times, including 40 in 1951 and 42 in 1954. On the flip side, he was often among the league leaders in strikeouts. He fell 79 hits shy of 2,000 for his career, but was a three-time Gold Glover at first base and a reliable 150+ game and 600+ plate appearances man for much of his career. Hodges was an Indiana high school star and has a bridge named after him in the Hoosier State, but he truly found his home in Brooklyn. Hodges' heart remained in the borough even after the Dodgers moved to LA in 1958. He won another World Series on the West Coast in 1959, and then returned to his beloved New York to finish out his playing

Miracle Worker

career with the 1962–1963 Mets. After a woeful stint as manager of the Senators from 1963 to 1967, Hodges was hired to skipper the Mets. The club finished in ninth place in 1968, but then won the 1969 Series in one of the most Amazin' turnarounds in baseball history. Hodges never had the chance to lead the Mets to another pennant in 1973. In the spring of 1972, he died of a coronary after a round of golf at the young age of 47. The adopted son Brooklyn, Gil Hodges will always be remembered in New York as one of the Dodgers' greats and for his winning spirit that drove the Mets to baseball glory.

PSA/DNA Authentication Services Says:

Gil Hodges proudly placed a beautiful, flowing autograph on everything he signed, and his style remained largely consistent throughout his adult life. Known for being a willing signer throughout his life, due to his early passing in 1972, authentic Hodges autographs can be more challenging than others to locate. Unlike most other players and coaches of the era, Hodges died prior to the industry boom of the 1980s and beyond. In addition, Hodges did have a clubhouse attendant sign on his behalf during his years with the Dodgers and his tenure as Mets manager, so collectors need to be aware of these non-malicious forgeries as well as the forgeries penned for financial gain.

BASEBALL'S GOLDEN AGE 139

Rogers Hornsby

The word Rajah means an Indian king or prince. This could be the most appropriate nickname in sports history because Rogers "Rajah" Hornsby was truly baseball royalty. He played 23 seasons for the Cardinals, Giants, Braves, Cubs, and Browns, but let's focus on the years between 1920 and 1931. In that time span, Hornsby was the best player EVER in baseball. He batted over .400 three times (1922, 1924, 1925), and led the league in OBP nine times, highlighted by an astonishing .507 mark in 1924. Seven times, he eclipsed the 200 hit plateau, and he won seven batting crowns. Hornsby dominated OPS when OPS was just the last three letters of the word bops, and oh yeah, he hit a few of those too, topping 300 home runs for his career and crunching a National League best 42 blasts in 1922, one of the greatest individual seasons in baseball history. That year, Hornsby hit .401, scored 141 runs, smacked 46 doubles, had 250 hits, an OBP of .459, and slugged .722—all league highs.

A second sacker by trade, Hornsby played every outfield and infield position except catcher. He also ran the gamut of critics. After batting just .246 as a 19-year-old Cardinal rookie in 1915, manager Miller Huggins suggested he be "farmed out." A few years later, manager John McGraw called the clean-living Texan, "a better hitter than Babe Ruth." He won Triple Crowns in 1922 and 1925, and was named MVP in 1925 and 1929. Hornsby saw postseason play that year with the 1929 Cubs, who lost to the Athletics in the World Series.

Rajah

"*He's the only guy I know who could hit .350 in the dark.*"

- Frankie Frisch

From 1925 on, Hornsby was player-manager of his teams, but his abrasive personality created problems with management and players and was the cause of several trades. His greatest success as manger was leading the Cards to the 1926 world championship. In the 1930s he played sparingly while managing the Cubs and Browns, and retired as a player in 1937. His .358 career average is still a record for NL right-handed hitters, and his 1924 batting average of .424 is the highest single-season average in the 20th century. Hornsby managed in the minors for several years, returned to the majors to manage the Browns and the Reds in the early 1950s, and continued on to coach for the Cubs and Mets until he passed away in 1963, at age 66. He was inducted into the Baseball Hall of Fame in 1942.

PSA/DNA Authentication Services Says:

At times, Rogers Hornsby had the reputation of being a fiery personality who sometimes clashed with management, but you would never guess that from his signing habits over his lifetime. Hornsby, one of the more passionate players to ever step on the field, channeled that energy in a positive way when answering fan requests both during and after his playing days were over. Even the vast majority of team-signed baseballs that surface contain a real Hornsby autograph versus a clubhouse version. From some of the earliest examples found in the mid-1910s to his passing in 1963, you will notice no major changes to his signatures over time. Just like he was as a hitter, Hornsby was remarkably consistent. As accommodating as Hornsby was, there was a period in the 1940s and 1950s when the Hall of Famer sought the assistance of his girlfriend to answer some of the mail requests from fans. These non-malicious forgeries appear from time to time in the marketplace.

BASEBALL'S GOLDEN AGE

Chuck Klein

One of the more underrated Hall of Fame members, Chuck Klein was a dominant National League force from the late-1920s to the mid-1930s. The Indianapolis native worked in the Indiana steel mills for several years, which developed his strength and stamina. "The Hoosier Hammer" was signed by the Philadelphia Phillies in 1928, and quickly developed into a strong, talented outfielder who could hit for power and play flawless defense. In 1929, his first full season in the majors, the 24-year-old Klein batted .356 and smacked an amazing 43 homers to win the National League home run crown. Interestingly, Klein's teammates helped guarantee that home run title. On the last day of the 1929 season, the Phillies played the New York Giants in a doubleheader. Klein and Giants superstar Mel Ott were tied for the home run lead. In the first game, Klein homered, which put him one ahead of Ott. In the second game, Ott was walked FIVE times by Phillies pitchers, and one of those walks was with the bases loaded. How is that for teamwork?

Defensively, Klein led the league in 1930 with 44 outfield assists, which is still a record. A beast on the basepaths, he also led the league in stolen bases in 1932, and was named National League MVP that year. Klein played a total of 15 seasons with the Phillies interrupted by a three-year stint with the Cubs and part of a season with the Pittsburgh Pirates. Although he batted .300 or better 11 of his 17 Major League seasons, Klein's glory days were between 1929 and 1934. During that period, he won the 1933 NL Triple Crown, was a two-time All-Star (1933, 1934), a four-time NL home run leader, and also led the league

The Hoosier Hammer

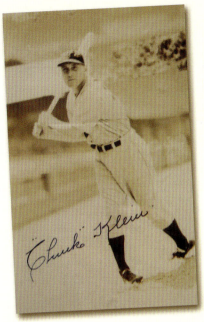

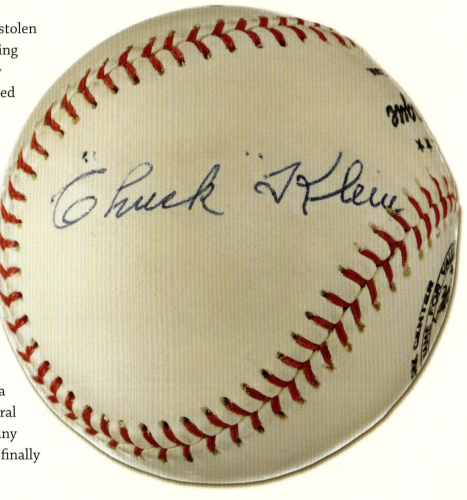

at various points in stolen bases, RBI, and batting average. In the early 1940s, Klein was used mostly as a pinch hitter, and was also a coach for the Phillies. He retired as a player in 1944 and as a coach in 1945, when he was 40 years old. After retiring, Klein had a tavern in Philly until 1947, when he suffered a stroke caused by physical issues aggravated by drinking and poor diet. After that, Klein had difficulty walking and speaking, and he moved back home to Indiana to live out his days with family. He died of a cerebral hemorrhage at age 53 in 1958. Overlooked for many years by Cooperstown, Charles Herbert Klein was finally inducted into the Hall of Fame in 1980.

PSA/DNA Authentication Services Says:

If you consider the era Chuck Klein played in, the terrific hitter's signature is relatively easy to find compared some of his contemporaries. Collectors will often encounter Klein's signature in the form of album pages, government postcards, and multi-signed baseballs. Most of the time, the Hall of Famer would sign "Chuck Klein" with quotation marks around his first name. Since he was such an active signer, both in person and through the mail, you don't see many examples of clubhouse or secretarial signatures in his place. As a key figure in both the Philadelphia Phillies and Chicago Cubs lineups during his prime, Klein remains popular with collectors. In 1947, Klein suffered a stroke and there are very few autographs that date from that period until the end of his life in 1958.

> *One reason why I've been able to play baseball well is because it's fun to me. Many players find it work.*
>
> – Chuck Klein

BASEBALL'S GOLDEN AGE

Stan Musial

Stan Musial's nickname, "Stan the Man," was more than just a rhyme. Throughout his illustrious 22-year career, all with the Cardinals, he was The Man, not only in St. Louis, but in all of baseball. The son of hardworking Polish immigrants, Stanley Frank Musial signed a Minor League contract while still attending high school in Donora, Pennsylvania. The young outfielder came up to the Cardinals in 1941 to hit .426 in 12 games. Musial blossomed in his second season with 10 home runs and 72 RBI in 140 games. In 1943, he won his first of seven batting crowns and led the National League in hits, doubles, triples, OBP, and slugging. Musial won the MVP Award that season, a feat he would duplicate two times in his next four seasons. After a year of military service in 1945, Musial led the NL with a .365 batting average in 1946. He hit over 20 home runs in 10 consecutive seasons (1948–1957), and in 1948, he hit 39 home runs with 230 hits, 131 RBI and a .376 average, all career highs.

In one of the great hitting runs of all time, Musial never batted lower than .310 between 1941 and 1958, and eclipsed the 200 hit plateau six times in that span. He backboned the Redbirds to the World Series in 1942, 1943, 1944, and 1946, winning three titles and hitting .304 in the 1944 Fall Classic versus the crosstown rival St. Louis Browns. A consistent doubles and triples man, Musial was the rock in the Cardinals lineup, playing in 3,026 career games, tied for 6th all-time with Eddie Murray. When he retired after the 1963 season, the 42-year-old Musial had amassed 475 career home runs, 1,951 RBI, and 3,630 hits. In one of baseball's great statistical wonders, Musial had exactly 1,815 hits at home

Stan the Man

and 1,815 hits on the road, proving that regardless of the ballpark or the city, Stan Musial truly was The Man. As General Manager in 1967, he led the Cards to their 4–3 World Series win over the Red Sox, and then continued on with the Cardinals in various front office capacities through 1980. He was inducted into the Baseball Hall of Fame in 1969 and passed away in 2013 at age 92.

PSA/DNA Authentication Services Says:

Stan Musial was one of the friendliest and most accessible superstars of his era. In fact, long after his playing career, when the hobby blossomed from a niche field into a nationwide industry, Musial helped create Stan the Man, Inc., a company that provided autographs direct to the public for many years, nearly up until the time he passed away in 2013. Early in his career, Musial's facsimile signature would occasionally be stamped on baseballs, photos, and GPCs in response to autograph requests. In fact, this was a fairly common practice used by the St. Louis Cardinals organization during that era.

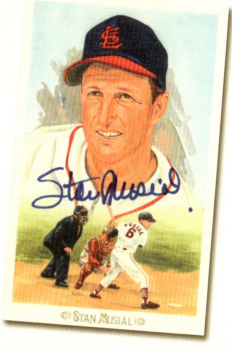

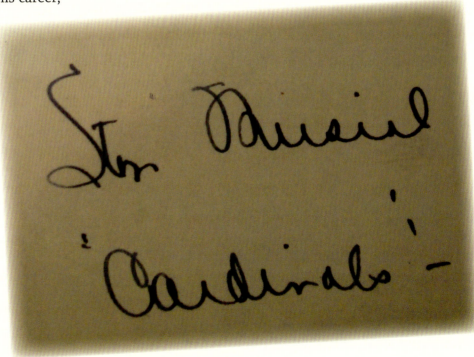

> " *I could have rolled the ball up there against Musial, and he would have pulled out a golf club and hit it out.*"
> – Don Newcombe, Brooklyn Dodgers All-Star

BASEBALL'S GOLDEN AGE 145

Satchel Paige

In the annals of baseball, there are few players who can match Leroy Robert "Satchel" Paige for personality and performance. Paige starred in the Negro Leagues before finally making it to Major League Baseball in 1948 at the age of 41. That season, he bolstered the Indians staff and helped them win the American League pennant and World Series, becoming the first African-American to pitch in the Fall Classic. He played for Cleveland, the St. Louis Browns, and Kansas City A's, and was a two-time All-Star. Paige's career MLB record of 28–31 belies his true greatness. If not for baseball's color barrier, which precluded African-Americans from the game until 1947, he could have easily been the best to ever pitch.

Born in 1906 in Mobile, Alabama, Paige broke into the Negro Leagues at age 20 and pitched for Birmingham, Chicago, Cleveland, Pittsburgh, Kansas City, New York, and the Homestead Grays. Because Negro League stats are sketchy at best, it is unclear how many untold games Paige actually pitched and won. Still, the lanky 6-foot, 3-inch, and 180 pound Paige was considered the best pitcher of his time and faced incredible talent among his Negro League brethren. A real showman, Paige brought his blazing fastball to any field, in any town, for a chance to show his stuff and earn a buck. He often left his Negro League team mid-season to barnstorm throughout the United States and Latin America.

Satchel

Paige came of age at a time of intense racial segregation in Alabama. It was in reform school that he first played baseball. He then reformed the game itself with his talent. Beneath all of Paige's showmanship and bravado, there was a true love of the game. It was all about pitching and dominating hitters. He pitched for several Minor League teams well into his 50s, and in 1965 at 59 years old, Paige pitched three shutout innings for the Kansas City A's in one last MLB appearance. In 1966, he played for the Carolina League's Peninsula Grays. That club included the young future Hall of Famer Johnny Bench. Imagine Paige firing a pitch to Bench, a battery for the ages. He was inducted into the Hall of Fame in 1971 and passed away in 1982, at age 75. Paige is known for his quote, "Don't look back. Something might be gaining on you." In truth, he had no such worries. Nothing could ever catch up to the great Satchel Paige.

PSA/DNA Authentication Services Says:

Paige was filled with life and had a youthfulness about him, even as he aged. Fans were drawn to Paige and he obliged them by being a friendly, gracious signer. With a very deliberate and neat appearance, his autograph was penned with great care, from his playing career throughout his life. Although he passed away in 1982, Paige did sign a reasonable amount of items in the 1970s and right up until the hobby started to blossom. While many of the single-signed baseballs you encounter are signed on the side panel, Paige also signed on the sweet spot from time to time. Finding a Paige autograph that dates to his time in the Negro Leagues is an entirely different story. Locating an example from that period is rare and the most desirable type of autograph from this MLB pioneer.

"*The best and fastest pitcher I've ever faced.*"

– Joe DiMaggio

BASEBALL'S GOLDEN AGE

Herb Pennock

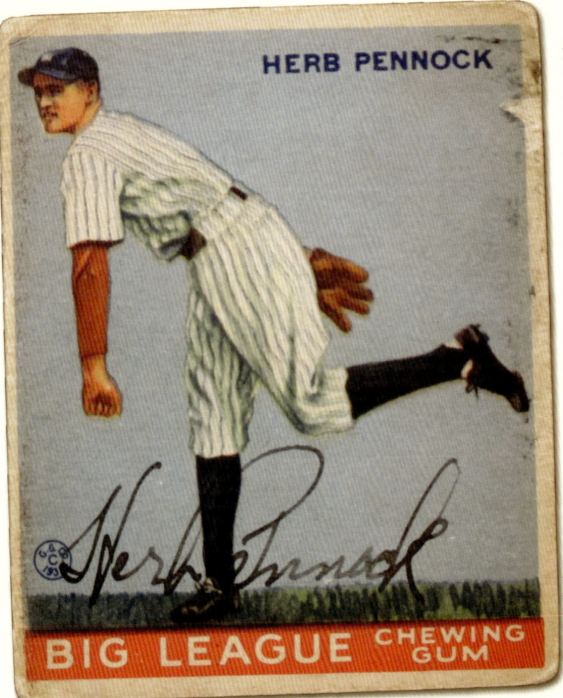

Considered one of the great lefties in baseball history, Herb Pennock had the bulk of his success with the New York Yankees. The lanky 18-year-old Kennett Square, Pennsylvania, native came up to the Philadelphia Athletics in 1912 and in 1914 posted a nifty 11–4 record with a 2.79 earned run average. Pennock was the opening day pitcher in 1915, but his effortless pitching and relaxed confidence on the mound was too laid back for Connie Mack's liking, and he was dealt to the Red Sox in June. Pennock spent some seasoning time in the minors and served in the Navy in 1918, so it was not until 1919 that he became a regular member of the Red Sox pitching staff. He went on to finish that season with a 16–8 record and for the next three seasons was fairly successful. During the 1922 off-season, Pennock was traded to the Yankees and his career as a dominating left-handed pitcher took off. His "rag-arm" style and big sweeping curveball worked for the Yanks and Pennock went 19–6 in 1923 to help New York to their first World Series Championship. He established himself as a gutsy high-pressure hurler in that Series, winning Game Two, coming in for the save in Game Four, and winning Game Six pitching on one day's rest. Over the next several years, Pennock dominated the American League, highlighted by a 23–11 season in 1926. Part of the 1927 Murderers' Row Yankees, Pennock helped his team to the Series Championship that year, and in 1928, he led the league in shutouts, but by 1929, father time

The Squire of Kennett Square

and various injuries caught up with Pennock. He became a relief pitcher with various measures of success, but was never the same. In the 1932 Series, Pennock is credited with the save in both Game Three and Game Four, helping the Yankees to a 4–0 win over the Cubs. In 1934, the 40-year-old Pennock went back to the Red Sox as a reliever and finished his 22-year pitching career that year retiring with a 241–162 record. He continued in several capacities for the Red Sox until 1943 when he became general manager of the Philadelphia Phillies. There, Pennock began to put together the team that would eventually become the 1950 "Whiz Kids." In 1948, the Squire of Kennett Square collapsed and died in New York City at the age of 53. Herbert Jefferis Pennock was elected to the Hall of Fame in 1948.

PSA/DNA Authentication Services Says:

As a part of several championship clubs, Pennock was often asked to sign many team-oriented items during his lifetime. Although his career started in 1912, you will not often encounter dated Pennock autographs until those signed in the early 1920s. Pennock was an accessible person during and after his career, both in person and through the mail. At different points during his lifetime, his autograph varied from "H. Pennock" to a full-name autograph "Herb Pennock." In addition, Pennock's signature was tall in stature and usually had a quickly-signed appearance. Despite passing away at the fairly young age of 53, there is a good supply of authentic Pennock signatures as a result of his consistent activity. He was so active that Pennock rarely employed the use of a clubhouse attendant or secretary to sign in his place.

" *Alway pitch to the catcher and not the hitter.*"

– Herb Pennock

BASEBALL'S GOLDEN AGE 149

Branch Rickey

In 1945, Brooklyn Dodgers general manager Branch Rickey signed Negro Leagues star Jackie Robinson. Two years later, Robinson joined the Dodgers, breaking baseball's long-embraced color barrier. It was the single most significant happening in the history of Major League Baseball and perhaps all of sports. Bringing Robinson to Brooklyn will always be the legendary Rickey's greatest contribution to the game. With Robinson, the Dodgers dominated the National League to the tune of six pennants and the 1955 World Series Championship. While players like Robinson, Pee Wee Reese, Roy Campanella, Duke Snider, Gil Hodges, and countless others certainly played key roles in Brooklyn's success, the foundation of the club was Rickey.

Young Branch Rickey hit .284 for the St. Louis Browns in 1906, and that was the highlight of his playing career. Eventually, he became player-manager of the Browns, and later, would remain in the Gateway City but jump to the National League's Cardinals as manager. He spent a decade managing in St. Louis, but never garnered a single pennant. In fact, he never finished higher than third place in any season. Despite his lack of success, Rickey was always building. The Cardinals franchise would go on to win six NL pennants and four world championships after Rickey moved from field manager to the front office. Much of the steel that girded the Cards' run to glory was forged by Rickey, with his establishment of the modern farm system to nurture and hone young talent.

As part-owner and general manager of the Dodgers from 1942 to 1950, The Mahatma, as Rickey was known, was the first executive to use statistical analysis to evaluate ballplayers, fostered the use of batting helmets for safety, and developed a state-of-the-art spring training facility in Florida. However, breaking MLB's color barrier is Rickey's greatest legacy. Rickey departed Brooklyn in 1950 after a power struggle with owner Walter O'Malley. What did he do then? He simply brought his tool box to Pittsburgh where, from 1950 to 1955, he constructed the roster of a team that would eventually win the 1960 World Series. Player, manager, general manager, humanitarian, innovator...after 60 years of involvement in the game, Wesley Branch Rickey died in 1965 at the age of 83, and was inducted to the Hall of Fame in 1967.

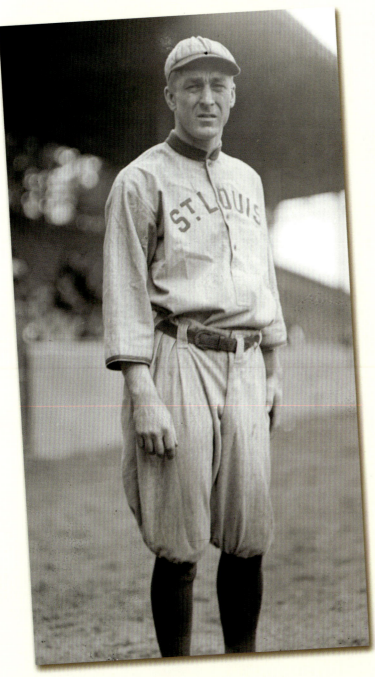

The Mahatma

PSA/DNA Authentication Services Says:

As a result of Rickey's position in baseball, many of his signatures can be found on documents, ranging from official contracts to letters. Beyond his official duties and the signatures that emanated from that role, Rickey was also an obliging signer on a personal level. Collectors will encounter an ample number of Rickey autographs, ranging from signed index cards to multi-signed items, but you don't tend to see many dated examples until you get to the 1930s. For collectors of single-signed baseballs, Rickey examples do exist, but in relatively small numbers. Since Rickey worked in baseball for many years, collectors may encounter an occasional secretarial signature that was used to help deal with the heavy amount of correspondence sent his way.

"*The thing about him [Branch Rickey] was that he was always doing something for someone else. I know, because he did so much for me.*"

– Jackie Robinson

BASEBALL'S GOLDEN AGE 151

George Sisler

Considered among the best first basemen to ever play the game, George Howard Sisler is one of the first sports greats to come out of the University of Michigan. The lefty pitcher and hitter played for Wolverines coach Branch Rickey, who brought Sisler up to the St. Louis Browns after he graduated in 1915. One of the most dominant ballplayers of the early 20th century, Sisler is not to be confused with Gorgeous George, the famous professional wrestler. This Gorgeous George excelled with his bat, not with body slams. Arguably the all-time greatest St. Louis Browns player, Sisler hit for high averages, was stellar defensively, and could run like a deer.

Branch Rickey started the 22-year-old rookie as pitcher, but soon moved Sisler to first base to benefit from his remarkable hitting. Rickey left for the Cardinals soon after, but Sisler remained with the Browns for 12 years. Although never postseason contenders, during Sisler's years with the Browns they did finish as high as second place in the American League. Consistently excellent, Sisler batted over .300 thirteen of his fifteen MLB seasons. In 1920, he led the league with an amazing .407 BA and his 257 hits total stood as the single-season record for 84 years until Ichiro Suzuki shattered it in 2004. In 1922, Sisler again led the league with an incredible .420

Gorgeous George

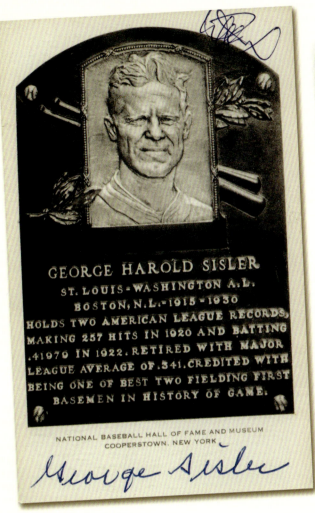

batting average, 246 hits, and 51 stolen bases. That year, he hit in 41 straight games, a record that stood until Joe DiMaggio broke it in 1941. To top it off, Sisler was voted the American League's Most Valuable Player in 1922.

After a stint as player-manager of the Browns from 1924 to 1926, Sisler finished up his playing career with the Boston Braves, retiring with a career .340 BA in 1930 at 37 years old. In the 1930s, he helped found the American Softball Association and developed the first lighted softball park, located in St. Louis. Sisler then worked in various capacities for Branch Rickey's Brooklyn Dodgers in the 1940s, and coached for Rickey's Pittsburgh Pirates in the 1950s. Along the way, he mentored greats like future Hall of Famers Duke Snider, Jackie Robinson, and Roberto Clemente.

With his offensive prowess, great defense, and base-running abilities, Gorgeous George solidified his place as one of the great ballplayers of the 20th century. George Howard Sisler, AL MVP, two-time batting champ, and four-time stolen base champ, was elected to the Hall of Fame in 1939. He passed away in 1973, two days after his 80th birthday.

PSA/DNA Authentication Services Says:

Accommodating and accessible, Sisler was one of the more productive signers of his era, even frequently responding to mail requests. Since Sisler stayed close the game, working for different organizations after his playing days, this provided fans with more opportunities to acquire his signature in public settings. As a result, most mediums containing Sisler autographs are attainable, especially items such as index cards and even Hall of Fame postcards. The great hitter's early signature "Geo. H. Sisler" evolved into "George Sisler" relatively quickly as the 1920s progressed. One interesting note about Sisler's signing habit is that he would vary from signing on the sweet spot or side panels of baseballs throughout his life. The Hall of Fame postcard shown above is signed by Sisler and also by Ichiro Suzuki, who broke Sisler's single-season hits record in 2004.

BASEBALL'S GOLDEN AGE 153

Casey Stengel

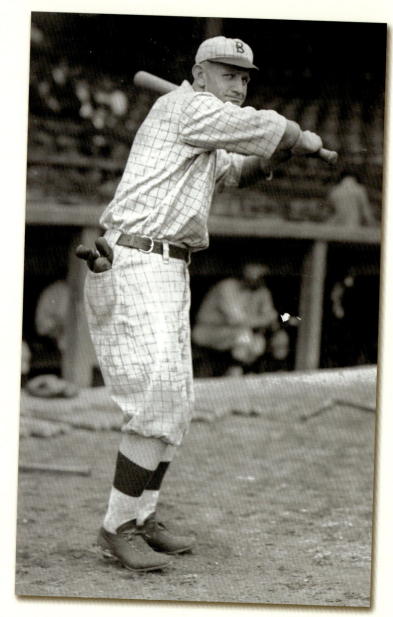

One of the most colorful individuals in baseball history, Casey Stengel managed some of the all-time greatest teams, and some of the all-time most pitiful teams. A solid outfielder, Charles Dillon Stengel played for the Dodgers, Pirates, Phillies, Giants, and Braves from 1912 to 1925, compiling a .284 batting average over his 14-year career. Along the way, he saw World Series play in 1916 with Brooklyn, and with New York in 1922 and 1923, winning the championship in 1922.

His career as a Major League manager started uneventfully. Over his three years with the Brooklyn Dodgers and six years with the Boston Braves, he reached the .500 mark only one season. He then managed in the minors with some success, but everything changed for Stengel when he became skipper of the New York Yankees in 1949. In his 12 years at the helm, Stengel's Yankees merely won 10 American League pennants and seven World Series Championships. Stengel joked about how smart he became overnight, to lead the Yanks to American League domination. In reality Stengel was an excellent manager. His philosophy was to think outside the box, regularly using innovations like platooning, making defensive substitutions at critical times, and using his bullpen. Stengel's run with the Yanks was one of the greatest in baseball history. Through it all, he kept his unique

" *The secret of managing is to keep the guys who hate you away from the guys who are undecided.*"

– Casey Stengel

154 BASEBALL'S GOLDEN AGE

The Old Perfessor

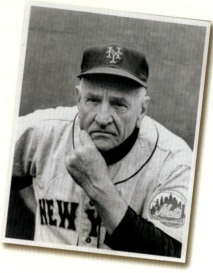

sense of humor, delighting the press and fans with colorful quotes.

After losing the Series in 1960, the 70-year-old Stengel was released, supposedly because he was too old. Stengel resurfaced in 1962 to manage the new expansion team in New York. The most famously awful team in modern baseball history, Stengel called his team the "Amazin' Mets," because they were so bad. The Mets finished dead last the entire four years Stengel steered the ship, but to fans everywhere they were the "Lovable Losers." Not afraid to verbalize just how incompetent his team really was, Stengel quipped, "We [the Mets] are a much improved ball club, now we lose in extra innings!" After breaking his hip in a fall, Stengel packed it in after the 1965 season and was elected to the Hall of Fame in 1966. When the Amazin' Mets won the Series in 1969, they presented Casey Stengel with a World Series ring which he proudly wore until his death in 1975 at age 85.

PSA/DNA
Authentication Services Says:

While Casey Stengel had the reputation of being a hard-nosed personality on the field, he was nothing but a cooperative signer with fans. Stengel stood out as a fantastic signer through the mail, especially later in his life. The legendary manager rarely deviated from signing his name "Casey Stengel," but sometimes signed his full name "Casey Dillon Stengel" on legal documents.

It is not uncommon to see clubhouse versions of his signature on team balls from his managing days with the Yankees and Mets. Stengel's wife, Edna, did respond to a small portion of mail requests, but this was not a frequent practice.

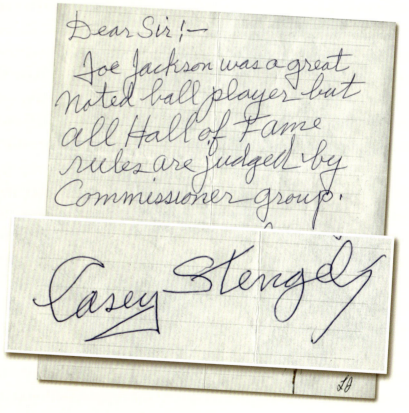

BASEBALL'S GOLDEN AGE 155

Hack Wilson

Lewis Robert "Hack" Wilson could be considered the poster boy for The Roaring Twenties. Prosperity, prohibition, speakeasies, and excessive behavior became the norm, and Hack Wilson bought into all of it.

Built like a barrel, Wilson stood 5-foot, 6-inches, weighed 190 pounds, and could hit for tremendous power, walloping tape measure home runs all over the National League. One of the most colorful players in the history of baseball, he was a prolific hitter, but was also a power drinker and brawler. In 1924, his first full season in the majors with the New York Giants, Wilson batted .295 with 10 homers and 57 RBI. Although he played for four different teams during his 12-year career, his glory days were with the Chicago Cubs. As a Cubbie from 1926 to 1931, Wilson was one of the most feared hitters in baseball, batting .300 or better for five consecutive seasons. He led the NL in home runs four times and in RBI twice. The pinnacle of his career came in 1930, when he batted .356 and blasted 56 home runs with an amazing 191 RBI, still the single season RBI record today. Hack Wilson developed a fondness for the bottle, and this sometimes spilled onto the field and into the stands. He had no problem mixing it up with players and fans alike. In 1928, Wilson jumped into the stands at Wrigley to fight a heckling fan, and it is said nearly 5,000 spectators got involved in the fracas.

Hack

As Wilson became more famous and made more money, he also drank more. At the height of his popularity, he played in Vaudeville and modeled men's clothing for a Chicago clothier. Although Wilson claimed he never played drunk, he was known to play with a hangover on many occasions. As a result of his hard living, Wilson's skills diminished after those five great seasons. The Cubs tired of his off-the-field antics and reduced productivity. He was traded to the Brooklyn Dodgers in 1932 and finally to the Philadelphia Phillies in 1934 where his colorful career came to an end. After baseball, Wilson was involved in several businesses that failed, worked in manufacturing and later as a city laborer. In the end, the bottle won. Hack Wilson died, virtually penniless, at the age of 48 in 1948. Hack Wilson's comet flamed out, but not before he left his mark on the game of baseball. For five memorable years Wilson dominated the National League. The Veterans Committee elected him to the Hall of Fame in 1979.

PSA/DNA Authentication Services Says:

As one of the most unique characters in the game and a fearsome hitter for the Chicago Cubs, Wilson has always been popular with collectors. His autograph changed over time as the barrel-chested slugger moved away from his full name "Lewis R. Wilson" and embraced his nickname, often signing "Hack Wilson" by the late-1920s. There are some post-retirement examples in the marketplace signed "Lewis 'Hack' Wilson" as the Hall of Famer started blending both styles together. Wilson appears to have been a good signer for fans, making himself available to the public. After retirement, he moved around quite a bit, making requests by mail difficult. However, Wilson remained social and often rewarded autograph seekers with a very attractive signature. While some Wilson single-signed baseballs do exist, they remain a challenge for the collector.

The Modern Era
(1960–Present)

★ ★ ★ ★ ★ ★ ★ ★ ★ ★ ★ ★ ★

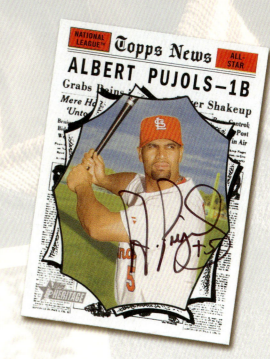

Expansion teams, TV revenues, and BALCO. This period in baseball history has been turbulent but exciting. Hammerin' Hank Aaron unseated the Babe. Players like Johnny Bench, Tony Gwynn, Willie Mays, Mike Schmidt, and Nolan Ryan showed us how the game should be played. Who can forget the Amazin' Mets or The Impossible Dream Red Sox? The 1980s saw the explosion of the autograph industry, providing more opportunities for fans to acquire signatures from their favorite players. Baseball today continues to thrive with a huge fan base. Meet the players from the Modern Era of baseball who have made, and continue to make, our National Pastime the only game in town.

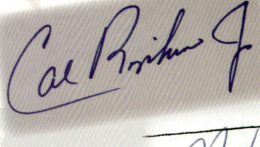

Hank Aaron

On April 8, 1974, in front of a national audience, Henry Louis Aaron hit a shot off of Dodgers pitcher Al Downing that changed baseball history. That April evening, with much of America watching, Hank Aaron hit his 715th home run, shattering the record held by the immortal Babe Ruth. Who can forget the image of those two teenagers who jumped onto the field to run alongside Aaron as he circled third base into the arms of his teammates?

By the time Aaron ended his 23-year playing career in 1976, he had amassed 755 homers. Thirty-one years later, Barry Bonds broke Hammerin' Hank Aaron's home run record. However, Bonds' feat has been clouded by the stigma of performance enhancing drugs and steroids, and allegations linger to this day. On the other hand, Hank Aaron's body of work was without controversy, and he has been held in the highest esteem as a person and ballplayer. In some eyes, Bonds is the true home run champ. In others, it is Aaron. The debate will probably continue for the rest of baseball eternity.

Besides walloping 755 and shattering Babe Ruth's record, Hank Aaron holds MLB records for RBI (2,297), total bases (6,856), extra base hits (1,477), and also holds the record for most All-Star Game selections (25). He was named the National League MVP in 1957, won three Gold Glove Awards, was the NL Home Run Champ

Hammerin' Hank

PSA/DNA Authentication Services Says:

Hank Aaron has always been considered very fan friendly when it comes to signing autographs. Even at the height of his fame when he was chasing Ruth's career home run record, Aaron often took the time to accommodate his fans. His signature has evolved over the years, transforming from a smaller version to a very large one, which can often take up the entire sweet spot of a baseball today. Hammerin' Hank was very active at memorabilia shows during the 1980s and 1990s, and even today the great slugger will show up periodically at a signing event. While Aaron autographs are more common than most others within our "Top 100," his stature in baseball history cements his place in the hobby.

four times and the NL Batting Champ two times. Oh yeah, he also banged out 3,771 hits.

Signed by the Braves out of the Negro American League, Aaron quickly learned to handle racial slurs with poise and dignity when he was assigned to the Braves' South Atlantic League affiliate. The 19-year-old phenom focused on performing up to his potential and was named MVP in 1953, the South Atlantic League's first desegregated season. Aaron again endured racial taunts and threatening letters when he closed in on the Babe's record, but he continued on in hopes of inspiring others to follow their dreams.

After his landmark achievement in 1974, Aaron left the Braves for the new AL Milwaukee Brewers and retired in 1976 at 42 years old. Later, as Vice President of Player Development for the Atlanta Braves, Aaron became one of the first African-American executives in MLB. Over the years, he has been a great ambassador for the game. Besides his stellar baseball career, Aaron has been successful in business with BMW dealerships and a restaurant chain. He was elected to the Hall of Fame in 1982.

" *The pitcher has got only a ball. I've got a bat. So the percentage in weapons is in my favor and I let the fellow with the ball do the fretting.*"

– Hank Aaron

THE MODERN AGE

Ernie Banks

The *C* on Ernie Banks' uniform signified that he played for the Cubs. But when it comes to Banks, the *C* could easily have stood for Class, Charisma, or even Cool. To the fans, Ernie Banks was simply "Mr. Cub." Coming up from the Negro Leagues in 1953, Banks became one of the most prolific players in MLB history. As the first African-American player for the Cubs franchise, he paved the way for other players of color in the organization. However, Banks was not interested in being a pioneer. He was simply a ballplayer who loved the game.

Voted the 27th greatest player of all time by the Society for American Baseball Research (SABR), Banks was a two-time NL RBI Champ and won the Gold Glove in 1960. He was a two-time National League MVP, made 14 All-Star game appearances, and smacked 512 home runs over his illustrious career. At the time of his retirement in 1971, Ernie Banks was the all-time leader in home runs by a shortstop (277), and to this day he still holds several Cubs records.

Stellar defensively as a shortstop, Banks made the move to first base during the second half of his career in order to preserve a bad wheel. A Cub for his entire career, Banks became the face of the franchise, and in 1969 Cubby fans voted him the "Greatest Cub Ever." He was a first ballot Hall of Famer in 1977 and was named to the MLB All-Century Team as shortstop in 1999. Banks became the first Cubs player to have his uniform number retired in 1982, and in 2008 a statue of

Mr. Cub

> "There's sunshine, fresh air, and the team's behind us. Let's play two."
>
> – Ernie Banks

Banks, "Mr. Cub," was placed at the entrance to Wrigley Field.

After his playing days, Banks coached for the Cubs and continued on as ambassador for the franchise. An astute businessman, he became the first African-American to own a Ford dealership in America. He was also active in several charitable endeavors.

On January 23, 2015, Ernest "Ernie" Banks died after suffering a heart attack at the age of 83. Banks never lived to see his Cubs win a World Series. His passion for the game was unsurpassed and it's a bit sad he never got to play in the Fall Classic.

> "He [Banks] was one of the greatest players of all time. He was a pioneer in the Major Leagues. And more importantly, he was the warmest and most sincere person I've ever known."
>
> – Tom Ricketts, Cubs chairman

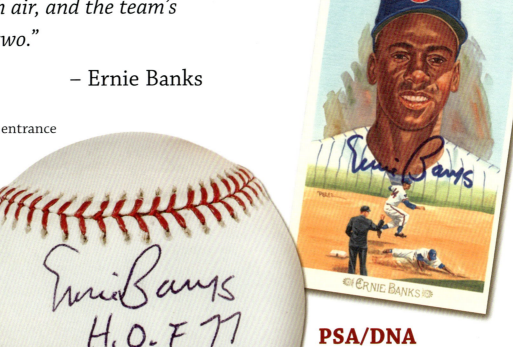

PSA/DNA Authentication Services Says:

Ernie Banks had the reputation for being a gregarious and enthusiastic player, and he carried that part of his personality into his signing habits. Known for being an approachable signer, both in person and through the mail, if you were fortunate enough to meet Banks in person, he would often initiate the conversation with you. There are some secretarial and stamped signatures in the marketplace, most of which made it into circulation during the latter portion of his career. For the majority of his life, Banks' signature was legible and neat. Earlier in his career, Banks' signature had a slower, more deliberate appearance. As he gained confidence and experience signing his name, Banks' signature evolved into a more flowing autograph. While certainly not one of the most scarce autographs on the list, the demand for his autograph has always been strong due to his immense popularity.

THE MODERN AGE

Johnny Bench

> "When you're in a big sweat and nervous, he [Bench] can calm you down more ways than I have ever seen."
>
> – Jim Maloney, pitcher

Considered by many to be the greatest catcher of all time, Johnny Bench is arguably the best defensive catcher in history. Berra, Campanella, Cochrane, Fisk, and Piazza fans may dispute either point, but Johnny Bench is certainly in the conversation.

The 17-year-old kid from Oklahoma was drafted by the Reds in 1965 and made his MLB debut late in the 1967 season. In 1968, Bench became the first catcher to receive the National League Rookie of the Year award, and in 1970 he was the youngest player to be named NL Most Valuable Player. He again attained NL MVP distinction in 1972. The backbone of the 1970s Cincinnati "Big Red Machine," Bench led his team to four pennants and two World Series Championships (1975, 1976). The "Little General" won 10 Gold Gloves, was a 14-time All-Star, and set the standard for durability, catching 100 or more games for 13 consecutive seasons from 1968–1980.

Stellar defensively, as catcher Bench led the league in putouts, assists, and fielding percentage at various points in his career. He perfected the one-handed catching technique, and is credited as the first catcher to wear a batting helmet for protection behind the plate. From an offensive standpoint, Bench could hit for power. His best year was 1970 when he hit .293 with 45 home runs and 148 RBI. When his storied 17-year career with Cincinnati ended in 1983, Bench retired as the all-time leader in home runs as a catcher with 389, a milestone that was later broken by Mike Piazza.

Bench's former manager, Sparky Anderson, summed up Johnny's great career by saying, "I don't want to embarrass any other catcher by comparing him with Johnny Bench." On many lists as the greatest catcher of all time, as an overall player, Johnny Lee Bench is ranked 16th by the *Sporting News* and 19th by the Society for American Baseball Research (SABR). In his post-baseball career, Bench maintained ties with MLB, appeared as a television and radio analyst, authored several books, played on the Senior PGA Tour, and has been active in charitable organizations. The Reds retired Bench's uniform number 5 in 1984, inducted him into the Cincinnati Reds Hall of Fame in 1986, and a statue of Bench was placed at the entrance to the Reds Hall of Fame in 2011. Elected to the Hall of

The Little General

Fame in 1989, his first year of eligibility, his plaque states Bench "redefined standards by which catchers are measured."

PSA/DNA Authentication Services Says:

Johnny Bench possesses one of the most visually-appealing autographs on our "Top 100" list. What his autograph may lack in scarcity, it more than makes up for in importance and flair. Bench's signature from his early playing days even has a measure of maturity and style to it. As Bench's popularity grew as a player and his achievements piled up in the 1970s, obtaining his autograph through the mail and in person became more difficult. That said, Bench has been one of the most active guests at sports collectibles conventions and private signings for four decades (1980s to the present). Bench even has his own website, which provides signed memorabilia to the public. As a result, autograph seekers have plenty of opportunities to add the former leader of "The Big Red Machine" to their collections.

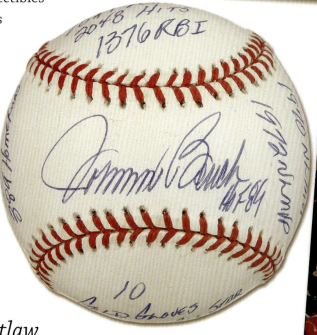

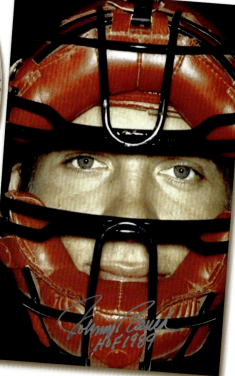

" *A catcher and his body are like the outlaw and his horse. He's got to ride that nag till it drops.*"

– Johnny Bench

Barry Bonds

On August 7, 2007, Barry Lamar Bonds stepped up to the plate and hit home run number 756, breaking Hank Aaron's record. Nevertheless, in September of that year, the Giants announced they would not renew the 43-year-old Bonds' contract, effectively ending a lengthy career filled with stellar achievement but surrounded by controversy. Here are some mind-blowing stats for you to digest. Barry Bonds was a 14-time All-Star, walloped 762 career home runs, went yard 73 times in a single season, won 8 Gold Gloves, was a seven-time National League Most Valuable Player, won 12 Silver Slugger Awards, and was walked 2,558 times in his career, with 688 of those walks being intentional. Bonds also had 2,935 hits to go along with a .298 lifetime batting average. However, at the time of this writing, Bonds cannot even get a whiff of the Baseball Hall of Fame. As magnificent a ballplayer as Bonds was, at this snapshot in time he is linked with the Bay Area Laboratory Co-Operative (BALCO) scandal and the alleged use of steroids and performance enhancing drugs.

Prior to the steroid allegation later in his career, Bonds' numbers were as good as the greatest players to ever don the flannels. Those numbers alone could qualify him for the hallowed halls of Cooperstown. Bonds was signed by the Pittsburgh Pirates out of Arizona State University in 1986 but it was not until 1990 that he became dominant, winning his first MVP, Gold Glove, and Silver Slugger, and making his first All-Star appearance that year. During his seven years with the Pirates, Bonds carried the team on his back as a player and was the main reason that ticket sales increased dramatically. He was signed as a free agent

Bonds

by the San Francisco Giants in December 1992 and spent the balance of his career there.

Part of the problem with the entire Barry Bonds mystique was his personality. Although his hometown fans loved him, Bonds had a surly attitude, an ego the size of the Grand Canyon, and no regard for the media. These traits certainly did not work to his advantage in combating the allegations of steroid use later in his career. In any event, you be the judge of what Barry Bonds actually accomplished in his 22-year MLB career. Does he follow the path that leads to Cooperstown, or does he turn at the bend and follow the road taken by Joe Jackson and Pete Rose? Time will tell.

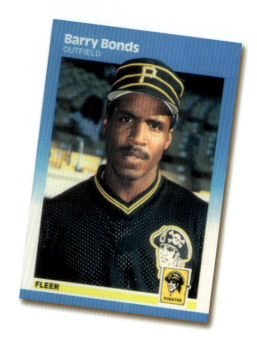

PSA/DNA Authentication Services Says:

In his early days with the Pittsburgh Pirates, Bonds was considered a fairly active signer, even responding frequently to mail requests. His early signature is considered his nicest from an aesthetic standpoint. He would even sign his full name "Barry L. Bonds" on occasion in neat fashion. Over time, as he gained popularity, Bonds' signature evolved and he ended up employing two different versions of his signature. One was tailored for memorabilia signings while the other was a more abbreviated version for in-person requests. In fact, Bonds provided genuine autographs and memorabilia through his own company for a period of time as a player. At the present, Bonds will typically personalize his autograph when asked to sign his name by the public. This is an approach that some players use to counter those seeking the autographs strictly for resale.

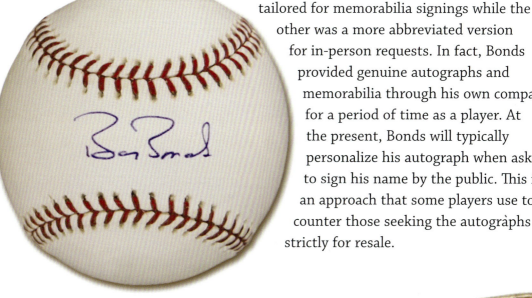

THE MODERN AGE 167

George Brett

face of the Red Sox. When it comes to the Kansas City Royals, no one has been more visible as the "face" than George Brett. As a three-time American League batting champ and 13-time All-Star, George Howard Brett is considered by many to be one of the top three greatest third basemen of all time. He banged out more than 3,100 hits over his illustrious career and was the first player to win batting titles in three decades (1976, 1980, 1990).

One of the great highlight films of all time is of "The Pine Tar Incident" during the Royals-Yankees game on July 24, 1983. Yankees manager Billy Martin, being Billy Martin, protested a two-run home run that Brett hit off reliever Goose Gossage. Martin maintained that the pine tar on Brett's bat exceeded the 18-inch limit. After umpire Tim McClelland measured approximately 24 inches of pine tar on the bat, he called Brett out. Brett charged the ump and had to be restrained from punching his lights out. After the Royals protested the loss, the President of the American League, Lee MacPhail, reversed the decision. Almost a month later, both teams resumed the game and the Royals won.

Most **Major League teams** have had a single player that is considered the "face" of their franchise. With all due respect to the likes of Lou Gehrig and Derek Jeter, Babe Ruth was the face of the Yankees, and Ted Williams was the

Mullet

> "If God had him no balls and two strikes, he'd still get a hit."
> – Steve Palermo, American League umpire

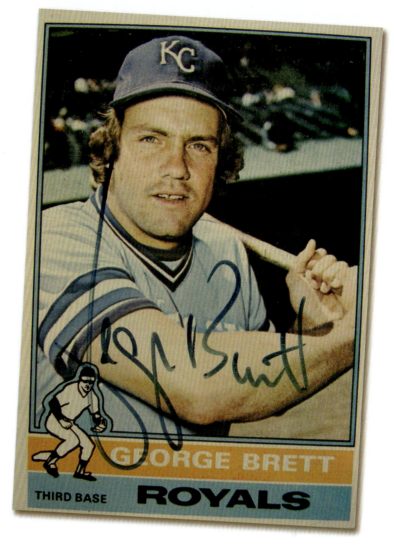

Arguably, Brett's best season was 1985 when he led the Royals to their first World Series Championship with a .335 average, 184 hits, and 30 homers to go along with a Gold Glove. Although he flirted with the .400 mark in 1980, his final average that season was .390. After playing his entire 21-year career with the Kansas City Royals, Brett retired in 1993 with a .305 lifetime batting average and numerous awards. He moved on to the Royals front office as Vice President of Baseball Operations, a position he still holds today, and remains the "face" of the franchise. In 1999, George Brett was elected to the Hall of Fame with the fourth-highest voting percentage at that time. His Hall of Fame plaque states George Brett "played each game with ceaseless intensity and unbridled passion."

PSA/DNA Authentication Services Says:

One of the most competitive players who ever stepped between the lines, George Brett has one of baseball's most distinctive autographs. Early in his career, Brett was an extremely cooperative signer, but that declined somewhat as the young third baseman became a star. As the demand for his time increased, Brett started having pre-printed postcards sent back to fans to help meet the increased demand through the mail. In public, Brett did sign for fans, but it became apparent that it wasn't something he enjoyed doing and he developed a reputation for being a bit surly at times. Unlike many of his contemporaries, Brett has not been a frequent guest on the show circuit. Brett has produced autographs over the years, such as some desirable signed and inscribed game-used bats from later in his career, but he remains a tougher autograph to find compared to most of the players from his generation.

Roger Clemens

Between the years 1984 and 1996, Roger Clemens was the dominant pitcher in the American League. During that period he collected three Cy Young awards, became the first pitcher to strike out 20 batters in a nine-inning game (a feat he performed on two different occasions), was a five-time All-Star, won the ERA title four times, led the American League in strikeouts three times, had three 20-win seasons, and won 192 games. Those numbers on their own merit consideration into the Hall of Fame, but, as we know, the story of William Roger Clemens certainly does not end there.

After 13 years with the Boston Red Sox, Clemens moved to the Toronto Blue Jays at age 34 as a free agent, and launched the second part of his career, which some look at with an asterisk next to his stats. Between 1997 and 2007, with the Blue Jays, Yankees, and Houston Astros, Clemens won four more Cy Young Awards, participated in six more All-Star games, and won another 162 games. With the Blue Jays, he won two Triple Crowns (1997, 1998) and took home two World Series rings with the Yankees (1999, 2000). However, from 1997 to the end of his career in 2007, some people linked Clemens to anabolic steroids and human growth hormones. Some Clemens detractors maintain that, after he left the Red Sox, he gained significant muscle and body mass that added velocity to his fastball, allowing him to

The Rocket

perform in his 30s and 40s as well as he did in his mid-20s. Over the last decade of his career, he had three more 20-win seasons, and with Houston at the age of 42, Clemens won 13 games with a gaudy 1.87 ERA. When you take a look at Clemens' entire career he goes down as one of the greatest pitchers of all time with 354 wins, a .658 win percentage, and 4,672 strikeouts. You decide if an asterisk should be placed next to his name.

In 2013, his first year of eligibility, Clemens received only 37.6% of the Hall of Fame votes. A player needs at least 75% of the votes to gain entrance. At the time of this writing, Clemens is the only 300-game winner not inducted to the Hall. The details of the steroid investigation are well known, but just looking at his pure numbers, Clemens was as good as any pitcher who ever stepped on the mound. Whether or not he had a little help will always be debated.

> " *It's been said before, but it's true: for Red Sox fans, watching Clemens thrive as a Yankee is the equivalent of watching your ex-wife marry your sworn mortal enemy – then live happily ever after.*"
>
> – Sean McAdam, sportswriter

PSA/DNA Authentication Services Says:

When it comes to "The Rocket's" signing habits, they are not unlike many other players from the same generation. Early in his career, Clemens was very accessible to fans and collectors. As he gained popularity and stature on the field, Clemens became overwhelmed with autograph requests. As a result Clemens became more guarded, which is common for many superstar players as their careers progress. While his signature changed over time, becoming shorter and quicker in appearance, elements of its basic structure were retained. Some collectors tend to seek out earlier Clemens examples based on their scarcity and eye-appeal. During his post-career days, Clemens has provided authentic signatures to the hobby during private and public signings in conjunction with memorabilia companies such as TRISTAR productions.

Don Drysdale

A **no-nonsense pitcher, Don** Drysdale would not hesitate to plunk a hitter or brush him back in order to maintain complete control of the strike zone. The eight-time All-Star hit a total of 154 batters over his 14-year career. Drysdale once stated his philosophy in this way. "My own little rule was two for one. If one of my teammates got knocked down, then I knocked down two on the other team."

In the 1960s, Dodgers Don Drysdale and Sandy Koufax became a dominant pitching tandem that owned the

National League hitters of the day. Drysdale won the Cy Young Award with a 25–9 record and 2.83 ERA in 1962, and in 1968, he set a Major League record by hurling six consecutive shutouts and an amazing 58 consecutive scoreless innings. A two-time 20 game winner, Drysdale was also one of the best hitting pitchers of all time and was sometimes called upon to pinch hit for the Dodgers. As a matter of fact, in 1965, Drysdale batted .300 with seven home runs and was the only .300 hitter on the Dodgers World Series roster.

A torn rotator cuff forced a 32-year-old Drysdale to retire during the 1969 season with a career 209 wins and a nifty 2.95 ERA. The tall, dark, and handsome Drysdale had appeared on several television shows during the 1960s. After his playing days, he worked as a broadcaster for a number of teams and networks. Drysdale even worked as a color commentator broadcasting Los Angeles Rams football. He later

Big D

teamed up with the legendary Vin Scully and became the color commentator for the Dodgers.

On July 3, 1993, Don Drysdale was found dead in his Montreal hotel room. He was only 56 years old. The previous day he had worked a Dodgers vs. Montreal Expos game. During that game, Drysdale noticed that the young Dodgers pitcher, Pedro Martinez, was tipping batters off with his glove positioning. After the game, he came down from the broadcast booth to teach the young pitcher how to better hide his pitches. Martinez believes that little piece of advice by Drysdale helped him significantly improve as a pitcher. Donald Scott Drysdale was elected to the Hall of Fame in 1984.

teammate Sandy Koufax, since they were the one-two punch for the Dodgers. Drysdale's unique signature is one of the more stylish autographs in the hobby, and it rarely varied throughout his playing days or beyond. As a player, Drysdale was diligent about answering mail requests and continued that practice long after his retirement. Collectors will occasionally encounter ghost signatures, but these non-malicious forgeries are not nearly as prevalent as they are with other names on our list.

PSA/DNA Authentication Services Says:

Don Drysdale was one of the most intimidating men to ever set foot on the mound, but his off-the-field personality and demeanor with fans was the polar opposite. A very personable individual, Drysdale was a gracious signer throughout his life, which ended way too soon at the age of 56 in 1993. The hard-throwing righty did live long enough to participate in the hobby boom of the 1980s, which resulted in some volume of Drysdale-signed baseballs and photos. This includes some dual-signed items, along with his former

"*I hated to bat against Drysdale. After he hit you he'd come around, look at the bruise on your arm and say, 'Do you want me to sign it?'*"

– Mickey Mantle

THE MODERN AGE 173

Ken Griffey Jr.

Considered by most to be the greatest home run hitter of the 1990s, George Kenneth Griffey Jr. was the proverbial five-tool player. He could do it all. In a career spanning 22 years, "Junior" hit 630 home runs, had 1,836 RBI, banged out 2,781 hits, made 13 All-Star appearances, won 10 Gold Gloves and 7 Silver Slugger awards. He was the 1992 All-Star MVP and in 1997 he led the league with 125 runs, 56 homers, and 147 RBI, earning the American League MVP award. Ken Griffey Jr. was one heck of a ballplayer, and he has never been linked to performance enhancing drugs, which makes his accomplishments even greater.

Griffey Jr. and his dad, former Major League great Ken Griffey Sr., were the first father and son duo to play together on the same team at the same time. Griffey Jr. came up to play centerfield for the Seattle Mariners in 1989, at 19 years old. He quickly rose to the top of the ranks as a superstar with his dependable bat and standout defensive play. His amazing over-the-shoulder and above-the-fence catches made him a fan favorite. The 39-year-old Griffey Sr. was patrolling the outfield for the Cincinnati Reds at the time. In 1990, Griffey Sr. left the Reds mid-season to join his son in the Mariners outfield, and Junior batted directly behind Senior in the lineup. On August 31, 1990, their first game together, they hit back-to-back singles and on September 14, 1990, they both hit dingers, becoming the first father-son duo to hit back-to-back home runs in a Major League game. The Griffeys played 51 MLB games as teammates before Griffey Sr. wrapped up his great 19-year career at the end of the 1991 season.

In 2000, Griffey Jr. joined his father's old team, the Cincinnati Reds. As a matter of fact, Griffey Sr. was a Reds coach at the time. During the second half of his career, Griffey Jr. worked through injuries to be named the NL Comeback Player of the Year in 2005. After a brief stint with the White Sox, Griffey Jr. returned to the Mariners in 2009 and retired in 2010 at age 40, as one of the few members of the 600 home run club. After retirement, Griffey Jr. accepted a position with the Mariners as a special consultant. He was elected to the Seattle Mariners Hall of Fame and the Cincinnati Reds Hall of Fame, and is ranked in the *Sporting News* Top 100 Greatest Players of All Time. An exclamation point to this illustrious career took place in January 2016 when Ken Griffey Jr. was elected to the Hall of Fame with an historic 99.3% of the vote.

Junior

PSA/DNA Authentication Services Says:

Unlike many of the sluggers who excelled during his era, Griffey was never linked to PEDs, which cast a shadow over so many stars of the 1990s and 2000s. As a result, a renewed respect has emerged for what Griffey accomplished, which ultimately has increased the desirability of his autograph. While Griffey was not known as an overly accommodating signer at the ballpark or in public, he has provided a large number of authentic autographs through various companies over the years, including notable hobby entities such as Upper Deck. The demand for his autograph started early since Griffey performed at a high level almost immediately. Griffey's autograph, which often has a light, flowing appearance, has remained relatively similar since his early days as a player.

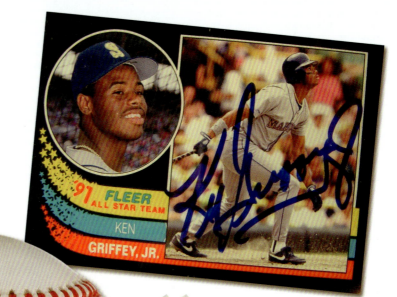

" *As long as I have fun playing, the stats will take care of themselves.*"

– Ken Griffey Jr.

" *He was the best player in baseball. There is nothing he couldn't do on a baseball field. And he did it so gracefully. Wonderful hitter that could hit for average. He could hit for power. He could drive in runs. He could steal a base. He could score from first on a double. Good RBI guy, and then at the same time you put him out there defensively, and he was as good of a center fielder as there was in baseball. Junior was one of the finest young men I've ever had the opportunity to manage.*"

– Lou Pinella, Seattle Mariners manager

Tony Gwynn

After the Ted Williams era, Tony Gwynn carried the torch as baseball's best pure hitter. Like Williams, Gwynn was meticulous about refining his stroke. He studied hitting techniques and reviewed film in order to maintain high standards as a batsman. An outstanding athlete, Gwynn excelled at both baseball and basketball at San Diego State University. He was a two-time All-Star for the Western Athletic Conference in basketball, and a two-time All-American baseball player. He was such a standout that both the MLB and the NBA drafted him in 1981.

Gwynn chose baseball, and thus began his stellar 20-year career with the San Diego Padres. In his first full season, 1984, Gwynn batted a league-high .351, banged out 213 hits, and won the National League batting title. This was just the beginning of a 19-year streak where he hit .300 or better.

Over his outstanding career, the great lefty hitter was a 15-time All-Star, and an eight-time NL Batting Champ. Gwynn won five Gold Gloves and ended his career in 2001 with 3,141 hits and .338 BA. During the strike-shortened 1994 season, he approached the lofty .400 mark with his .394 BA. Gwynn played in both the 1984 and 1998 World Series, posting a .371 average. Defensively, he was excellent, often leading all right fielders in putouts, assists, double plays, and fielding percentage.

Mr. Padre

Along with success, came some controversy. Some teammates felt Gwynn sacrificed the good of the team to beef up his stats. Gwynn believed he put the Padres first, and this was just a personality conflict with a few teammates, most notably Jack Clark. He also battled a weight problem, which was a contributing factor to several injuries, but Gwynn managed to maintain his high standards.

The affable slugger was passionate about the game and passionate about his team. Known as "Mr. Padre," Gwynn was beloved by fans. After retirement, Tony Gwynn spent 12 years as head coach at his alma mater, San Diego State. He also worked as a broadcaster on both television and radio. In 2004, the Padres retired his number 19 jersey, and in 2007 they unveiled Gwynn's statue in Petco Park. Gwynn was diagnosed with salivary gland cancer in 2010, which was attributed to his long-time chewing tobacco use. Anthony Keith Gwynn passed away at the young age of 54 on June 16, 2014. Mr. Padre was elected into the Hall of Fame in 2007 with almost 98% of the vote.

PSA/DNA Authentication Services Says:

Tony Gwynn has long been considered one of the most fan-friendly players who ever donned a Major League uniform. This is especially true when compared to players of his stature, during the same era. You often hear first-hand accounts of Gwynn spending a half-hour to an hour with fans after games, signing everything they had to give the great hitter. While Gwynn did make subtle changes to his autograph over time, the neatness and legibility of his signature was always of excellent quality. Later on, as his career started to wind down, Gwynn did start generating a higher volume of autographs through various notable hobby enterprises. In some cases, authentic autographs were provided direct to the public via his own company, which also offered game-used memorabilia.

> *"I'm a chemistry guy. I believe you've got to play together to have a chance to win."*
>
> – Tony Gwynn

Rickey Henderson

Baseball fans love to argue. Could this player have flourished in that era? Could that player have been successful in this era? When it comes to 10-time All-Star and 2009 first ballot Hall of Famer Rickey Henderson, there is no argument. The all-time leader in runs scored and stolen bases would have been a legend in any baseball epoch. The word that most comes to mind regarding Henderson is fear. His sculpted physique was intimidating. When he stepped to the plate, the all-time leader in leadoff home runs elicited nervous perspiration from pitchers, and if Henderson got on base, deep anxiety ensued as he goaded any hurler into throw after throw to first base. Minutes later, Henderson would be standing on second or third, smiling, and what a smile he had. No one enjoyed the game more than Rickey Henderson. Through 25 years, nine teams, and 3,081 games, Henderson lived to play ball.

> "*If my uniform doesn't get dirty, I haven't done anything in the baseball game.*"
>
> – Rickey Henderson

Born in Chicago in 1958, and raised in Oakland, California, the "Man of Steal" attended Technical High School where he was a multi-sport star. He was drafted by his hometown A's, the first of four stints with the club, in the fourth round of the 1976 draft. Rickey Nelson Henley Henderson debuted in 1979 with the Athletics in a free fall to last place. His flash, dash, and smash style would awaken the dynasty and return it to eventual glory. Henderson stole 100 bases in 1980, breaking Ty Cobb's AL record of 96. His career statistics are confounding, 1,406 steals including a record 130 in 1982, 297 home runs, and 13 seasons with 100-plus runs scored, including an amazing 146 in 1985. In 1990, Henderson was an All-Star, American League MVP, and a Silver Slugger Award winner. That year, he scored 119 runs, hit 28 home runs, and had an OBP of .439. He stole 30-plus bases seven times after the age of 35, including a league-leading 66 in 1998 at age 39. Henderson played in 14 postseason series and hit .284 with 33 steals in 60 games. In 1989, he hit .400 and was the MVP of the ALCS. He then led the A's to the World Series title and would win another ring with Toronto in 1993. Henderson played in Oakland, New York, Toronto, San Diego, Anaheim, Seattle, Boston, and LA, but more than travel, he walked. He drew a free pass to first base more than 2,000 times in his career and, more often than not, he ended up right back where he started.

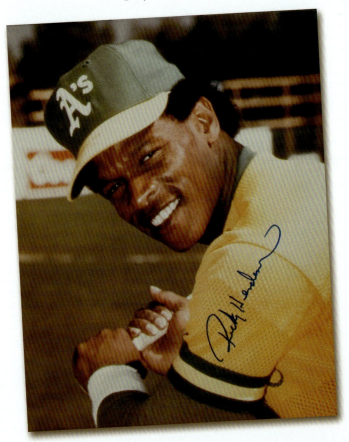

Man of Steal

PSA/DNA Authentication Services Says:

In addition to being widely considered the greatest leadoff hitter of all time, Henderson was one of the real characters of the game. While his signing habits for fans were somewhat inconsistent throughout his career, Henderson did sign a large number of items through various companies during his playing career and beyond. The appearance of his autograph has remained remarkably consistent for over three decades. You will see some variation to his signature during his first few years in Oakland and these examples are often considered the most desirable by advanced collectors. Henderson remains a fixture on the show circuit for those still seeking an in-person signature from baseball's all-time stolen base leader.

> "There was only one Rickey Henderson... he was the greatest leadoff hitter of all time."
> – George Steinbrenner

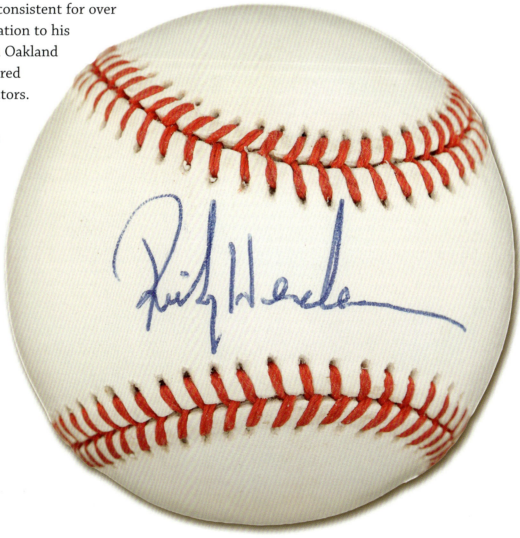

THE MODERN AGE 179

Elston Howard

During the early years of his career, Elston Gene Howard, one of the great catchers in MLB history, could not crack the Yankees starting lineup as catcher. Why? He happened to be backing up Yogi Berra, considered one of the top catchers of all time. After three seasons in the Negro Leagues, the quiet, gentlemanly Howard was drafted by the Yankees in 1950, and promptly sent to the minors. He served Uncle Sam during the Korean War and after a few more Minor League seasons, Howard finally emerged in 1955 as the first African-American to don Yankee pinstripes. After inheriting the catching position from Berra in 1960, Ellie Howard became an elite American League catcher and perennial All-Star. With both his offense and defense, Howard became one of the quiet leaders on some great Yankees teams.

Before his career came to an end, Howard made 12 All-Star appearances, won two Gold Gloves, and enjoyed six World Series wins—four as a player and two more as coach. His crowning achievement came in 1963 when he was voted the American League Most Valuable Player, the first African-American to be so honored.

After 13 years with the Yankees, Howard was traded to the Boston Red Sox midway through the 1967 season, and his leadership behind the dish helped the young Sox pitching staff improve significantly. In what became known as the Impossible Dream, the Sox won the pennant that year, but lost the Series to St. Louis in seven games. Ironically, earlier that season, while still a Yankee, Howard broke up

Ellie

rookie Sox pitcher Billy Rohr's no-hit bid in his MLB debut at Yankee Stadium. Facing the great Whitey Ford, Rohr was in the ninth inning when Carl Yastrzemski made an historic catch, robbing Tom Tresh of extra bases, to preserve the no-hitter. However, Howard stroked a single to break up Rohr's nearly historic moment.

After his playing career ended, Elston Howard rejoined the Yankees as first-base coach, becoming the first African-American to coach in the American League. He held that position from 1969 to 1978, winning World Series titles in 1977 and 1978. Howard remained with the Yankees until his health began to decline. Diagnosed with a rare heart ailment, he was only 51 years old when he died of heart failure in 1980. Howard's jersey number 32 was retired in 1984 and a plaque was dedicated to him in Yankee Stadium. It reads, "A man of great gentleness and dignity. One of the all-time Yankee greats."

PSA/DNA Authentication Services Says:

The first African-American catcher in New York Yankees history, Elston Howard, added to the legacy of All-Star talent behind the plate for the Bronx Bombers. Howard was considered a very obliging signer throughout his playing and coaching career. In addition, his signature is one of the more visually-appealing autographs on our "Top 100" list, which adds to its appeal. Howard's autograph is tougher to find compared to other stars who played during the same era, due to his early passing. Like fellow Yankee catcher Thurman Munson, Howard died right before the hobby explosion of the 1980s.

THE MODERN AGE

Reggie Jackson

On October 18, 1977, Reggie Jackson hit three home runs on three pitches from three different Dodger pitchers (Burt Hooten, Elias Sosa, Charlie Hough) in a World Series clinching game in Yankee Stadium. That night, his star power, burning since the early 1970s, absolutely exploded. Simply put, Jackson is one of the most intriguing, enraging, captivating, and polarizing figures in baseball history. After a stellar run at Arizona State, he was selected by the Kansas City A's with the second pick in the 1966 draft. Jackson debuted for KC in 1967, hitting just .178 in 35 games. In 1968, with the A's now in Oakland, he blossomed into the most talented player on a star-studded team that would win three straight World Series (1972–1974). Jackson's 1969 season was epic: 123 runs, 47 homers, 118 RBI, a .410 OBP, and .608 slugging percentage. In the 1971 All-Star Game in Detroit, Jackson jacked a pitch from Dock Ellis off the transformer high above right field, further burgeoning his legend.

In 1976, Jackson signed a lucrative free agent contract with the Yankees and began one of baseball's greatest soap operas. His gregarious personality grated on manager Billy Martin and teammates Graig Nettles and Thurman Munson. The infamous "straw that stirs the drink" parlayed his media magnetism into a television and film career. In a 1977 game at Fenway Park, Jackson appeared to loaf on a fly ball to right field prompting an enraged Martin to replace him with backup Paul Blair. A now legendary dugout melee ensued with the ever-bellicose Martin having to be restrained. Despite the non-stop vitriol, the Yankees won the World Series again in 1978, restoring the team's domination.

Jackson, who would finish his 21-year career with the Angels and A's, is the all-time leader in one major

182 THE MODERN AGE

Mr. October

statistical category: strikeouts. He fanned 2,597 times, most often with a violent swing that twisted him into the dirt. When he did connect, however, it was majestic. Jackson clubbed 563 career dingers and had 1,702 RBI. He hit 20-plus home runs in 13 straight seasons (1968–1980), leading the AL four times. Between 1969 and 1984, he played in 14 of 16 All-Star Games. Jackson was named World Series MVP in 1973 and 1977, and batted over .400 in three different postseason series. He was elected to the Hall of Fame in 1993. On that short list of players who transcended the game and dominated the psyche of a generation, we had not seen before and shall not see again the charismatic likes of Reginald Martinez Jackson.

PSA/DNA Authentication Services Says:

Reggie Jackson has a reputation for being an extremely confident and proud guy, and you can see that through his signature. While he may not have been consistent about obliging fans in person, his signature has been very consistent over the years. Jackson was also known for using a ghost signer to help answer mail requests, especially as he marched towards 500 career home runs in the 1980s. In addition, a clubhouse attendant would often add Jackson's name to team balls when he wasn't available to sign. This practice was evident during his early years with the A's and extended into his tours with other teams such as the Yankees and Angels. When the hobby blossomed in the 1980s and 1990s, Jackson was one of the first players to provide authentic signed memorabilia to collectors through various companies, which included his own at one point in time.

> "The thing about Reggie is that you know he's going to produce. And if he doesn't, he's going to talk enough to make people think he's going to produce."
>
> – Catfish Hunter

THE MODERN AGE

Harmon Killebrew

One of the great home run hitters of all time, Harmon Clayton Killebrew became the face of the Twins during his 14 seasons in Minnesota. With a compact swing and a lot of muscle, "Killer" Killebrew's home runs were majestic, high, and deep.

A farm boy from Idaho, Killebrew built his strong, muscular physique by hauling 10-gallon cans filled with milk. An All-American Quarterback for Payette High School who excelled in both football and baseball, he was signed right out of high school by the Senators in June of 1954, just days before his 18th birthday. Killebrew made his Major League debut that year, but struggled during his first few seasons. His breakout year was 1959 when, after some seasoning in the minors, he became the Washington Senators regular third baseman, smacked 42 home runs, and made the All-Star Team.

In 1961, the Senators moved to Minnesota and changed their name to the Twins. The Minnesota climate evidently agreed with Killebrew as that year he slammed 46 home runs with 122 runs batted in. For the next 10 years he was a veritable home run machine. Of his eight seasons of 40 home runs or better, seven were with Minnesota. Over his 22-year MLB career, Killebrew was a 13-time All-Star, led the American League in home runs on six different occasions, and was named the AL Most Valuable Player in 1969. His career total of 573 dingers stood as an American League record for right-handed batters until Alex Rodriguez bested it in 2009.

Killebrew was the driving force for the Twins right up to the

Killer

early 1970s. The Twins won the AL pennant in 1965 and were AL West Champs in 1969 and 1970. His last big season was 1971, when he led the league in RBI. His numbers started to decline and in 1974 the Twins released Killebrew, retiring his number 3 jersey. He finished up with one last season in Kansas City with the Royals in 1975, after which he was a television broadcaster for the Twins and had business interests in the automotive and insurance industries. One of the most well-respected men in baseball, Killebrew was quiet and unassuming, the polar opposite of his "Killer" nickname. He was elected to the Hall of Fame in 1984. Killebrew was diagnosed with esophageal cancer in 2010 and passed away in 2011, at age 74.

> *Killebrew can knock the ball out of any park, including Yellowstone"*
>
> – Paul Richards, Orioles manager

PSA/DNA Authentication Services Says:

Once the hobby became a full-fledged industry in the 1980s, Killebrew became a fixture at conventions across the country, gaining the reputation for being one of the friendliest stars a collector could hope to encounter. In addition to his genial demeanor, he took obvious pride in his autograph. Killebrew had one of the most consistently beautiful autographs you will ever see, forming every letter of his name in flowing form. While often overshadowed by the likes of Mickey Mantle and Ted Williams, Killebrew's autograph is a necessary component for everyone looking to complete the esteemed 500 Home Run Club. As a result of his regular attendance at shows and private signings, Killebrew's autograph is one of the more common on our "Top 100" list, but it is also one of the best looking.

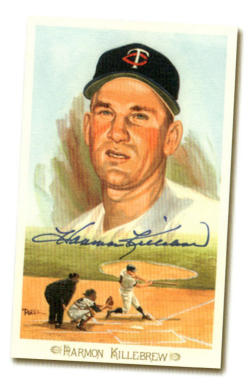

> *There was nothing subtle about the Idaho strongboy and it was always his intention to mash a pitched ball as hard and as far as he could."*
>
> – Donald Honig, author, *The Power Hitters*

THE MODERN AGE 185

Willie Mays

With a .302 lifetime batting average, 3,283 hits, 660 home runs, 24 All-Star appearances, 12 Gold Gloves, two All-Star MVP awards, and two NL MVPs, it is almost impossible to find an equal to the "Say Hey Kid." The phrase "five-tool player" is sometimes used a bit too liberally. However, Willie Howard Mays Jr. really was the prototypical five-tool player. The guy could hit for both power and average, run like a gazelle, had a cannon for an arm, and was an amazing fielder.

Coming out of the Negro Leagues to the Giants in 1951, Mays initially had trouble hitting in the majors. After an inauspicious debut going 1–26, manager Leo Durocher told him to pull the legs of his pants up higher to create a smaller strike zone. That piece of advice worked so well that Mays ended up with the Rookie of the Year Award. Mays was drafted by the U.S. Army and ended up playing stateside baseball for Uncle Sam most of 1952 and 1953. When the Giants young center fielder returned in 1954 he exploded as a player, batting .345 with 41 home runs, earning the National League MVP title. From that point on, Mays had some monstrous seasons. After the Giants relocated to San Francisco, he continued to dominate the National League. Along the way, the charismatic, likeable Mays gained the reputation of being very accessible to fans. He was even known to play stickball in the streets with kids of all ages.

In the final stages of his career, the Giants sent Mays to the New York Mets in May of 1972. This was a win-win trade for both organizations as the Giants were losing money, and the Mets needed a shot in the arm at the gate. Still beloved in New York,

Say Hey Kid

> "If he could cook, I'd marry him."
>
> – Leo Durocher

Mays helped attendance, but may have hung on a little too long. Mays had played in three World Series with the Giants (1951, 1954, 1962) and played in his fourth and final World Series in 1973 as a Met, retiring at the end of the Series at 42 years old.

In addition to working in the entertainment field, Mays continued to work in various capacities for the Mets and the Giants, and has remained an ambassador for the game.

He was elected to the Hall of Fame in 1979 with 95% of the vote. The 5% that did not vote for him on that first ballot probably slept through his career.

PSA/DNA Authentication Services Says:

Willie Mays is one of the legends who signed his fair share of autographs during the 1980s hobby explosion, but vintage examples of his signature remain much tougher to locate and are very desirable. Early examples of Mays' signature are neater and smaller in appearance than those penned later on during public and private events. When it comes to vintage, team-signed baseballs, Mays often added his name, but many team balls feature a clubhouse Mays autograph. Early in his career, Mays appeared to be more responsive to mail requests, but by the early 1970s he often used a ghost signer to handle them. Much like contemporary star Hank Aaron, Mays virtually disappeared from the show circuit during the 2000s.

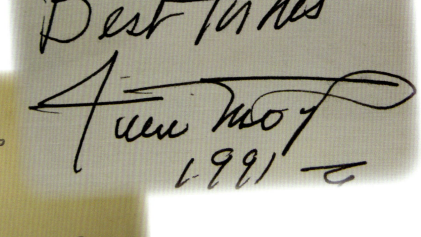

Thurman Munson

" *He has just the right cockiness, he's a born leader.*"

– Billy Martin, Yankees manager

On August 2, 1979 a Cessna Citation I/SP jet crashed at the Akron-Canton Regional Airport. The official cause of the crash was attributed to pilot error. Evidently, the approach to the landing strip was too low, causing the plane to undershoot the runway, clip a tree, and crash. Ironically, the man behind the controls of that Cessna was a guy who could not tolerate error of any kind when it came to playing baseball. Thurman Lee Munson, the heart and soul of the New York Yankees in the 1970s, died that day, having crashed his own plane because of pilot error.

The three-sport star athlete for Lehman High School in Canton, Ohio, and Kent State University baseball star was drafted by the Yankees in 1968. Munson quickly proved his worth both offensively and defensively, batting .302 and winning the 1970 Rookie of the Year Award. The seven-time All-Star, three-time Gold Glove winner, and 1976 American League Most Valuable Player was a no-nonsense, hard-nosed competitor who wore his emotions on his sleeve. Munson's confrontations with archrival Boston catcher, Carlton Fisk, made for great conversation at local taverns as they both played the game with a "take no prisoners" mentality. Named team captain at the start of the 1976 season, the first captain since Lou Gehrig, Munson led his team to three consecutive Fall Classics and the World Series Championships in 1977 and 1978. Throughout the 1970s, Munson was considered one of the best catchers in the game. A consistent hitter, he always hovered around the .300 mark and averaged 140 hits per season. He batted a career .292, with

Tugboat

a postseason average of .357. An excellent catcher defensively, Munson led the league in various categories over his 11-year career.

It all came to an end on that day in 1979 when he died in that fiery crash. After playing in the August 1 Yankees' win over the White Sox in Chicago, Munson flew home to Ohio to see his wife and children. The homesick Munson had purchased the plane in July so he could spend more time with his family on off-days during the season. The tragic crash took place while he was practicing landings in his new plane. The day after the tragedy, in an emotional pre-game tribute with over 51,000 in attendance, Munson's Yankee teammates took their positions, but left the catcher's box empty in honor of their 32-year-old team captain.

PSA/DNA Authentication Services Says:

Obtaining a Thurman Munson autograph is a tough proposition. Getting him to sign during his playing days was difficult because he was an extremely focused athlete at the ballpark. As his career heated up and he received more requests, Munson handed off some of them to clubhouse attendants. As a result, there are many forgeries, both malicious and non-malicious, on single-signed baseballs as well as trading cards. One of the most desirable Munson signed cards is his 1979 Topps issue. His tragic death in 1979 cut short his great career. Since he passed away before the 1980s hobby boom, authentic Munson autographs were never produced from typical private and public signings.

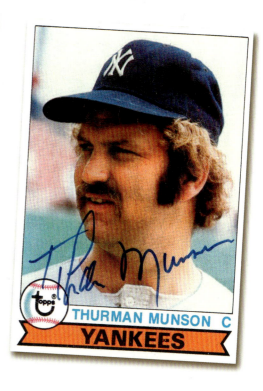

THE MODERN AGE

Sadaharu Oh

The Japanese consider the slugging tandem of Sadaharu Oh and Shigeo Nagashima, nicknamed the "O-N Cannon," as the Ruth and Gehrig of Asia. Both hitters combined for 1,312 home runs over their brilliant careers. Oh alone hit an amazing 868 career homers in his native Japan. There is much discussion of the level of play in Japan vs. the level played in the U.S. during the 1960s and 1970s. No matter, Oh became an iconic superstar in Japan.

Born in Tokyo in 1940, Sadaharu Oh was crazy about baseball as a child, and went against his father's wishes to play the game professionally. He played his entire 22-year career for the Yomiuri Giants in the Japan Central League. The 19-year-old rookie first baseman was a disappointment in 1959, batting just .161 in 94 games, and his 72 strikeouts earned him the mocking nickname of the "Strikeout King." Oh finally broke out in 1962, his fourth season, after diligently working to develop his new "flamingo" stance at the plate, which corrected a hitch in his swing. That year he blasted 38 home runs and kept going to lead the league in home runs 15 times. His best season was in 1973 when he batted .355 with 51 home runs. The nine-time Central League Most Valuable Player led his team to 11 championships and ended his playing career in 1980 with a .301 career batting average, 2,786 career hits, and those incredible 868 dingers. The acknowledged

SADAHARU OH

The Japanese Babe Ruth

> "I had strong legs that would have made me a good sumo wrestler and I used that to my advantage, but my home runs were achieved by technique."
> – Sadaharu Oh

home run king in Japan, Oh struck up a friendship with U.S. home run king Hank Aaron when they took part in a Home Run Derby in Tokyo's Korakuen Stadium in 1974. Aaron had recently bested Babe Ruth's record, but the contest was close. Oh and Aaron went head-to-head with Aaron winning 10–9.

After retirement, Oh became assistant manager of his Giants team until he was named manager in 1984, a position he held until 1988. He later managed the Fukuoka Daiei Hawks of the Japan Pacific League from 1995 to his retirement in 2008 at age 68. He led the team to Pacific League pennants in 1999, 2000 and 2003, and managed Japan's national team to the inaugural World Baseball Classic title in 2006. In his 19 years and 2,508 games as manager, Oh won 1,315 games with a .540 winning percentage. He was elected to the Japanese Baseball Hall of Fame in 1994.

PSA/DNA Authentication Services Says:

While he played his entire career in Japan, Oh has a global appeal as his stature has grown with time. More Japanese players have entered MLB over the past few decades, providing a reminder of Oh's legacy. As a result of that crossover appeal, you will find Oh autographs signed in both Japanese and English. In some cases, Oh will provide both versions on the same item if requested. In recent years, more forgeries have been spotted in the marketplace as he gains popularity. One of his more popular autographed items features Oh and Hank Aaron, both home run hitting icons from their respective leagues. While Oh has been an active signer for years, finding vintage-signed items has been more challenging for the collector.

Albert Pujols

When Stan Musial retired after a 22-year career with the St. Louis Cardinals, it signaled the end of an on-field love affair between a city and a ballplayer. While the Cardinals remained a factor in the National League, none of their subsequent players gripped the city quite like Stan the Man. In 2001, a 21-year old kid from the Dominican Republic did just that. Jose Alberto Pujols, Prince Albert, assumed Musial's throne and set the rabid Cardinal fan base into an 11-year frenzy. His Rookie of the Year numbers in 2001 were staggering: 194 hits, 47 doubles, 37 homers, 130 RBI, and a .329 batting average. The kid became an All-Star and finished fourth in MVP voting. That season set the tone for a career that rivals any of baseball's all-time greats. In his first 15 seasons, Pujols had already surpassed the 500 home run and 1,600 RBI milestones. He batted .312 and won three National League MVP Awards, finishing in the top five of MVP voting in seven other seasons from 2001 to 2011. Pujols was selected to play in eight straight All-Star games from 2003 to 2010. In each of those seasons, he registered an OBP of over .400 while leading the league in runs five times and slugging three times. Beyond mere stats, Pujols became royalty in St. Louis, a city that worships its baseball gods. In his 11 years in the Gateway City, the Cards qualified for the postseason seven times. Pujols hit well over .300 in the playoffs and was named MVP of the 2004 NLCS. In both 2006 and 2011, Pujols led the Cardinals to the World Series title cementing the franchise as second only to the Yankees in MLB championship lore. Following the 2011 season, the unthinkable became a stark reality. Prince Albert of St. Louis took his first baseman's mitt and sure-fire Hall of Fame resume and signed a free agent contract with the Los Angeles Angels of Anaheim. He immediately provided leadership to the Halos, not to mention 50 doubles, 30 homers, and 105 RBI. The Angels made it to the playoffs in 2014 and Pujols became a two-league All-Star in 2015. When it is all said and done, Albert Pujols will breathe that rarified air of baseball's best, a true legend among the game's immortals.

> "*He is the whole package as far as a player. He commits to defense just like he does offense. He has a natural talent.*"
> – Tony LaRussa, St. Louis Cardinals manager

Prince Albert

PSA/DNA Authentication Services Says:

Since becoming one of the most desirable autographs of the post-2000 era, Pujols' signature is also one of the most heavily-forged of the current period. The slugger has not been a big part of the public show circuit, preferring to participate in private signings instead. Pujols has provided a reasonable quantity of authentic autographs to the hobby via these private events. Like many professional athletes, as Pujols' status grew in the game, his autographs became more difficult to obtain in person. Early in his career, Pujols signed his name "Jose. A. Pujols," but that evolved into "A. Pujols" as time went on. On occasion, Pujols will add a cross sign and his uniform number to signed items.

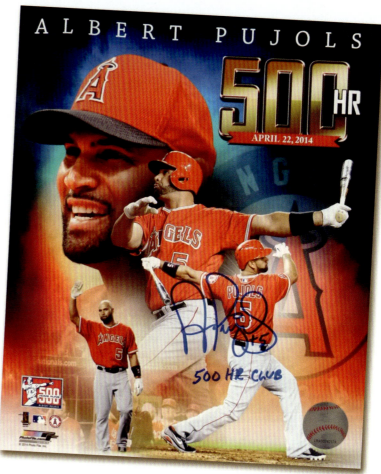

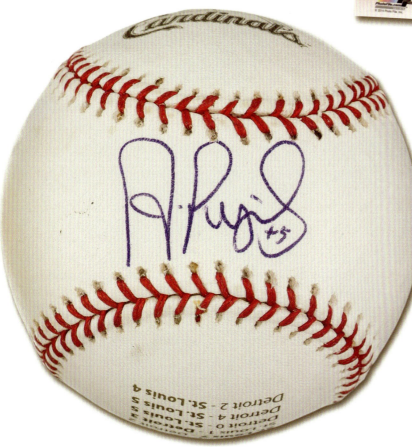

"*You don't have to scout a guy like Albert. He draws attention to himself. He has such inner confidence, without being cocky.*"

– Jim Leyland, former Major League manager

THE MODERN AGE 193

Cal Ripken Jr.

For 21 seasons, Cal Ripken Jr. represented everything that is good about baseball. His amazing 2,632 consecutive games streak surpassed the late Lou Gehrig's record of 2,130 on September 6, 1995, and is credited for restoring the fans' faith and interest in the game following the bitter 1994–1995 players' strike. Gehrig and Ripken share not only an unfathomable durability, but their credo of honesty, family, and integrity made us feel good about being baseball fans.

Born into Baltimore baseball royalty in 1960, Ripken, the son of Orioles coach and manager Cal Sr., was selected by the Orioles in the second round of the 1978 draft. With the Rochester Red Wings on April 18, 1981, Ripken played every inning in the longest game in professional baseball history. The Red Wings and Pawtucket Red Sox played to a 2–2 tie in 32 innings before the game was halted in the wee hours of the morning. Pawtucket won the continued game in 33 innings on June 23. Ripken debuted August 10, 1981, to hit just .128 in 23 games, but on May 30, 1982, the shortstop began his incredible streak that would run until September 20, 1998. He won the Rookie of the Year award in 1982 with 28 homers and 93 RBI. Ripken had 431 career dingers, drove in nearly 1,700 runs, and hit .300 or better five times. He led the American League in games played nine times and made the All-Star Team every year between 1983 and 2001. In that 1983 season, Ripken led the Orioles to a world championship and was named league MVP with his 211 hits, 47 doubles, 27 home runs, 102 RBI, and .318 batting average. He garnered another MVP award in 1991, along with the first of two Gold Gloves. At 6-foot, 4-inches, and 200 pounds, Ripken was not the prototypical shortstop, but what he lacked in quickness, he made up for with intelligence. The consummate team player, Ripken graciously moved to third base and DH later in his career, remaining productive until retiring in 2001. A lifetime Oriole, Ripken remains a baseball ambassador with his youth

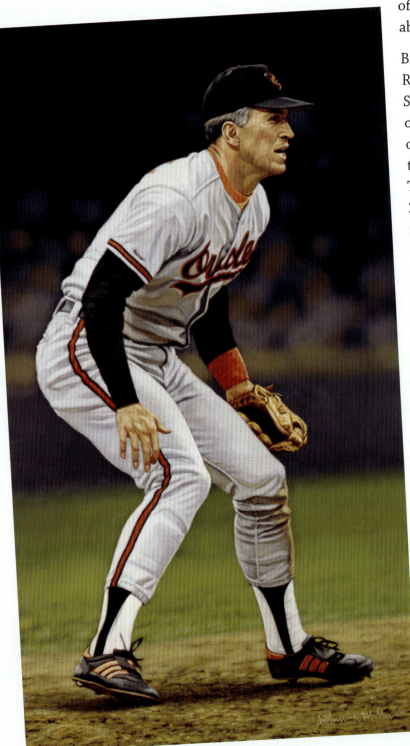

Iron Man

> *"He's been loyal to his team, his fans, the community and professional sports every phase of his career. His determination and talent has been great for baseball and America."*
>
> – President Bill Clinton

baseball league and many charitable endeavors. Calvin Edwin Ripken Jr. was inducted into the Hall of Fame in 2007 and will be remembered as the man with the streak of iron and a heart of gold.

PSA/DNA Authentication Services Says:

One of the most gracious, active signers of the post-1980s era in baseball, Ripken would sign for hours at a time at the ballpark during his playing career. As his popularity grew, Ripken remained accessible to the fans and would often interact with them while signing. The Hall of Famer was very consistent with the care and precision of his autograph, taking obvious pride in his penmanship. Today, Ripken has become a fixture on the show circuit, giving fans more opportunities to obtain genuine, in-person autographs. One of the areas that Ripken has been very particular about is the signing of his game-used equipment. It is well known within the hobby that Ripken will not add inscriptions such as "gamer" or "game used" to equipment unless those items originated from his personal collection.

CAL RIPKEN JR.

> *"Stubbornness is usually considered a negative, but I think that trait has been a positive for me."*
>
> – Cal Ripken

THE MODERN AGE 195

Mariano Rivera

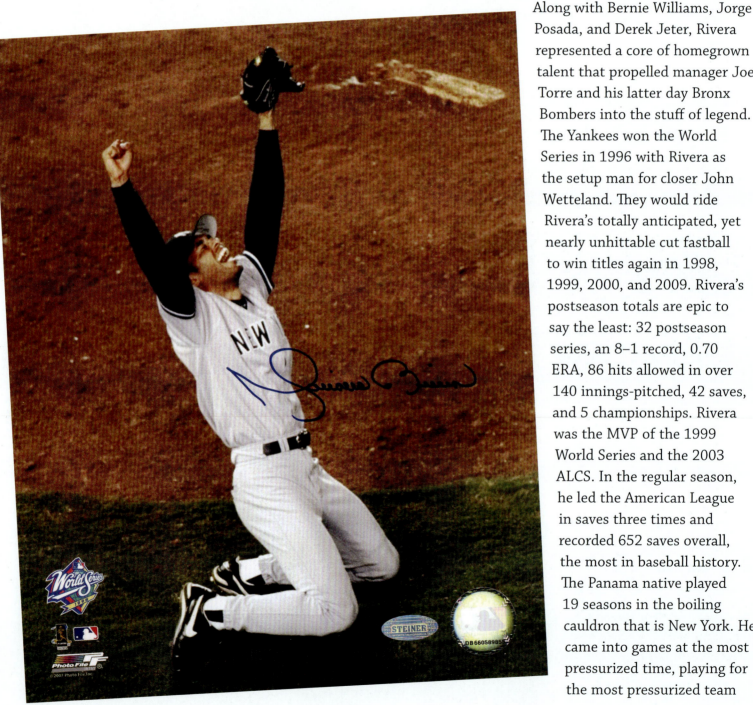

The moniker "best ever" in baseball is subject to opinion and perspective. There may be just one exception. Mariano Rivera is the best closer in the history of baseball. Trevor Hoffman, Dennis Eckersley, Lee Smith, and several others merit mention, but Rivera tops them in almost every category, and his postseason numbers obliterate any argument. Granted, Rivera did have the good fortune to join the Yankees in 1995, just as the New York dynasty of the late 20th and early 21st century was beginning. Nonetheless, he was one of the major reasons that the dynasty existed at all.

Along with Bernie Williams, Jorge Posada, and Derek Jeter, Rivera represented a core of homegrown talent that propelled manager Joe Torre and his latter day Bronx Bombers into the stuff of legend. The Yankees won the World Series in 1996 with Rivera as the setup man for closer John Wetteland. They would ride Rivera's totally anticipated, yet nearly unhittable cut fastball to win titles again in 1998, 1999, 2000, and 2009. Rivera's postseason totals are epic to say the least: 32 postseason series, an 8–1 record, 0.70 ERA, 86 hits allowed in over 140 innings-pitched, 42 saves, and 5 championships. Rivera was the MVP of the 1999 World Series and the 2003 ALCS. In the regular season, he led the American League in saves three times and recorded 652 saves overall, the most in baseball history. The Panama native played 19 seasons in the boiling cauldron that is New York. He came into games at the most pressurized time, playing for the most pressurized team

Sandman

> "When Rivera takes the mound, the other team is sitting in the dugout thinking, 'We've got no chance. It's over.'"
>
> – Rich Gossage, Hall of Fame closer

in the most pressurized city. He had a smile that put teammates at ease and a cutter that put opponents on waivers. In 11 different seasons, he registered an ERA under 2.00. Choosing Rivera's best season is nearly impossible. Was it 2004 when he had 53 saves and a 1.94 ERA, 2001 with 50 saves, or 2005 with a 1.38 ERA and 43 saves? There are other choices, to be sure. The 13-time All-Star came back from a devastating injury to play one last season in 2013. At age 43, he posted a 6–2 record with an ERA of 2.11 and 44 saves. The sure-fire Hall of Famer holds a hallowed spot in Yankee history and inspired respect from foes and teammates alike.

an apparent measure of care into every letter. Like many players, Rivera's autograph evolved with time and experience. Becoming the star closer for the most popular sports franchise on the planet thrust Rivera into the spotlight, but he was as accommodating to autograph seekers as they come. Like teammate Derek Jeter, Rivera also signed items for hobby entity Steiner Sports, which produced various collectibles over the years.

PSA/DNA Authentication Services Says:

During an era when many players have developed very rushed, abbreviated, or illegible autographs, Rivera has been a standout and an exception to the rule. Possessing one of the most visually-appealing autographs of the past 30 years, Rivera's signature reflects his sensitive nature, placing

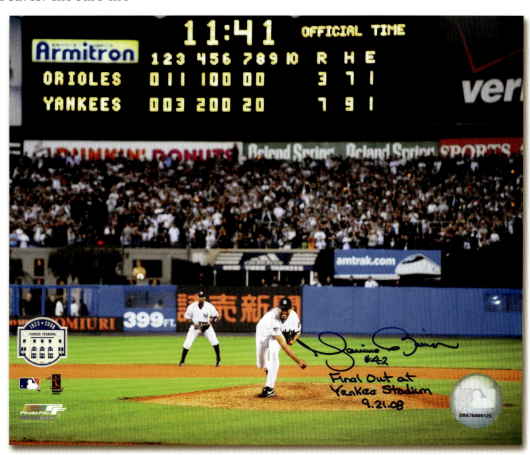

Frank Robinson

One of the most feared sluggers in the history of the game, Frank Robinson cut his sports teeth at Oakland's McClymonds High School and debuted with the Reds in 1956. He posted one of the greatest rookie seasons ever with 38 home runs, 83 RBI, and a .290 batting average. For the man known as "The Judge," the verdict was in early. Robinson led the National League in runs scored, made his first of 12 All-Star Teams, and won Rookie of the Year honors. In 10 seasons with Cincy, Robinson clouted 324 home runs and drove in over 1,000 runs while batting .303. He was league MVP in 1961 and was a run-scoring, doubles, OBP, and slugging percentage machine. After a 1965 season in which Robinson hit 33 home runs and drove in 113 runs, the Reds orchestrated one of the most ill-advised trades in history, shipping Robinson to the Orioles. A man of intense pride, Robinson responded with the best season of his 21-year playing career. His Triple Crown-winning 1966 numbers are staggering: 49 homers, 122 RBI, a .316 batting average, 122 runs, .410 OBP, and a .637 slugging percentage. Robinson won his second MVP award, the first player to win it in both leagues, and lifted Baltimore to the world championship while winning World Series MVP honors. In his six seasons in Baltimore, the Orioles took the pennant four times. In 1970, Robinson led the Orioles to another World Series win with his 25 home runs and a .306 batting average that season. Following a 1971 season in which he hit 28 dingers and knocked in 99 runs, Robinson was once again traded, this time

The Judge

to the Dodgers. After one season in LA, he reinvented himself yet again with the California Angels, swatting 30 homers in 1973 and 22 more in 1974 with the Angels and Indians at age 38. Frank Robinson hit 586 career home runs in a record 32 different MLB parks and once hit grand slams in successive innings. While playing for Cleveland, Robinson became the first African-American manager in the major leagues in 1975. In his sixteen years as a MLB manager he took the helm in Cleveland, San Francisco, Baltimore, Montreal, and Washington. The Judge was inducted into the Baseball Hall of Fame in 1982. Whether it was the bat against the baseball or the social advancement of the sport he loved, the name Frank Robinson is synonymous with the word impact.

PSA/DNA Authentication Services Says:

Robinson's autograph has remained remarkably consistent throughout his life. With the exception of subtle changes, the core structure of Robinson's bold and powerful-looking signature has stayed the same, which is very different from other superstars of the era such as Mickey Mantle and Willie Mays. While an active player and manager, clubhouse attendants would fill in his name on team-signed items on occasion and secretaries would answer fan mail from time to time. Over the past few decades, Robinson has participated in public and private signings, which has helped provide a healthy number of authentic autographs to the hobby.

" *Going over the hitters it was decided that we should pitch Frank Robinson underground.*"

– Jim Bouton

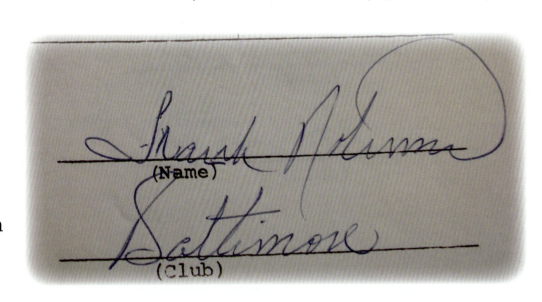

Pete Rose

In 1989, Pete Rose was banned from baseball for life by Commissioner Bart Giamatti after a comprehensive investigation determined Rose bet on baseball games, including his own, as manager of the Cincinnati Reds. In 2015, with baseball Commissioner Rob Manfred considering Rose's appeal of the decision, reports surfaced that Rose had also bet on the Reds and other teams as a player. This is the sad truth about Peter Edward Rose. Still beloved by fans, he essentially wrecked an exemplary career in which he was a 17-time All-Star as outfielder, third baseman, and first baseman, and the all-time leader in games, plate appearances, at-bats, and hits with 4,256. Rose's devil-may-care style endeared him to baseball followers. Even when he viciously bulldozed Indians catcher Ray Fosse for the game-winning run in the 1970 All-Star Game, Rose was revered as a man who played each game as if it were his last.

In 1973, Rose won the NL MVP award with a .338 batting average and 230 hits. He was the piston that motored Cincinnati's Big Red Machine to four pennants and back-to-back World Series titles in 1975 and 1976. In that epic 1975 classic vs. Boston, Rose hit .370 and took home MVP honors. Rose left the Queen City in 1979 via free agency and added another World Series crown with the Phillies in 1980. Overall, he batted .321 in 14 postseason series. Rose scratched, clawed, kicked, and fought his way to ten 200-hit seasons. He led the league in hits seven times, doubles five times, runs four times, batting average three times, and won two Gold Gloves. The kid from Cincy broke in with the Reds in 1963 and won Rookie of

Charlie Hustle

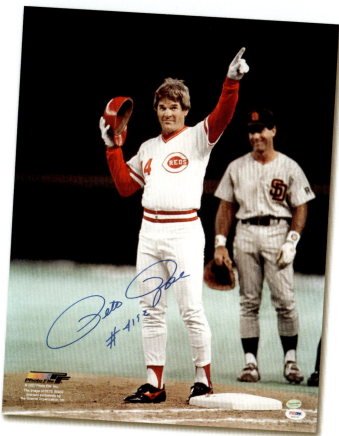

the Year honors. That preseason, he was sarcastically nicknamed "Charlie Hustle" by Yankees great Whitey Ford after sprinting to first base on a walk, a practice Rose continued throughout his 24-season career. In 1984, after a brief stint with the Expos, Rose returned to the Reds as player-manager and broke Ty Cobb's all-time hits mark in 1985. He played his last game in 1986 but the 45-year-old Rose remained the team's manager until his banning in 1989, winning 412 games in six seasons. In the end, one of the great winners in baseball history made one bet too many and, in doing so, lost his name, reputation, and rightful place amongst the game's immortals.

> *Does Pete hustle? Before the All-Star Game he came into the clubhouse and took off his shoes and they ran another mile without him."*
>
> – Hank Aaron

PSA/DNA Authentication Services Says:

Quite simply, Rose is the most prolific signer in the history of baseball. More than the great Babe Ruth and more than the incredibly active Bob Feller during the boom of the hobby, Rose has signed more autographs than anyone. Beyond the countless public appearances at shows and private signings with dealers, Rose has become a fixture in Las Vegas inside The Forum Shops at Caesars Palace. Early in his career, Rose had a simplistic-looking autograph, but his autograph slowly evolved into the distinctive signature collectors are accustomed to seeing today. From the 1970s onward, while the sizing of his letters has fluctuated, Rose maintained this often-seen signature style. During the height of the "Big Red Machine," Rose did use a clubhouse attendant to help meet demand. While he has experienced his share of controversy, Rose remains one of the most accommodating signers you could ever encounter, often willing to inscribe virtually anything requested by the customer.

Nolan Ryan

As a pitcher, Nolan Ryan's modus operandi was not hard to figure. He threw the baseball hard and fast. Still, Ryan himself stands as an enigma. When the topic shifts to the greatest pitcher of all-time, Ryan's name seldom comes up first. Perhaps this stems from the fact that Ryan played for predominantly unremarkable teams throughout his 27-year career with the Mets, Angels, Astros, and Rangers. He won 324 games, but also lost 292. In addition, Ryan won more than 20 games just twice (1973, 1974). He was a sub-.500 pitcher in nine seasons, led his league in walks eight times, and is the game's all-time leader in walks with 2,795. There are many reasons why Ryan does not get his all-time due, but there are even more reasons why he should.

For more than a quarter-century, he put up staggering statistics. The Ryan Express is baseball's all-time leader in strikeouts, logging an amazing 5,714 Ks through the age of 46. Despite his nearly 300 losses, Ryan had a career ERA of 3.19, and an ERA under 3.00 eight times. The eight-time All-Star led his league in strikeouts a whopping 11 times, including 1990 when he was 43 years old. Six times, he topped the 300 strikeout milestone in a season, perhaps the most impressive in 1989 when he fanned 301 batters, won 16 games, and had an ERA of 3.20 for the fourth place Rangers. Ryan made his final All-Star Team that year at the age of 42. His numbers show consistent domination over the long haul. A physical fitness fanatic, Ryan could blow baseballs by big league batters at an age when most pitchers are long retired. Among all of Ryan's stats, the number 7 stands alone. Ryan tossed a record 7 no-hitters in his career, the final one at age 44 in 1991. While no baseball record is safe, Ryan's magnificent 7 is almost assured to stand the test of time. After retiring in 1993, Ryan owned Minor League teams and was president of the Texas Rangers. Born in Refugio, Texas in 1947, Lynn Nolan Ryan was inducted into the Baseball Hall of Fame in 1999. The years between went by really, really fast. Just ask any batter who faced him.

The Ryan Express

> "*You don't face Ryan without your rest. He's the only guy I go against that makes me go to bed before midnight.*"
>
> – Reggie Jackson

PSA/DNA Authentication Services Says:

As fan-friendly as they come, Nolan Ryan has been one of the all-time most obliging signers. Known to sign for long periods before and after games as a player, Ryan was also great about responding to mail requests and remained available to fans even when his popularity increased. During the early part of his career, Ryan's signature appeared more rushed, but as he became more comfortable, the flamethrower's signature became more structured and consistent. At the height of his player popularity with the Texas Rangers, Ryan sent out autopen or pre-printed facsimile signatures to cope with the overwhelming demand. Since 1990, he has provided genuine autographs direct to the public through The Nolan Ryan Foundation, where fans can request personalized signatures in exchange for a donation.

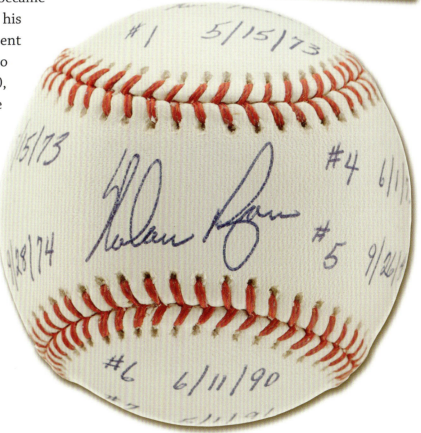

THE MODERN AGE 203

Mike Schmidt

> "If you could equate the amount of time and effort put in mentally and physically into succeeding on the baseball field and measured it by the dirt on your uniform, mine would have been black."
>
> – Mike Schmidt

With all due respect to George Brett, Home Run Baker, Brooks Robinson, Eddie Mathews, Wade Boggs and the rest, Mike Schmidt is considered by most to be the greatest third baseman of all time. He was a 12-time All-Star, won 10 Gold Gloves, six Silver Slugger awards, and was a three-time National League MVP. Schmidt hit for power, leading the National League in home runs eight times, and finished his 18-year career in the vaulted 500 club with 548 dingers.

With the Philadelphia Phillies for his entire career, the Ohio University graduate struggled a bit in 1973, his first full season, but he showed good power potential, whacking 18 home runs. In 1974, it all came together for Schmidt when he batted .282 with a league-leading 36 home runs and made his first NL All-Star Team.

Schmidt won his first Gold Glove in 1976, firmly establishing himself as the best third baseman in the National League. The Dayton, Ohio, native led the Phillies to the World Series Championship in 1980 and was voted Most Valuable Player of that Fall Classic. Schmidt continued his assault on NL pitchers until a torn rotator cuff caused him to miss the last part of the 1988 season. Because he was unable to play at his former level of excellence when he returned in 1989, Schmidt decided to call it a career in May, retiring at age 39 with a .267 BA and 1,595 RBI. He retired holding records for the most RBI and most home runs as third baseman, and most home runs in the 1980s.

Voted the all-time greatest Phillies player by fans in 1983, Schmidt was also named the Player of the 1980s Decade by the *Sporting News*. In retirement, he dabbled in coaching and broadcasting for the Phillies, and authored several books about baseball. As a philanthropist, Schmidt has raised awareness and significant funding for the Cystic Fibrosis Foundation with his annual Winner Circle Invitational Fishing Tournament. Michael Jack Schmidt was elected to the Hall of Fame in 1995 on the first ballot with 96.52% of the vote which, at the time, was the fourth-highest voting percentage in HOF voting history. The greatest

Schmitty

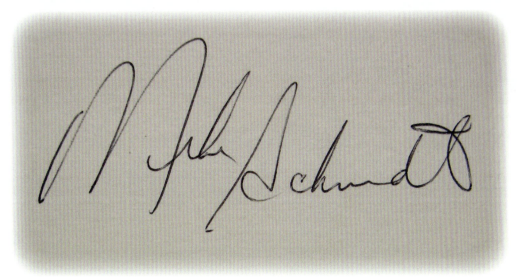

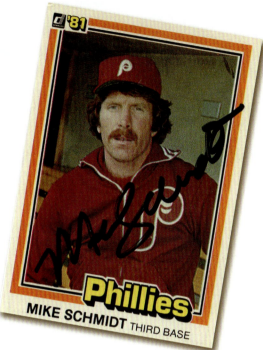

third baseman of all time? In the opinion of most, there is absolutely no argument. Mike Schmidt gets the nod at the hot corner on the team that includes Ruth, Cobb, and the rest of the truly great players.

PSA/DNA Authentication Services Says:

Compared to some of his contemporaries, Schmidt was considered a relatively tough autograph to obtain throughout his career. When he did sign, Schmidt's early autograph style had a flowing appearance where you could discern every letter of his name. Over time, Schmidt's autograph became more condensed in nature, but it has always been very distinctive. While some players have been extremely active in the hobby during their post-playing careers, Schmidt has remained an exception. The great third baseman has made appearances and signed autographs in different settings, but has not been nearly as active as several superstars of his generation like Johnny Bench or Reggie Jackson. In recent years, Schmidt's health has contributed to the decline in his public appearances, but his show activity has never been consistent.

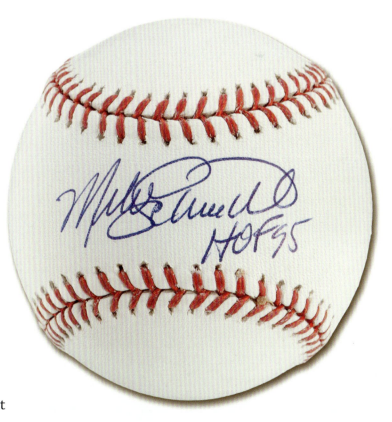

THE MODERN AGE

Ichiro Suzuki

> "When Ichiro steps into the batter's box, no one – the pitcher, the shortstop, the fans, even his teammates – has any idea what he is planning. . . . He may be the Madonna of baseball, reinventing himself periodically to keep people guessing."
>
> – *Baseball Digest*, November 2002

After nine seasons in the Japan Pacific League, racking up seven consecutive batting titles, seven Gold Gloves, and three MVP titles, the phenomenon known as Ichiro Suzuki brought his amazing talent and work ethic to the United States. As a 27-year-old rookie with the Seattle Mariners in 2001, Suzuki led the league with 242 hits, 56 stolen bases, and a .350 batting average, earning both the Rookie of the Year and American League Most Valuable Player awards. This began an incredible streak of 10 consecutive 200-hit seasons, 10 consecutive Gold Gloves, and 10 consecutive All-Star Game appearances, effectively putting an end to any debate about the level of talent in the Japan Pacific League vs. MLB.

By the end of the 2015 season, Suzuki had 2,935 hits to go along with his .314 batting average accumulated over 15 MLB seasons. These statistics do not include his achievements over his nine seasons in Japan. Had he played his entire career in the United States, it is quite possible that Suzuki would now be the all-time leader in hits in MLB history. Nicknamed "Wizard" and known simply as Ichiro, he broke the legendary George Sisler's record, set in 1920, for most hits in a single season when he reached 262 hits in 2004. The two-time AL batting champ slammed the first inside-the-park home run in All-Star Game history in 2007, and was named the All-Star MVP that year.

After 12 seasons with the Mariners, Suzuki was traded to the Yankees in 2012 and moved on to the Miami Marlins outfield in 2015 at 41 years old. A living baseball legend in his own rite, Ichiro Suzuki has honored the players of the past by visiting the graves of some of the greats to pay his respects. He is known for the meticulous, almost reverent care he gives to his bats, keeping them in a special humidor case to keep moisture out of the wood. The list of Suzuki's achievements goes on and on: most consecutive stolen bases not caught stealing (45), most seasons with 200 or more hits (10), most singles in a season (225), most consecutive seasons leading the league in singles (10). Players like this are few and far between. Ichiro Suzuki will most likely be a first ballot candidate for the Hall of Fame. As fans, we have been blessed to see this gift from Japan perform over the years.

Wizard

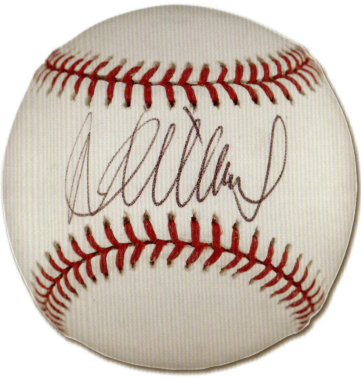

PSA/DNA Authentication Services Says:

While Sadaharu Oh may be the most legendary Japanese baseball player in the country's history, it is hard to imagine any player being more popular today than Ichiro Suzuki. With an established fan base in both the United States and Japan, Ichiro has strong crossover marketability and has provided a solid number of authentic autographs to the public with the help of hobby retailers. He possesses a fast-paced, flowing signature, often appearing as "Ichiro S." and he will add his uniform number "51" to items from time to time. His full-name signature is usually reserved for official documents, such as contracts or checks, and this variation of his autograph is very legible, with each letter of his name carefully executed. Today, Ichiro rarely signs his name in Japanese for fans, but you can find a good number of these autographs from his early playing days.

" *I'm not a big guy and hopefully kids could look at me and see that I'm not muscular and not physically imposing, that I'm just a regular guy. So if somebody with a regular body can get into the record books, kids can look at that. That would make me happy.*"

– Ichiro Suzuki

THE MODERN AGE

Index

★ ★ ★ ★ ★ ★ ★ ★ ★

Aaron, Henry "Hank," 160
Alexander, Grover C. "Pete," 44
Anson, Adrian "Cap," 46
Banks, Ernest "Ernie," 162
Bender, Charles "Chief," 48
Bench, Johnny, 164
Berg, Morris "Moe," 116
Berra, Lawrence "Yogi," 118
Bonds, Barry, 166
Brett, George, 168
Brouthers, Dennis "Dan," 50
Brown, Mordecai, 52
Burkett, Jesse, 54
Campanella, Roy, 120
Cartwright, Alexander, 56
Chadwick, Henry, 58
Chance, Frank, 102
Charleston, Oscar, 122
Chesbro, John "Jack," 60
Clarkson, John, 62
Clemens, William Roger, 170

Clemente, Roberto, 12
Cobb, Tyrus "Ty," 16
Cochrane, Gordon "Mickey," 124
Collins, Edward "Eddie," 64
Collins, James "Jimmy," 66
Comiskey, Charles "Charlie," 68
Connor, Roger, 70
Davis, George, 72
Dean, Jay "Dizzy," 126
Delahanty, Edward "Ed," 74
Dihigio, Martin, 128
DiMaggio, Joseph "Joe," 130
Drysdale, Donald "Don," 172
Evers, John "Johnny," 102
Ewing, William "Buck," 76
Foxx, James "Jimmie," 26
Gehrig, Henry "Lou," 10
Gibson, Joshua "Josh," 6
Greenberg, Henry "Hank," 132
Griffey Jr., George "Ken," 174
Grove, Robert "Lefty," 134
Gwynn, Anthony "Tony," 176
Hamilton, William "Billy," 78
Heilmann, Harry, 136
Henderson, Rickey, 178
Hodges, Gilbert "Gil," 138
Hornsby, Rogers, 140

208   THE 100 GREATEST BASEBALL AUTOGRAPHS

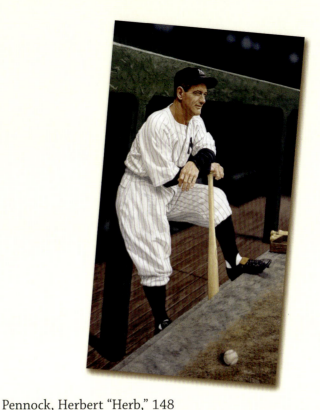
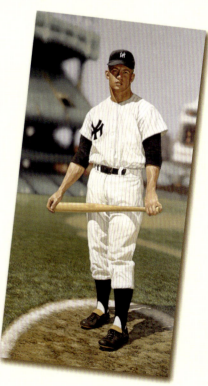

Howard, Elston "Ellie," 180
Huggins, Miller, 80
Jackson, Joseph "Shoeless Joe," 8
Jackson, Reginald "Reggie," 182
Jennings, Hugh "Hughie," 82
Jeter, Derek, 32
Johnson, Walter, 28
Joss, Adrian "Addie," 34
Keefe, Timothy "Tim," 84
Keeler, William "Willie," 86
Kelly, Michael "Mike," 88
Killebrew, Harmon, 184
Klein, Charles "Chuck," 142
Koufax, Sanford "Sandy," 36
Lajoie, Napoleon "Nap," 30
Mack, Cornelius "Connie," 90
Mantle, Mickey, 20
Maris, Roger, 38
Mathewson, Christopher "Christy," 4
Mays, Willie, 186
McGinnity, Joseph "Joe," 92
McGraw, John, 94
Munson, Thurman, 188
Musial, Stanley "Stan," 144
Oh, Sadaharu, 190
Ott, Melvin "Mel," 14
Paige, Leroy "Satchel," 146

Pennock, Herbert "Herb," 148
Plank, Edward "Eddie," 18
Pujols, Jose Alberto "Albert," 192
Rickey, Wesley "Branch," 150
Ripken Jr., Calvin "Cal," 194
Rivera, Mariano, 196
Robinson, Frank, 198
Robinson, Jack "Jackie," 22
Rose, Peter "Pete," 200
Rusie, Amos, 96
Ruth, George "Babe," 2
Ryan, Lynn Nolan, 202
Schmidt, Michael "Mike," 204
Sisler, George, 152
Spalding, Albert "Al," 98
Speaker, Tristram "Tris," 100
Stengel, Charles "Casey," 154
Suzuki, Ichiro, 206
Tinker, Joseph "Joe," 102
Waddell, George "Rube," 104
Wagner, Johannes "Honus," 106
Walsh, Edward "Ed," 108
Weaver, George "Buck," 110
Williams, Theodore, "Ted," 40
Wilson, Lewis "Hack," 156
Wright, William "Harry," 112
Young, Denton "Cy," 24

THE 100 GREATEST BASEBALL AUTOGRAPHS

About the Authors and Contributors

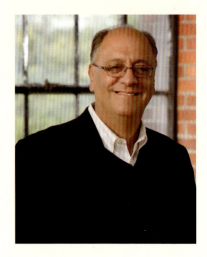

Tom Zappala is a businessman in the greater Boston area who is passionate about maintaining the traditions and historical significance of our National Pastime. He is co-author of the award-winning books *The T206 Collection: The Players & Their Stories* and *The Cracker Jack Collection: Baseball's Prized Players*, and he co-hosts a popular talk radio show that broadcasts in northern Massachusetts and southern New Hampshire. As co-owner of ATS Communications, a multimedia and consulting company, he handles publicity and personal appearances for several authors and a variety of artists in the entertainment field. He enjoys collecting vintage baseball and boxing memorabilia using the simple philosophy of collecting for the love of the sport. Proud of his Italian heritage, Zappala recently authored *Bless Me Sister*, a humorous book about his experience attending an Italian parochial school. He loves spending time with his children and grandchildren, and enjoys an occasional martini with two baseball-sized olives.

Ellen Zappala is president of ATS Communications, a multimedia marketing and consulting company. Co-author of the award-winning books *The T206 Collection: The Players & Their Stories* and *The Cracker Jack Collection: Baseball's Prized Players*, Zappala also worked with former welterweight boxing champ Tony DeMarco on his autobiography *Nardo: Memoirs of a Boxing Champion*. Zappala was publisher of a group of six newspapers in Massachusetts and New Hampshire for many years and served as president of the New England Press Association. She works closely with various publishing companies on behalf other authors, and handles publicity in both print and electronic media. She especially enjoys bringing the stories of the Deadball Era and Golden Age players to life.

Joe Orlando is president of Professional Sports Authenticator and PSA/DNA Authentication Services, the largest trading card and sports memorabilia authentication service in the hobby. Editor of the nationally distributed *Sports Market Report* (SMR), a Juris Doctor, and an advanced collector, Orlando has authored several collecting guides and dozens of articles for Collectors Universe, Inc. He is the author of *The Top 200 Sportscards in the Hobby* (2002) and *Collecting Sports Legends* (2008), and contributed the foreword and last chapter to the award-winning *The T206 Collection: The Players & Their Stories* and *The Cracker Jack Collection: Baseball's Prized Players*. As a hobby expert, Orlando has appeared as featured guest on numerous radio and television programs, including ESPN's *Outside the Lines*, HBO's *Real Sports*, and on the Fox Business Network.

John Molori is a columnist for *Boston Baseball Magazine*, *Patriots Football Weekly*, and *New England Golf Monthly*, and he contributed to the award-winning book, *The Cracker Jack Collection: Baseball's Prized Players*. Molori has also written for

ESPNW.com, *Boston Metro*, *Providence Journal*, *Lowell Sun*, and *The Eagle-Tribune*. His radio and TV credits include: ESPN, SiriusXM, Fox, Comcast, NESN, and NECN. A writing and media professor at Lasell College, Molori has lectured at Emerson College, Boston University, and Curry College. His awards include: New England Emmy Award, CableACE, Beacon Award, and the New Hampshire Association of Broadcasters Award. For his contributions as a sports journalist, Molori was inducted to the Methuen, MA, Athletic Hall of Fame in 2011, along with 1987 Cy Young Award winner Steve Bedrosian.

Steve Grad is the principal authenticator for PSA/DNA Authentication Services and, over the years, has authenticated some of the hobby's most prestigious autographed items. A renowned expert in his field, Grad is also the expert authenticator for the History Channel's hit program *Pawn Stars*. In addition to authenticating, Grad has an extensive, high-grade Star Wars autograph collection and has traveled throughout the world in search of elusive autographs. Before getting involved in autograph authentication, Grad was anchor/reporter and show host with One on One Radio Network, now known as Sporting News Radio. Steve lives in southern California with his wife, Claire, and daughters, Mikayla and Isabel.

Arthur K. Miller is an award-winning portrait artist specializing in historical sports figures and pop culture icons. A graduate of the School of Visual Arts in New York City, Miller assisted famed artist/designer David Edward Byrd before focusing on his own talents. His work has been exhibited internationally for over 30 years, including a five-year solo exhibition at the National Baseball Hall of

Fame & Museum. Miller's exacting portraits regularly appear on the cover of *Sports Market Report* (SMR) and are featured in permanent collections of the Baseball Hall of Fame, the New-York Historical Society, and the Louisville Slugger Museum. His recent work includes large faux-antique pop culture banners that evoke entertainment and promotional posters of the early to mid-twentieth century. Miller's original designs, typography, and canvas distressing technique give these works the feel of an actual antique found in the attic.

Tony Dube is president of White Point Imaging in Windsor, Connecticut. One of the first to embrace digital photography, he has extensive knowledge of leading-edge equipment and techniques. His images depicted in *The T206 Collection: The Players & Their Stories* and *The Cracker Jack Collection: Baseball's Prized Players* received critical acclaim for set design, styling, and lighting. In addition to product and collectibles photography, Dube works on lifestyle and model photography, as well as non-professional subjects. He also enjoys coaching baseball, playing racquetball, inventing products, and working on his photographic series called "Collectographs™," the art of collecting.

COLLECTIBLE DEALER SPOTLIGHT

Memory Lane Inc. THE LEADER IN VINTAGE SPORTS CARDS & COLLECTIBLES

The leading dealer of sports collectibles in the country, Memory Lane Inc. treats each customer individually and in complete confidence. With over 120 years of combined experience in the collectibles industry, the staff at Memory Lane will make your transaction both enjoyable and profitable, whether it is an estate liquidation, a small collection, or one individual piece.

Sports, historic Americana, and entertainment memorabilia are our specialty, and we are also available for appraisals and private consultations. As you flip through each page of this book, shades of our National Pastime's glorious past will overwhelm you. Babe Ruth, "Shoeless" Joe Jackson, Christy Mathewson, Ty Cobb, Lou Gehrig and Honus Wagner are just a few of the iconic figures that come to life through the narratives and autographs in these pages.

alongside the incomparable "Big Six," and rekindle thoughts of Gehrig's "Luckiest Man on the Face of the Earth" speech as you glance at his ultra-desirable signature.

Memory Lane offers wonderful signatures, similar to those featured in this beautiful publication, to our vast customer base. We give the collector an opportunity to transcend time, so you can own a piece of baseball history. Imagine standing alongside the "Sultan of Swat" as he proudly scripted one of his colossal bats or holding an extremely rare "Shoeless" Joe signed document that was painstakingly scripted by this remarkable yet illiterate slugger. As you view the great Christy Mathewson's articulate script, we invite you to "toe the rubber"

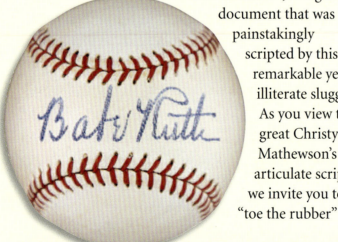

The list of legendary greats presented in this beautifully designed hardcover is seemingly infinite, synonymous with our ongoing goal of providing the collecting community with the finest memorabilia available. Whether you choose Memory Lane for our world-class auction services or for a private sale, the discerning collector as well as the novice will certainly be pleased with our unparalleled service.

CALL US FOR YOUR AUTOGRAPH BUYING & SELLING NEEDS

12831 Newport Ave., Suite 180 | Tustin, CA 92780

TOLL FREE: 877.606.5263 (LANE) | Office: 714.730.0600 | FAX: 714.730.0602
Email: contactus@memorylaneinc.com | Website: memorylaneinc.com